About Pfeiffer

Pfeiffer serves the professional development and hands-on resource needs of training and human resource practitioners and gives them products to do their jobs better. We deliver proven ideas and solutions from experts in HR development and HR management, and we offer effective and customizable tools to improve workplace performance. From novice to seasoned professional, Pfeiffer is the source you can trust to make yourself and your organization more successful.

Essential Knowledge Pfeiffer produces insightful, practical, and comprehensive materials on topics that matter the most to training and HR professionals. Our Essential Knowledge resources translate the expertise of seasoned professionals into practical, how-to guidance on critical workplace issues and problems. These resources are supported by case studies,

with CD-ROMs, websites, ... easier to read, understand, and use.

Essential Tools Pfeiffer's Essential Tools resources save time and expense by offering proven, ready-to-use materials—including exercises, activities, games, instruments, and assessments—for use during a training or team-learning event. These resources are frequently offered in loose-leaf or CD-ROM format to facilitate copying and customization of the material.

Pfeiffer also recognizes the remarkable power of new technologies in expanding the reach and effectiveness of training. While e-hype has often created whizbang solutions in search of a problem, we are dedicated to bringing convenience and enhancements to proven training solutions. All our e-tools comply with rigorous functionality standards. The most appropriate technology wrapped around essential content yields the perfect solution for today's on-the-go trainers and human resource professionals.

Pfeiffer
www.pfeiffer.com

Essential resources for training and HR professionals

THE **COLLABORATIVE WORK SYSTEMS** SERIES

Building collaborative capacity in the world of work

OTHER **COLLABORATIVE WORK SYSTEMS** SERIES TITLES

£31.50

GUIDING THE JOURNEY TO COLLABORATIVE WORK SYSTEMS

A STRATEGIC DESIGN WORKBOOK

Michael M. Beyerlein

Cheryl L. Harris

Pfeiffer
A Wiley Imprint
www.pfeiffer.com

Published by Pfeiffer
An Imprint of Wiley
989 Market Street, San Francisco, California 94103-1741   www.pfeiffer.com

For additional copies/bulk purchases of this book in the U.S., please call (800) 274-4434.

Pfeiffer books and products are available through most bookstores. To contact Pfeiffer directly, call our Customer Care Department within the U.S. at (800) 274-4434, outside the U.S. at (317) 572-3985, fax (317) 572-4002, or visit www.pfeiffer.com.

Pfeiffer also publishes its books in a variety of electronic formats. Some content that appears in print may not be available in electronic books.

ISBN: 0-7879-6788-2

Acquiring Editor: Matthew Davis
Director of Development: Kathleen Dolan Davies
Developmental Editor: Susan Rachmeler
Editor: Rebecca Taff
Production Editor: Carolyn Uno, Tigris Productions
Manufacturing Supervisor: Bill Matherly
Interior Design and Cover Design: Bruce Lundquist
Illustrations: Lotus Art

Printed in the United States of America

Printing   10 9 8 7 6 5 4 3 2 1

CONTENTS

LIST OF FIGURES, TABLES, AND TOOLS

FIGURES

TABLES

ASSESSMENTS

WORKSHEETS

MIKE dedicates this book to the next generation in hopes that their workplaces will be more effective and healthy.

CHERYL dedicates this book to her family. Mom and Dad, you show me love and support in countless ways. I can never repay all you have given me. To my grandmothers, Ethel and Evelyn, who will always be role models for their strength, wisdom, and grace, thank you for all that you have taught me. To my sisters and brothers-in-law, Wende, Teresa, Bryan, and Brandon, who are not just family but also friends, thanks for making me laugh and being there to lend a helping hand. I love you all!

IN LAUNCHING THIS SERIES, it is the editors' intention to create an ongoing, dynamic forum for sharing cutting-edge ideas and practices among researchers and those practitioners involved on a day-to-day basis with organizations that depend on collaborative work systems (CWSs) for their success.

Proposed publications in the CWS series include books devoted to specific topics, workbooks to guide planning and competency development, fieldbooks that capture lessons learned in organizations experimenting with collaborative work systems, software for facilitating learning, training materials, and assessment instruments. The goal of the series is to produce four new products per year that will build a foundation for a perspective on collaboration as an essential means of achieving high levels of performance in and across organizations. Our vision for the series is to provide a means for leveraging collaborative work practices around the world in for-profit, government, and not-for-profit entities.

Collaborative work systems are those in which conscious efforts have been made to create strategies, policies, and structures as well as to institutionalize values, behaviors, and practices that promote cooperation among different parties in the organization in order to achieve desired business outcomes. While many organizations vocalize support for teamwork and collaboration, collaborative work systems are distinguished by intentional efforts to embed the organization with work processes and cultural mechanisms that enable and reinforce collaboration. New forms of organization continue to emerge with CWSs as an essential facet. Team-based organizations and self-managing organizations represent types of collaborative systems. The computer revolution has made possible network, cellular, and spherical forms of organizing, which represent more transorganizational forms of collaboration.

Why the urgency? The challenges organizations face seem to be escalating rapidly. The number of global issues that affect an organization have proliferated, including the terrorist threat, continued deforestation of ancient lands by debtor nations, wars, famine, disease, the accelerating splitting of nations' consciousness into the haves and the have-nots around the globe, which fuels hatreds—all aspects of interrelated political, social, economic, environmental challenges that will ultimately reduce quality of life on a worldwide scale if not addressed. These are the systemic, wicked problems that depend on many minds lodged in a common value set committed to improving human welfare in all settings. The business community must work with city, county, and state governments, with nation states, and with transnational organizations, such as the United Nations and the World Bank, to bring enough intellectual and financial capital to bear on the problems to do something about them—demanding collaborative initiatives at all levels.

Individuals working well together—this seems like a relatively simple proposition. Yet barriers abound in organizations that tend to inhibit collaboration at every turn. Social barriers are erected for a variety of reasons, including turf wars and mindsets that lead to hoarding of specialized knowledge rather than sharing. Fear of loss seems to get amplified during economic downturns as operating budgets are trimmed, fueling a multiplicity of negative personal scenarios, including loss of jobs, promotional opportunities, titles, and perks, which in turn can threaten self-esteem and professional identity. Barriers to establishing effective collaborative work systems can also reflect lack of cross-training, cultural norms and reward systems that reinforce individual performance, organizational political realities that reinforce competition for scarce resources among units, and differing technical languages that make communication challenging. However, despite these difficulties, some companies appear to overcome the significant barriers and benefit from the positive consequences of effective collaboration.

People in and around organizations have been experimenting with and learning about designing effective work processes for millennia. Researchers and practitioners have been capturing the lessons learned since the early part of the 20th century. That process continues as we embark on the 21st century. There will be much to document as changes in global business practices and new generation technologies enable more effective ways of organizing, operating, competing, innovating, and collaborating. Technical developments during the next quarter century will create unheralded challenges and opportunities in an increasingly interdependent world.

The move from muscle-based work to knowledge-based work has been so profound that some writers have called it the age of the knowledge economy. It demands new levels of collaborative expertise and a shift in focus to intangible forms of capital.

Knowledge grows through the development of organizational routines. Knowledge includes knowing what, but also knowing how and why. Each employee carries a somewhat different library of knowledge and a unique perspective on how to apply it—termed intellectual capital. The network of interaction among knowledge workers creates a rich environment where ideas can grow and blossom in stair-step fashion—termed social capital—and where there is widespread competence in teamwork at all levels of the organization in various forms—termed collaborative capital. This form of capital provides the foundation for leveraging what the other forms contribute, but it demands radically different ways of organizing work and involving employees in its design and practice.

In summary, collaborative work systems provide one of the key competency areas that organizations can focus on for building vitality and excellence, including competitive and collaborative advantage. On a daily basis, people come together to make decisions, solve problems, invent new products and services, build key relationships, and plan futures. The effectiveness of those gatherings and the effectiveness of the systems that emerge from them will depend greatly on the collaborative capacity that has been built in their organizations. A high level of collaborative capacity will enable more effective work at the local and daily levels and at the global and long-term levels. We can solve our immediate problems more effectively and we can cooperate more effectively to take on the emerging global issues that threaten us in the 21st century when we have the skills, values, and processes for effective collaboration. This series of publications is intended as a catalyst in building that collaborative capacity at both local and global levels.

Michael M. Beyerlein, Ph.D.
Susan T. Beyerlein, Ph.D.
Center for the Study of Work Teams
University of North Texas

James Barker, Ph.D.
United States Air Force Academy

ACKNOWLEDGMENTS

WE HAVE LEARNED from hundreds of people during the past seven years. Some were researchers, some consultants, some book or article authors, and others were team members and managers. Some were presenters at the Center for the Study of Work Teams' conferences. Others were managers and employees in the organizations or teammates on project teams with which we were involved. Much of the understanding and scope we bring to this book comes from our contact with these people. They are too numerous to mention, but a few had truly notable influences, and we will single them out for acknowledgment.

Chris Hall is a former teammate whose research profoundly expanded our view of organizational support systems. Susan Mohrman is an author and conference presenter who expanded our horizons on every contact.

Sarah Bodner contributed to the book in so many ways. She helped develop the concepts and applications through partnering in consulting projects. She co-authored with Cheryl two book chapters that further developed the concepts in this book. She spent countless hours reviewing and commenting on drafts of the workbook, providing feedback that enhanced the quality. We especially appreciate her ability to take concepts to practical application and her knack for developing relevant exercises. Cheryl thanks Sarah for "meeting her under a bridge in Paris" and hopes to return the favor someday!

Special thanks go to all the colleagues at the Center for the Study of Work Teams we have worked with over the years. This book could not exist without the benefits of their collaboration. Our thanks include, but are not limited to, Rodger Ballentine, Doug Johnson, Chris Hall, Eric Simpson, Karon Tedford, Frances Kennedy, Michael Kennedy, Mikhail Koulikov, Cynthia Cantu, Katina Davenport Wilkins, Cheryl Zobal, and Ron Lynch.

We especially thank colleagues at the Center for the Study of Work Teams who took extra steps to help make our vision a reality. Lori Bradley and Bob Francoeur provided developmental feedback. Thanks to Lori for reviewing the Guiding Assessment and to Bob for development of definitions to improve the conceptual foundation.

Nicole DeJarnett, Jodi Longo, and Lindsey Straka graciously critiqued each chapter, completed a big-picture review of the book, and helped in the development of resource lists, all with little guidance from the authors (thank you!). Jon Turner completed the arduous task of creating an index for the book; we sincerely appreciate that!

Our special thanks go to Nancy Gorman at the Center for her assistance with the manuscript preparation and submission. Her organization kept us from making major blunders in the process. Her initiative led to supplemental feedback that raised the quality of the manuscript. Her patience with our fast-paced and fragmented e-mailing of dozens of files to be deconstructed and reassembled for submission spread a sense of calm over an otherwise hectic project.

Cheryl would like to thank the Center for Creative Leadership for their support during part of the research that contributed to the concepts in this book. Judith Steed and Gina Hernez-Broome were instrumental in providing feedback and dialogue, David Loring championed the project, and many friends helped along the way, including, but not limited to, Linda Hunter, Carol Vallee, Rachael Carr, Stephanie Trovas, Erin Yount, and Karen Hajek. Twenty-one experts in the field of organization development participated in phone interviews during Cheryl's time at the Center for Creative Leadership. Thank you for sharing your expertise and experience.

Cheryl would like to thank her family and friends for their patience and support during the journey. Mom, Dad, Teresa, Wende, Brandon, Bryan and Burke, you can never be thanked enough! Thanks to AC and the Packham and the Harris families, Beth Zeinert (and Richard, James, and Hannah), "brother" Rick Emery, Mike and Katina Wilkins (and Katelyn), and the "dream-day" gang—Keith, Lisa, Larry (and Ashley), Brant, Ray, Ron, Delia, and Herb (and Dottie). Now that the book is done, I can return those phone calls!

Mike would like to thank his family, Sue and Marisa, for their patience and support. Long hours at the computer cut into family time even during holidays, so they shared in the pain of this project and deserve special attention now that it's over.

Support at Pfeiffer has been outstanding throughout this project. We want to single out Susan Rachmeler, our developmental editor, for her incredible work on the sequence of drafts we created. Susan's knowledge of organizations, her skill at dissecting a manuscript, and her care in sharing her ideas in a clear, thorough, and inspiring manner enabled us to improve both our vision of the book and the manuscript itself—at least a full quantum leap, probably two. Susan's words and ideas are peppered throughout the book to such an extent that we consider her our invisible co-author.

We thank Carolyn Uno, our production editor, who fearlessly pulled together the hundreds of details necessary for production of the workbook.

Finally, our thanks to Kathleen Dolan Davies and Matthew Davis at Pfeiffer, for guidance and support, and to three anonymous reviewers whose critical feedback helped lift this book to a higher plane of quality.

Bringing our vision of the workbook to reality was truly a collaborative effort!

IF YOU BELIEVE THAT YOUR ORGANIZATION would benefit from people working together more effectively and you want to do something about it, this book is for you. If you believe there are opportunities to work across the boundaries of the organization to enhance the flow of work and information, read on. If you believe resources can be leveraged to multiply their value by the way people work together, you will find value in this book.

Guiding the Journey to Collaborative Work Systems guides members of the change leadership team through a planning process, using a strategic approach to transform the organization to support collaboration. Unique features of the workbook include:

- Organization around the critical success factors that a successful collaborative work system initiative depends on

- Cutting-edge treatment of support system alignment with collaborative work units

- Comprehensive coverage of the topics that change leadership teams must address in planning the initiative

- Dozens of new assessment and planning tools to enable the change leadership team to translate the abstract plan into a practical implementation process

After reading the book, readers will be able to:

- Create an effective change leadership team for teams or groups

- Design in-depth plans for change, improving the collaborative practices and processes in their organization's work systems

- Generate and maintain support for the initiative

- Launch a thoroughly planned change program

- Communicate the plan to the rest of the organization

- Integrate change efforts across functions and levels

- Assess progress during implementation

- Review and revise the plan as circumstances change

Our qualifications for authoring this workbook include the following:

- Working with change leadership teams

- Publishing fifteen other books on teams

- Seven years of research together and other research prior to that

- In-depth interviews with 610 team members and managers and with twenty-one experts

- Surveys with over two hundred teams

- Sponsoring twenty-nine conferences on teams

- Giving numerous conference presentations and workshops

Our intent is for the book to be very practical, so the readers walk away saying, "Yes, that book really helped us make real change." We hope readers will:

- See the value of building an environment that enhances collaboration

- See collaboration as a means to results

- See teams and team-based organizing as part of a menu of options in designing for effective collaboration

- Understand the importance of alignment for organizational success

- See ways to leverage the resources in the organization

- Understand how to manage this major change intelligently

- Understand the value of collaboration and alignment

- Understand how to put those concepts into practice

We hope you find the workbook to be a valuable resource in your work to build collaborative capability in your organization.

Michael M. Beyerlein
Cheryl L. Harris

Understand the Strategic Design Process

IN THIS INTRODUCTION, we describe the strategic design process for developing organizations to support collaboration, a key to business success. We provide an overview of the workbook and techniques for using it (Chapter 1), then review the basic concepts of collaborative work systems (Chapter 2). Next, we introduce the Guiding Assessment (Chapter 3), a tool that will help you tailor the strategic design process to your organization and set your priorities for working through the rest of the chapters in the workbook.

Key Questions in Each Chapter

Chapter	Key Question
1 How to Use This Workbook	
2 Learn the Basics of Collaborative Work Systems	What are the different types of collaborative work systems?
3 Start with the Guiding Assessment	How can we learn about the strategic design process and apply it to our organization?

## CHAPTER 1

How to Use This Workbook

Rationale for the Workbook

Organizations seeking competitive advantage look for new ways to leverage resources, creative ways to harness the hearts and minds of members, and innovative methods of building market share or customer delight. Many approaches have aided leading-edge companies, including continuous quality improvement, lean manufacturing and Six Sigma, business process re-engineering, enterprise resource planning, knowledge management, team-based organizations (Harris & Beyerlein, 2003b, 2003c), leadership development, joint ventures, and so on. The approach that receives the least attention is collaboration. Although it plays a key role in making all of the approaches successful and receives special attention in team-based methods, there are few organizational examples of world-class levels of collaboration. Hence, this area represents one of the primary sources of competitive advantage for the 21st century.

A great deal of preparatory work is essential to set the stage for design and implementation of the collaborative work system (CWS) initiative. Many leading the change underestimate the scope of this part of the work and try to rush it to conclusion too quickly. Design is also often rushed. Taking time to do these things well pays off in more rapid and effective implementation and richer business results.

This workbook is a practical guide for people responsible for the design or redesign of organizations that want to reap more value from their potential for effective collaborative work. We will use the term *change leadership team* (CLT) to refer to the group leading the change. Other terms for CLT include steering team, design team, and guiding coalition.

The exercises, assessments, discussion points, and worksheets are designed for getting real work done. The workbook is a whole systems change guide appropriate for both organizations just beginning the CWS initiative and those wanting to take the next step in the evolution. It is also appropriate for change work in maintenance and problem diagnoses in work systems where collaborative capability can make a difference in achieving strategic goals.

The content of the workbook emphasizes the development of collaborative work systems. Collaborative work systems occur anywhere that working better together can improve performance, whether it is formal or informal, large or small, complex or simple, intentional or unintentional. Examples range in size from teams and communities of practice to team-based organizations and collaborative organizations (Beyerlein, Freedman, McGee, & Moran, 2002) and beyond. Collaboration occurs naturally, but organizations tend to create barriers. Intentional focus on CWSs helps to bring down those barriers. The goal of intentional focus on CWSs is individuals and groups effectively working together to achieve strategic goals.

The workbook makes the assumption that the CLT will focus on a single business unit, such as a single work site, project, program, or plant. Those focusing on a larger or smaller organization can adapt the material to other levels of operation, such as corporate or department change.

This workbook is primarily focused on developing the collaborative work system in a brownfield site (an existing operation), but much of it applies to greenfield sites (new organization, site, project, or start-up) as well. Also, most of the principles and exercises in the workbook apply to other change initiatives, since each is embedded in the set of social, cognitive, emotional, and cultural systems of the organization.

The workbook is organized around thirteen critical success factors (CSFs) (Harris & Beyerlein, 2003a)—each represented by a chapter in Part I or Part II. CSFs represent areas of attention, decision making, and action that play important roles in the success of any change initiative. When a CSF is ignored, the results are likely to be detrimental to the initiative, even resulting in failure. Our years of study on team failure, work with organizations, extensive searches of publications, and interviews with twenty-one experts has helped us determine the CSFs essential to planning, implementing, and sustaining collaborative work systems. Other factors may also play a role in success, particularly such local factors as political climate in the organization, economic conditions that demand rapid and radical alterations in the organization, or competing initiatives that may consume significant resources. Our list of CSFs is intended to be applicable to many types of organizations but also adaptable enough to fit with the local changes with which the CLT must deal.

Goals of the Workbook

We hope the workbook will help users achieve the following goals:

1. Establish a big picture, holistic framework for the collaborative work systems initiative. The workbook is intentionally sparse to allow a breadth of coverage, but users are encouraged to continue filling in the details through use of resources suggested at the end of each chapter.

2. Practice CWS principles through exercises and activities. The experience will provide a model for others and a learning lab for the change leaders.

3. Recognize the importance of building an environment that enhances collaborative practices. When facets of the environment punish people for working together, collaborative excellence is unattainable.

4. Pursue collaborative excellence primarily because it is a means for achieving business results. When that focus is lost, change initiatives tend to be abandoned.

5. Understand the importance of alignment and its relationship with collaboration.

6. Realize that this huge challenge is worth tackling and that the change leadership team has or can get the resources necessary to make a success of the undertaking.

Workbook Organization

This workbook is organized in three sections: Introduction, Part I: Create a Foundation for Change, and Part II: Align the Organization for Collaboration.

In the Introduction section, Chapter 1 focuses on an introduction to the workbook and techniques for using it. Chapter 2 reviews the basic concepts of collaborative work systems and provides an activity to guide users through preliminary understanding of the extent of the change desired. Chapter 3 provides a guiding assessment tool that links with the rest of the chapters in the workbook. Completing this guiding assessment provides users with basic knowledge of the CWS concepts and some understanding of the prioritization of working through the chapters of the workbook.

Part I, Create a Foundation for Change, concentrates on creating a foundation for the collaborative work system initiative. Constructing the foundation starts by developing the change leadership team (Chapters 4 and 5), then by teaching people how to think strategically about change and apply effective change principles (Chapters 6 and 7). Building the business case (Chapter 8) ensures approval from top leaders to ease the transition to Part II of this workbook. Finally, using assessment to identify needs and measure progress (Chapter 9) provides the tools necessary to understand whether the goals of the CWS initiative are being met.

Part II, Align the Organization for Collaboration, moves from the more internal change leadership team focus of creating the foundation for change to a broader organization focus on how to create the framework of plans to design or redesign your collaborative work system. Planning begins by understanding the environment outside the organization and creating ways to link and adapt to that environment (Chapter 10). Understanding current and ideal culture helps set guiding values and principles for the CWS initiative (Chapter 11). Understanding the work of the organization provides an anchor for the rest of the initiative by ensuring that the real reason for organizations—conducting business—is the focus (Chapter 12); designing structures to best fit that work ensures an effective organization design (Chapter 13). Visualizing and planning what employee behavior looks like at the ideal level of collaboration through an empowerment plan (Chapter 14), defining the new roles of leaders to support employee empowerment (Chapter 15), and developing support systems to support employee empowerment and new leader roles (Chapter 16) all work together to reinforce collaboration.

Finally, the conclusion (Chapter 17) provides activities for pulling together all the material generated in the workbook.

Elements in Each Chapter

Each chapter contains common elements for ease of use of the workbook. See Table 1.1 for a list of the elements and explanations.

Table 1.1. Elements in Each Chapter

Element	Explanation
Map of critical success factors	The CWS Design Model shows how the critical success factors (each represented by a chapter) fit together and serves as an organizing "roadmap" of the workbook process. The model is in the form of a house built on a brick foundation (see Figure 1.1) with the current chapter highlighted.
Key question	The central question for each chapter is provided at the beginning of the chapter and reviewed again in the chapter conclusion.
"Quick Look" introduction	The "Quick Look" introduction provides a quick overview of the chapter. It includes: • A brief overview of the contents of the chapter and the intended outcomes • A table listing chapter headings with icons to indicate the type of content included in that heading. Types of content include educational framework pieces, discussion questions, assessments, and planning activities. See Table 1.4 for icons that indicate each of these content types. • A second set of icons for collaborative principles, which help to link this book to others in the Collaborative Work Systems Series (see Table 1.6).
Keys to the chapter	A summary of the key points at the end of the chapter
Chapter wrap-up	Questions that help the users convert their learning into action steps (for more, see "Suggestions for Maximizing Use of the Workbook").
Resource list	A resource list for further help on the topic. The workbook intentionally provides broad, sparse coverage, so the resource lists will be valuable in getting more in-depth information to fill in the details of the plan.
Action planning sheet	A form for capturing decisions made while working through the chapter (for more, see "Suggestions for Maximizing Use of the Workbook").

The bricks in the foundation of the house in Figure 1.1 represent the chapter titles and CSFs for Part I of the workbook. The titles around the house itself represent the chapter titles and CSFs of Part II. The image of the shining sun represents the environment surrounding the organization. We chose this image to show the need to build a foundation for effective organizational change, to illustrate construction under way, and to reflect the complexity of the task; it takes about 25,000 decisions to build a house, some major and some minor.

Practical Focus

This workbook addresses practical concerns and includes many worksheets, charts, illustrations, and exercises to aid in utilizing the ideas presented here. Some rationale and explanation is provided around each activity connecting it to the key points in the

Figure 1.1.   Model of the Strategic Design Process

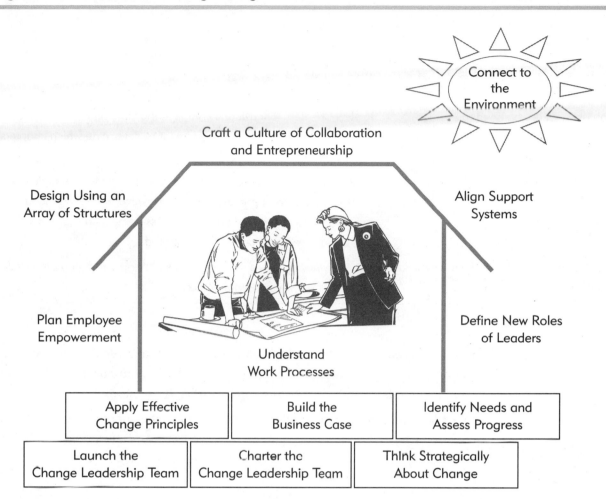

chapter. A CLT can work through the workbook by completing the exercises and building a roadmap for the collaborative work systems initiative to lay the foundation for change and plan the CWS initiative.

A complete list of all the exercises in the workbook can be found in Assessment 17.1.

Approaches to the Material
How to Read the Workbook

Ideally, the CLT members read the workbook together and work through the exercises as a team. The outcomes from the exercises contribute to the planning work for which the CLT is responsible.

Some general recommendations on reading the workbook are listed below. More specific recommendations are given in Table 1.2.

- In the Introduction, read Chapters 1 and 2 and do the exercise in Chapter 2 to develop a shared understanding of collaboration, the CWS initiative, and the workbook. Then complete the assessment in Chapter 3 to identify where CLT work needs to focus.

Table 1.2. Ways to Work Through the Workbook

Situation	Recommendation
Change leadership teams (CLTs) who are just beginning	Work straight through, chapter by chapter.
Established CLTs who need to evaluate progress and determine next steps	Review Chapters 1 and 2 and complete the Guiding Assessment in Chapter 3. Use the Guiding Assessment to determine which chapters to review next.
CLTs who have identified a specific issue	Read Chapter 1 and shop around in the workbook for the topic that fits the CLT's current primary concern. However, we recommend returning to Chapter 3 for the Guiding Assessment so that other issues that need attention can be surfaced.
The CWS initiative is well under way, and an unforeseen problem occurs.	Use the workbook as a reference or as a manual that can be pulled from the shelf when a problem occurs.

- In Part I, Create a Foundation for Change, the chapters build on each other to provide a solid foundation for the change work. We recommend that CLTs complete Part I in its entirety before moving to Part II, if possible.

- In Part II, Align the Organization for Collaboration, the chapters build on each other in parts, but, if necessary, can be reviewed as stand-alone segments. Use the Guiding Assessment in Chapter 3 to determine needs.

Change Is Nonlinear

In published form, we have to present the material linearly, but we recognize that the actual change process is nonlinear. There will be places where things will happen simultaneously or loop back to prior stages. Jump around as needed. The organization is a complete whole. Ideally, change work takes that into account. However, we can only work and write with a focus on one piece at a time, so always work to link the parts back to the whole.

Time Requirement

Different methods for organizing the time needed to work through the workbook are listed in Table 1.3. The choice of approach depends on such local conditions as how much time the CLT members can devote to meetings together and to follow-up work outside the meetings, the level of urgency for redesign, and the level of prior experience with change initiatives. The workbook should be viewed as a tool to use throughout the transformation journey, not as a mere classroom exercise. The work is so extensive that it is unlikely that a CLT can make major, successful changes in under two years, and the whole range of change will probably take five or more years—much of it with concurrent parts under way from several chapters. However, the process is designed to generate business-related benefits continually.

Table 1.3. Methods for Organizing Time Needed to Work Through the Workbook

Method	Explanation
Intensive two-week training/planning situation	An intensive two-week session provides time for the change leadership team to focus, build a strong team, and become immersed in the planning process, but allows little time for working outside the meeting to revise materials and obtain input from other stakeholders. A concentrated two-week exploration of the book's contents does not substitute for its use during the months of transformational work; it merely provides a thorough overview of the high-level change map. Such a workshop launches the collaborative work systems initiative, but action planning and implementation should occur concurrently, following along with the workbook.
A half-day per week over many months	This approach allows for time between meetings to reflect on the material, refine ideas, and collect information from other stakeholders. However, it is more difficult to sustain focus, as often the other details of business get in the way.
Intensive three-day workshop with weekly meetings as follow-up	This approach combines the strengths of the first two approaches. The three-day kickoff allows time for focus and immersion in the planning process, while weekly follow-up meetings provide opportunities for refining plans and involving other stakeholders. Additional one-day to three-day meetings may be appropriate.

Getting the Most from the Exercises

Getting the most from exercises depends on:

- Quality of the team process (see Chapters 4 and 5)

- Expertise of people in the group

- Knowing when to supplement your expertise with outside resources such as consultants and facilitators (see "Using a Facilitator" below)

- Time, effort, and concentration put into it

Using a Facilitator

Most CLTs will benefit from having either process or content facilitators for their meetings. Process facilitators manage the flow of the meeting for efficient and effective decision making. Content facilitators, such as organization development specialists and consultants, provide information on best practices, tools, and red flags to improve the strategic design plan and execution. Members of the CLT can take turns playing the facilitator role, but use of an experienced facilitator in the beginning will make the launch of the CWS initiative a smoother process.

Most of the instructions for planning activities and assessments are written as though a facilitator will be reading them. For each exercise, determine whether an outside facilitator will be used or if one of the CLT members will serve in that role. In some of the simpler activities, the members could share facilitation responsibilities, although it is preferable to have a designated person in the facilitator role to ensure that the process is smooth.

Suggestions for Maximizing Use of the Workbook

Mechanisms for converting learning into practice are intentionally placed throughout the workbook to maximize its use. Consider the following suggestions:

- Use the chapter wrap-up and action planning sheets at the end of each chapter to record (1) ideas for putting learning into practice, (2) actions that come out of the chapter, (3) person responsible, (4) due date for each task, and (5) key decisions made.

- Use the conclusion (Chapter 17) to review the outcomes of each chapter and compile the actions and key decisions created in the chapter wrap-up and action planning sheets.

- Use the conclusion (Chapter 17) to create a master timeline for goals and activities.

- Create a "CWS initiative handbook" to compile the most current versions of chapter outcomes and other relevant materials. This becomes a living document that can be used to communicate both with CLT members and others in the organization. Consider publishing versions of this in paper form or even on a Web site for sharing with other members of your organization. Consider it the CLT's project diary.

- Have CLT members read each chapter before the meeting to review that chapter, so they will be prepared with questions and comments for discussion. Consider other reading assignments from the resources lists.

Content Icons

The icons shown in Table 1.4 will be used to distinguish between different types of content in each chapter.

Special Terms

Table 1.5 identifies and defines some terms used in the workbook that may not be familiar to some readers.

In addition to these definitions that apply to the entire book, we will begin each chapter defining terms that apply specifically to that chapter.

The Collaborative Work Systems Series

This is the third book in the Pfeiffer Collaborative Work Systems Series. The first two books are *Beyond Teams: Building the Collaborative Organization* (Beyerlein, Freedman, McGee, & Moran, 2002) and *The Collaborative Work Systems Fieldbook* (Beyerlein, McGee,

Table 1.4.   Workbook Icons

 Key question for chapter

 Quick look at chapter includes an overview, chapter plan, and CWS principles used

 Educational framework pieces to introduce the reader to the content

 Discussion questions to help the reader understand the content

 Assessment tools to apply the content to the reader's organization. To better facilitate use of the assessment tools, each assessment lists the time requirement, supplies required, an overview, and instructions.

 Planning tools to help the reader apply the content to their change plans. To better facilitate use of the planning tools, each planning tool lists the time requirement, supplies required, an overview, and instructions.

 Chapter conclusion

 Keys to the chapter, included at the end of the chapter as a summary of key points to remember

 Chapter wrap-up. Includes a list of "things to do" at the end of each chapter.

 Resource list for further information on the topic

Table 1.5. Special Terms

Collaborative Work System (CWS)	Collaborative work systems occur anywhere that people depend on each other to get work done, whether it is formal or informal, large or small, complex or simple, intentional or unintentional. Examples range in size from teams and communities of practice to team-based organizations, collaborative organizations, integrated supply chains, and joint ventures. Collaboration occurs naturally, but organizations tend to create barriers. Intentional focus on CWSs helps to bring down those barriers. The goal of an intentional focus on CWSs is individuals and groups effectively working together to achieve strategic business goals.
CWS initiative	The focus of this workbook is to build collaborative capability through a change initiative focused on collaborative work systems. Most of the content applies to any major change initiative an organization adopts. To maintain a focus on CWSs, we are omitting the generic terms like "change initiative," "change effort," and so on.
Change Leadership Team (CLT)	The group responsible for leading the change effort—the primary audience for the workbook.
Critical Success Factor (CSF)	Each chapter title from Chapter 4 through Chapter 16 represents a factor that is critical to the success of a CWS initiative. Explanation of each CSF is found in Chapter 3. The points comprised in the CSFs are shared in the Guiding Assessment in Chapter 3. This Guiding Assessment helps the reader determine where to go in the workbook.

Klein, Nemiro, & Broedling, 2003). The fourth book in the series, *The Collaborative Work Systems Casebook,* will be published soon. Other books in the series will focus on various aspects of CWSs, such as the relationship to Six Sigma, creativity in virtual teams, and shared leadership. The four books are linked together by a system of icons representing the principles introduced in the first book, *Beyond Teams.* Table 1.6 lists the icons, the principles they represent, and the chapters in the workbook where specific principles appear. The icons facilitate the reader finding similar material in the other three books—explanations, examples, and tools. We recommend using the other books in the series as supplemental resources as needed.

 ## Conclusion

Use this workbook as a guide, as a tool, as a record of what your team does and as a reference and resource when problems in the CWS initiative arise. The work of the CLT will be challenging, interesting, and rewarding in many ways. Using the material in this workbook will reduce the frustration and ambiguity of the journey to a collaborative work system and greatly increase the probability of a successful conclusion.

Table 1.6. Collaborative Work Systems Series Principles Applied in Each Chapter

Icons	Collaborative Work Systems Series Principle	2	3	4	5	6	7	8	9	10	11	12	13	14	15	16	17
	Focus collaboration on achieving business results	X	X			X		X		X		X					
	Align support systems to promote ownership						X								X	X	
	Articulate and enforce "a few strict rules"										X				X		X
	Exploit the rhythm of divergence and convergence			X								X	X				
	Manage complex trade-off decisions					X		X		X		X					
	Create higher standards for discussion, dialogue, and sharing of information			X			X		X	X							
	Foster personal accountability									X	X			X			
	Align authority, information, and decision making				X		X	X	X		X			X	X	X	
	Treat collaboration as a disciplined process	X	X	X	X	X							X	X			X
	Design and promote flexible organizations that foster needed collaboration	X	X					X				X	X			X	

Resources

Armstrong, L. (1994). Evolution to a team-based organization. *Canadian Business Review, 21*(3), 14–18.

Beyerlein, M., Freedman, S., McGee, C., & Moran, L. (2002). *Beyond teams: Building the collaborative organization.* San Francisco: Jossey-Bass/Pfeiffer.

Beyerlein, M., Johnson, D., & Beyerlein, S. (Eds.). (1997). *Advances in interdisciplinary studies of work teams: Vol. 4. Team implementation issues.* Greenwich, CT: JAI Press.

Beyerlein, M., McGee, C., Klein, G., Nemiro, J., & Broedling, L. (2003). *The collaborative work system fieldbook.* San Francisco: Jossey-Bass/Pfeiffer.

Bishop, S. K. (1999). Cross-functional project teams in functionally aligned organizations. *Project Management Journal, 30*(3), 6–12.

Cabana, S. (1995, January/February). Participative design works, partly participative doesn't. *Journal for Quality and Participation,* 10–19.

Carroll, B. (1999). Self-managed knowledge teams simplify high-tech manufacturing. *National Productivity Review, 18*(2), 35–40.

Cross, R. L., Yan, A., & Louis, M. R. (2000). Boundary activities in "boundaryless" organizations: A case study of a transformation to a team-based structure. *Human Relations 53*(6), 841–869.

Dubois, T. C. (1999). The gradual transition to a team-based environment: The success story of a medium-sized manufacturing facility. *Hospital Materiel Management Quarterly, 21*(1), 31–41.

Dyck, R., & Halpern, N. (1999). Team-based organization redesign at Celestica. *Journal for Quality and Participation, 22*(5), 36–41.

Fanning, M. M. (1997). A circular organization chart promotes a hospital-wide focus on teams. *Hospital & Health Services Administration, 42*(2), 243–255.

Forrester, R., & Drexler, A. B. (1999). A model for team-based organizational performance. *Academy of Management Executive, 13*(3), 36–49.

Gerard, R. J. (1995). Teaming up: Making the transition to a self-directed, team-based organization. *Academy of Management Executive, 9*(3), 91–93.

Gerwin, D. (1999). Team empowerment in new product development. *Business Horizons, 42*(4), 29–41.

Hackman, R. J. (1990). *Groups that work and those that don't: Creating conditions for effective teamwork.* San Francisco: Jossey-Bass.

Harris, C. L., & Beyerlein, M. M. (2003a). Critical success factors in team-based organizing: A top ten list. In M. Beyerlein, C. McGee, G. Klein, J. Nemiro, & L. Broedling (Eds.), *The collaborative work systems fieldbook* (pp. 19–42). San Francisco: Jossey-Bass/Pfeiffer.

Harris, C. L., & Beyerlein, M. M. (2003b). Navigating the team-based organizing journey. In M. Beyerlein, D. Johnson, & S. Beyerlein (Eds.), *Advances in interdisciplinary studies of work teams: Vol. 9. Team-based organizing* (pp. 1–29). Oxford, England: Elsevier Science.

Harris, C. L., & Beyerlein, M. M. (2003c). Team-based organization: Creating an environment for team success. In M. A. West, K. Smith, & D. Tjosvold (Eds.), *International handbook of organisational teamwork and cooperative working* (pp. 185–210). West Sussex, England: Wiley.

Jones, S., & Beyerlein, M. (Eds.) (1998). *In action: Developing high performance teams* (Vol. 1). Alexandria, VA: ASTD Press.

Jones, S., & Beyerlein, M. (Eds.) (1999). *In action: Developing high performance teams* (Vol. 2). Alexandria, VA: ASTD Press.

Jusko, J. (2000). Paths for progress: World-class plants combine best practices, teamwork, and technology to achieve optimal performance. *Industry Week, 249*(20), 24–35.

Mohrman, S. A., & Quam, K. F. (2000). Consulting to team-based organizations: An organizational design and learning approach. *Consulting Psychology Journal: Practice and Research, 2*(1), 20–35.

Purser, R. E., & Cabana, S. (1998). *The self managing organization: How leading companies are transforming the work of teams for real impact.* New York: Free Press.

Sethi, R. (2000). New product quality and product development teams. *Journal of Marketing, 64*(2), 1–14.

Spreitzer, G. M., Cohen, S. G., & Ledford, G. E., Jr. Developing effective self-managing work teams in service organizations. *Group & Organization Management, 24*(3), 340–366.

Wageman, R. (1997). Case study: Critical success factors for creating superb self-managing teams at Xerox. *Compensation & Benefits Review, 29*(5), 31–41.

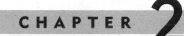

CHAPTER 2

Learn the Basics of Collaborative Work Systems

 Key Question of This Chapter

What are the different types of collaborative work systems?

 ## Quick Look

Overview

A *collaborative work system* (CWS) is an organizational unit that occurs any time that collaboration takes place, whether it is formal or informal or occurs intentionally or unintentionally. Intentional focus on CWSs requires the conscious and deliberate arrangement of organizational systems aimed at enabling collaboration and limiting impediments to collaborative work. Types of CWSs range from group to organization level and beyond. This chapter presents a typology of the organization level of CWS as both formal and informal collaborative practices. Outcomes of the chapter include an understanding of the different types of collaboration, identification of the type that closest fits the current organization, and a preliminary understanding of the CWS target that can be used to communicate with others.

Chapter Plan

Topic				
What Is a Collaborative Work System?	✓			
Types of Collaborative Work Systems	✓			✓
Understand the Current Organization	✓		✓	
Select the Collaborative Work System Target	✓			✓

Principles of Collaborative Work Systems Series

Focus collaboration on achieving business results

Treat collaboration as a disciplined process

Design and promote flexible organizations
that foster needed collaboration

What Is a Collaborative Work System?
What Is Collaboration?

Collaboration is the collective work of two or more individuals where the work is undertaken with a sense of shared purpose and direction that is attentive, responsive, and adaptive to the environment. In collaborative work relationships, the awareness of the environment develops through access to information and knowledge about how work done by a group influences individuals at every layer of context, a process that is often described in terms of effects on stakeholders and customers. Because of this awareness, people who collaborate are able to guide their work so that it meets the needs of those surrounding the work and optimally coordinate their efforts so that their capacity for creating positive change becomes a primary force for generating meaning and commitment.

What Is a Collaborative Work System?

A *collaborative work system* (CWS) is an organizational unit that occurs any time that collaboration takes place, whether it is formal or informal, or occurs intentionally or unintentionally. Intentional focus on CWS requires the conscious and deliberate arrangement of organizational systems aimed at enabling collaboration and limiting impediments to collaborative work. All work groups have elements of collaboration, but intentional focus on CWSs increases and improves collaborative capability.

CWSs come in many shapes and sizes. Some forms of CWSs are listed below; look in the "Types of Collaborative Work Systems" section for a full typology.

Group Level

- *Team.* A group of people who have interdependent tasks and a shared purpose and who are held mutually accountable for shared goals

- *Community of practice.* An informal group or network of people who have shared interests, stories, and a common language, but are not necessarily held mutually accountable (for example, a group of engineers sharing learnings informally)

Organization Level

- *Team-based organization.* Teams are the unit of work, managers are in teams, and the organization is designed to support teams.

- *Collaborative organization.* Both formal and informal collaboration is supported, teams are used where needed, and the organization is designed to support collaboration.

Collaboration occurs naturally, but organizations tend to create barriers. For example, in traditional functional organizations, often a decision has to be escalated from worker to supervisor to manager in one function, then across to a manager in another function and down to a supervisor to a worker, and so on, before a final decision is made and communicated. The result is a loss of decision-making quality and time. Knocking down functional barriers and allowing workers to talk directly to relevant parties and make their own decisions (when possible) enhances natural collaborative processes and results in better and faster decisions. The goal of intentional focus on CWSs is individuals and groups effectively working together to achieve strategic goals.

Why Focus on Improving Collaborative Work Systems?

Some reasons for focusing on CWSs are listed below:

- *To create a competitive advantage.* Organizations have to work collaboratively, and do it well, to succeed in today's environment.

- *To create a context for team success.* Teams and other collaborative structures have a much better chance of success if the organization is designed to support collaboration.

- *To promote lateral integration and alignment.* Focusing on CWSs means improving not only collaboration within groups, but between groups. This lateral integration promotes significant performance payoffs between teams and decreased failure of isolated teams.

- *To better connect to your environment.* Continual links to the environment create awareness of the need to change to survive and thrive.

- *To increase flexibility.* The ability to collaborate provides flexibility to meet the needs of the environment (including customers), which improves the success and longevity of the organization.

Improve Collaborative Work Systems Through Intentional Effort

The optimal collaborative work system occurs when group members are provided access to information, knowledge, and resources that allow them to participate in the design of unit-level methods for accomplishing the work and the construction of environmental support systems and enabling arrangements. The quality of the participation depends on the ability of group members to establish relationships with other individuals and groups so that decision making (formal authorization, empowerment) and accountability (structure) are clearly communicated and mutually understood within the context of support systems and enabling structures.

Individuals who are experienced in establishing collaborative work groups often have the ability to organize quickly and create rules and norms that support their work with minimal effort. Those without experience benefit from education, training, and procedures for incremental acceptance of authority and accountability and examples of activities or steps that have been associated with successful creation of collaborative work systems. Everyone benefits by having a shared approach for the expansion of collaborative work systems throughout an organization. All individuals and groups that experience the process of developing collaborative practices and who are supported by collaborative work systems share in personal and organizational learning that leads to higher levels of personal and organizational maturity.

There is no universal template for creating collaborative work groups and systems, but research into the experiences of other organizations (information about practices that have been successful as well as strategies that have failed to produce satisfactory results), knowledge about human behavior, and logical and creative problem solving contribute to minimizing pitfalls as well as increasing the probability and benefits of success. The purpose of this workbook is to bring together information and examples of steps that lead to higher levels of collaboration at any and every level of an organization. It is not a set of recipes, but a set of principles and suggestions intended to help navigate through the uncertainties of organizational change.

Types of Collaborative Work Systems

In this section, we will share our definitions of types of CWSs at the organization or site level. Please note that this is only one way to define organization types; many others have created alternate definitions.

Figure 2.1 depicts organization types as a function of use of formal and informal collaboration practices. Formal forms include temporary or permanent teams, single or multifunction teams, co-located or distributed teams, and cross-functional or function-specific teams. Informal forms include communities of practice, learning communities, and the "water cooler." Both formal and informal forms depend on structural support and cultural changes, but perhaps to different extents. Ideally, an

Figure 2.1. Formal and Informal Organization Types

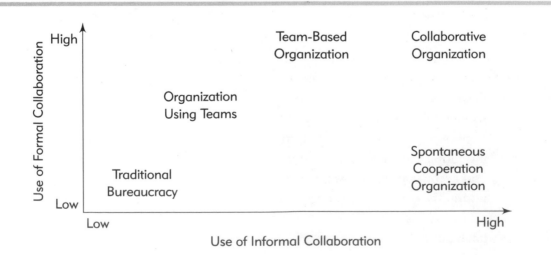

organization promotes both formal and informal forms (see Chapter 13 for more on types of collaborative structures), becoming what we call a collaborative organization. Each of the organization types in the framework is described briefly in Table 2.1. See Figure 2.2 for visual representations.

Table 2.1. Brief Descriptions of Organization Types

Type	Description
Traditional Bureaucracy	• No teams at any level • Norms, rules, and procedures inhibit informal collaboration (for example, discussing problems over the water cooler is seen as wasting time and is punishable by the rules) • Focus of systems (for example, rewards and compensation, performance management) is on the individual • Individuals are usually organized in functions (for example, engineering, production) • High level of hierarchy in reporting structure
Organization Using Teams	• Some teams used, but only at the worker level • Norms, rules, and procedures inhibit informal collaboration • Focus of systems is on the individual • Individuals are usually organized in functions • Medium to high level of hierarchy in reporting structure
Spontaneous Cooperation Organization	• Few to no teams used at any level • Norms, rules, and procedures support informal collaboration (for example, a norm that individuals consult with each other when they need help) • Focus of systems is on the individual • Individuals are usually organized in functions • Medium to low level of hierarchy in reporting structure
Team-Based Organization	• A variety of team types are used as the basic units of accountability and work; workers and managers are organized in teams • Norms, rules, and procedures do not actively support informal collaboration • Focus of systems is on individual, team, and organization • Teams are usually organized around processes, products, services, or customers • Low level of hierarchy in reporting structure
Collaborative Organization	• A variety of team types are used as the basic units of accountability and work; workers are organized in teams; managers may or may not be organized in teams • Norms, rules, and procedures actively support informal collaboration (for example, common spaces like lounges are created and employees are encouraged to meet there to discuss issues) • Focus of systems is on individual, team, and organization • Teams and individuals are usually organized around processes, products, services, or customers • Low level of hierarchy in reporting structure

Figure 2.2.   Visual Representations of Organization Types

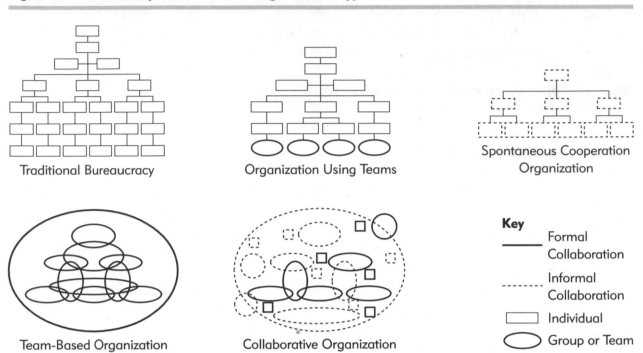

Traditional Bureaucracy   Organization Using Teams   Spontaneous Cooperation
                                                                              Organization

Team-Based Organization   Collaborative Organization

Key
———— Formal
        Collaboration

- - - - Informal
          Collaboration

☐ Individual

◯ Group or Team

Please note that there are other organization types that fall in the white spaces of Figure 2.1. For the sake of simplicity, the types with the most contrasts are shown. Your organization may fall somewhere between these types.

Activity: Understand Different Types of Collaboration

Time Requirement: Approximately 1 hour

Supplies: String, sewing needle, sharpened pencil, sewing thread, dime, roll of masking tape

Overview: This simulation is designed to create understanding about different types of collaboration—no collaboration, informal collaboration, and formal collaboration. Understanding different types of collaboration will help provide insight into the different organization types.

Instructions

1. Prepare for the activity. Designate a facilitator (a CLT member or an outside facilitator) to lead the exercise. Cut string into lengths of 8 feet, one for each participant. Tie knots at each end to prevent fraying. Insert the sewing needle straight down into the top of the sharpened pencil. Cut the sewing thread into one length of about 6 to 8 inches. Thread one end of the sewing thread through the eye of the needle. Tie each end of the sewing thread to the roll of masking tape so the pencil is suspended like a plumb line.

2. Getting started. Give each participant a length of string. Have participants loop their string through the roll of masking tape (the "ring") and hold it at full length, one end in each hand.

3. With the group surrounding the ring, have individuals try different actions and movements. For example, have one participant pull hard on both ends or on one of the ends; have a participant let his or her string go slack. Try having them close their eyes and move the strings, feeling the forces at play.

4. Now have them swap one of their strings with the person on their left, so they have one hand on their own string and one on another's. Repeat various movements and actions to feel the interdependence.

5. Create a simulation where the group has to work together to achieve a goal. For each of the rounds listed below, the task remains the same. Place a dime on the floor somewhere near the group. Placing the pencil point directly on the dime becomes the goal of the group. As the rounds progress, you may want to make the goal more challenging by moving the dime to a corner of the room.

   - Round 1: No collaboration. Ask for a volunteer. Tell the volunteer that he or she is now the leader of the group. The leader is responsible for getting the group to accomplish the goal of placing the pencil point directly on the dime. Other participants are not allowed to talk or communicate in any way.

   - Round 2: Informal collaboration. No leader is appointed. The group is allowed to communicate in any way they desire. The goal remains the same.

   - Round 3: Formal collaboration. Before the activity, ask the group to take 10 minutes to develop a plan for best accomplishing their goal. Encourage them to discuss what they have learned through the previous round, brainstorm methods to accomplish the goal, then finally agree on a solution. Conduct the activity with the same goal as before.

6. Explain that round 1 was intended to simulate a "no collaboration" situation, round 2 was "informal collaboration," and round 3 was "formal collaboration." Then use the following questions to debrief the exercise.

   - What are some of your observations about round 1? What was it like for the participants? What was it like for the leader? What parallels can you draw between this round and your organization?

   - What are some of your observations about round 2? What was it like not having a leader? Was round 2 easier or more difficult than round 1? Why? What parallels can you draw between this round and your organization?

   - What are some of your observations about round 3? What happened during the planning session? What happened during the activity? Did the planning session help or hinder goal achievement? What parallels can you draw between this round and your organization?

   - Which of the rounds was most like your organization now?

   - Which of the rounds was most like your ideal organization?

   - What learnings did you gain that relate to how your group works together?

   - What learnings did you gain that relate to how your organization works?

7. Capture the learnings and keep them in mind as you work on planning the CWS initiative.

Understand the Current Organization

There are a variety of design criteria that can be used to distinguish among organization types. Table 2.2 shows how the organization design criteria relate to the organization types.

As you begin or refresh your CWS initiative, it is important to determine where the organization is now and to start from that point. That can take some frank and honest self-appraisal. What are the strengths and weaknesses? Where are the opportunities and hurdles? What is a realistic time frame for achieving the vision, given these circumstances? (For more on this, see the Guiding Assessment in Chapter 3.) The next assessment helps determine the organization type that most closely resembles your current organization.

Assessment: Identify Current Organization Type

Time Requirement: Approximately 1 hour

Supplies: Assessment 2.1, flip chart, markers, transparency of Table 2.2 and projector or reproduction of Table 2.2 on flip chart, and colored dot stickers (all in one color)

Overview: Using the organization design criteria in Table 2.2 as your guide, determine which organization type most accurately represents your current organization.

Instructions

1. As a group, complete Assessment 2.1 using your current organization as the reference. If possible, try to circle only one answer, but if more than one answer truly applies, it is acceptable to circle more than one. List examples that support your answers. Please note, there are no "right" answers; this is simply meant as a discussion tool. Modify your answers from the current categories if necessary.

2. Transfer your answers from Assessment 2.1 to your reproduction of Table 2.2. For the flip chart option, place a colored dot in the cell or cells that best represent your answer. For the overhead transparency, indicate the cell or cell with a transparency pen.

3. Look at how the colored dots or marks cluster in Table 2.2. Which organization type has the most dots?

4. Given your answers, which organization type most closely represents your current organization?

Select the Collaborative Work System Target

Now that you have identified the CWS type closest to your current organization, it is time to think about the CWS target. Major change initiatives are major challenges. It is tempting to minimize awareness of the scope, challenge, and risk, so the anxiety of being overwhelmed doesn't emerge, but it is important to achieve and maintain a realistic view.

Identify the Next Step of the Evolution

There is no one right answer to the question of most effective organization design. Not every organization should strive to be a collaborative organization. Instead, it depends on the circumstances of the organization. Different designs fit different situations. Find the point that fits for your organization. Use the planning tool in the next section to start identifying that desired point in the evolution.

Ask, "Are the resources, skills, knowledge, and support available or developable for the organization to create and sustain the desired CWS target?" If the answer is no, attention should be redirected to what is appropriate for now. That may be readiness work—assessing the state of readiness of the organization for allocating attention and resources to the CWS initiative.

Work Closely with Key Decision Makers

Selecting the CWS target sets the high-level scope of the CWS initiative. Work closely with key decision makers for approval to start defining that scope.

Planning: Determine Collaborative Work System Target

Time Requirement: Approximately 1 hour

Supplies: Transparency or flip chart page used in "identify current organization type" assessment, overhead and transparency pens or flip chart and markers, colored dot stickers (in a different color than was used for the previous activity)

Overview: Use this planning activity to begin to identify your collaborative work system target and to start defining design goals for your CWS initiative.

Instructions

1. Look back at the transparency or flip chart page used in the "identify current organization type" assessment. Now use a different color dot or transparency pen to indicate your preferences for each criteria for your *ideal* level of collaboration.

2. Look at how the colored dots or marks representing the ideal level of collaboration cluster in Table 2.2. Which organization type has the most dots?

3. Given your answers, which organization type most closely represents your ideal organization?

4. Review your results with key decision makers in the organization to determine the scope of the CWS initiative.

Conclusion

The key question for this chapter is, "What are the different types of collaborative work systems?" A collaborative work system occurs any time collaboration takes place, but intentional focus on CWS results in more effective collaboration. This

Table 2.2. Design Criteria for Organizational Types

Design Criteria	Type of Organization				
	Traditional Bureaucracy	**Organization Using Teams**	**Spontaneous Cooperation Organization**	**Team-Based Organization**	**Collaborative Organization**
Type of work supported	Simple, routine	Moderately complex, moderately non-routine	Moderately complex, moderately non-routine	Complex, non-routine	Complex, non-routine
Appropriate environment	Slow change, local, certain	Medium change, moderate global, moderate uncertainty	Medium change, moderate global, moderate uncertainty	Fast change, global and local, uncertain	Fast change, global and local, uncertain
Levels of hierarchy	High	Medium	Medium	Low	Low
Use of formal collaborative structures	Low	High	Low	High	High
Use of informal collaborative structures	None	None	High	Medium	High
Unit of accountability	Individual	Individual and team	Individual	Team, individual, and organization	Team, individual, and organization
How managers are organized	Individuals	Individuals	Individuals	Teams	Individuals or teams
Organization design supports	Individual	Individual	Informal collaboration	Both formal and informal collaboration, leaning more toward formal	Both formal and informal collaboration
Integration costs*	Low	Medium	Medium	High	Very high
Potential collaborative results*	Low	Medium	Medium	High	Very high

*Integration costs refer to the time, money, and other resources needed to effectively integrate for collaboration. Integration does not just magically occur; it takes a lot of effort. However, the more that is spent on integration, the greater are the potential collaborative results.

Assessment 2.1. Description of Current Organization

Design Criteria	Current Organization	Example
Type of work	Simple Complex	
	Routine Non-Routine	
Environment	*Change* Slow Medium Fast	
	Local Global	
	Certain Uncertain	
Levels of hierarchy	Low Medium High	
Use of formal collaborative structures	Low Medium High	
Use of informal collaborative structures	Low Medium High	
Unit of accountability	Individual Team Organization	
How managers are organized	Individual Team	
Organization design supports	Individual Informal Collaboration Formal Collaboration	

chapter focuses on types of CWS at the organization level as a function of formal and informal collaboration, including traditional bureaucracy, organization using teams, spontaneous cooperation organization, team-based organization, and collaborative organization. Discussing the current type and ideal type with key decision makers until approval is gained garners their support for the CWS initiative.

Keys to the Chapter

- Collaboration is the collective work of two or more individuals where the work is undertaken with a sense of shared purpose and direction that is attentive, responsive, and adaptive to the environment.

- Intentional focus on CWS helps bring down the barriers to natural collaboration that organizations tend to create unintentionally.

- The goal of CWS is individuals and groups effectively working together to achieve strategic goals.

- Identifying your current organization type sets a baseline for the CWS initiative.

- The appropriate CWS type target depends on the situation of the organization. Find the point that fits for your organization.

- Work closely with key decision makers for approval to start defining the scope of change required in the CWS initiative.

Chapter Wrap-Up

- What ideas did this chapter trigger for you and your group? List them in the action planning worksheet at the end of this chapter.

- Review the ideas list. Which of these do you want to implement? List the action item, person or group responsible, and target due dates in the action planning worksheet.

- Were any significant decisions made? Include them at the bottom of the action planning worksheet.

- How can you communicate the pertinent material generated by your work on this chapter to different audiences? Discuss and consider adding action items based on your discussion.

- How can you use the resources list for additional help?

- What can you do tomorrow or within the next week based on what you learned in this chapter? Have each person share what he or she will do, and be sure to follow up.

- What is your biggest learning from this chapter? Ask each person to share. This is a nice way to end the session. Include any resulting ideas or action items in the action planning worksheet.

Resources

Beyerlein, M. (Ed.). (2002). *Work teams: Past, present, and future.* Hingham, MA: Kluwer.

Beyerlein, M., Freedman, S., McGee, C., & Moran, L. (Eds.). (2002). *Beyond teams: Building the collaborative organization.* San Francisco: Jossey-Bass/Pfeiffer.

Beyerlein, M., & Johnson, D. (Eds.). (1994). *Advances in interdisciplinary studies of work teams: Vol. 1. Theories of self-managing work teams.* Greenwich, CT: JAI Press.

Beyerlein, M., Johnson, D., & Beyerlein, S. (Eds.). (2003). *Advances in interdisciplinary studies of work teams: Vol. 9. Team-based organizing.* London: Elsevier Science.

Harris, C., & Beyerlein, M. (2003). Team-based organization: Creating an environment for team success. In M. West, K. Smith, & D. Tjosvold (Eds.), *International handbook of organisational teamwork and cooperative working* (pp. 187–209). West Sussex, England: Wiley.

Lawler, E. E., III. (1996). *From the ground up: Six principles for building the new logic corporation.* San Francisco: Jossey-Bass.

Lawler, E. E., III, Mohrman, S. A., & Ledford, G. E., Jr. (1998). *Strategies for high performance organizations—the CEO report: Employee involvement, TQM, and reengineering programs in Fortune 1000 corporations.* San Francisco: Jossey-Bass.

Lytle, W. O. (1998). *Designing a high-performance organization: A guide to the whole-systems approach.* Clark, NJ: Block Petrella Weisbord.

Miles, R. E., Coleman, H. J., Jr., & Creed, W. E. (1995). Keys to success in corporate redesign. *California Management Review, 37,* 128–145.

Mohrman, S. A., Cohen, S. G., & Mohrman, A. M., Jr. (1995). *Designing team-based organizations: New forms for knowledge work.* San Francisco: Jossey-Bass.

Orsburn, J. D., & Moran, L. (2000). *The new self-directed work teams: Mastering the challenge.* (2nd ed.). New York: McGraw-Hill.

Pasmore, W. A. (1988). *Designing effective organizations: The sociotechnical systems perspective.* Hoboken, NJ: Wiley.

Purser, R. E., & Cabana, S. (1998). *The self-managing organization: How leading companies are transforming the work of teams for real impact.* New York: The Free Press.

Ray, D., & Bronstein, H. (1995). *Teaming up: Making the transition to a self-directed, team-based organization.* New York: McGraw-Hill.

Action Planning and Summary Sheet

Ideas Generated from This Chapter

1	
2	
3	
4	
5	

#	Action Item	Target Date	Person/Group Responsible
1			
2			
3			
4			
5			
6			

Significant Decisions Made

1	
2	
3	
4	

Start with the Guiding Assessment

?

Key Question of This Chapter

How can we learn about the strategic design process and apply it to our organization?

Quick Look

Overview

This chapter reviews the strategic design process, defined by critical success factors for collaborative work systems, which is the framework for this workbook. The two parts of the strategic design process are (I) create a foundation for change and (II) align the organization for collaboration. The outcomes of this chapter include completion of the Guiding Assessment, an understanding of the appropriate order in which to use the rest of this workbook for your CWS initiative, and a list of the factors supporting or hindering your initiative.

Chapter Plan

Topic	![ABC]	![people]	![magnifier]	![clipboard]
The Strategic Design Process and Guiding Assessment	✓			
Part I: Create a Foundation for Change	✓		✓	
Part II: Align the Organization for Collaboration	✓		✓	
Summarize the Pressures For and Against Change	✓			✓

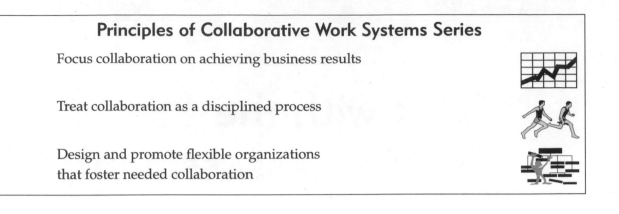

Principles of Collaborative Work Systems Series

Focus collaboration on achieving business results

Treat collaboration as a disciplined process

Design and promote flexible organizations
that foster needed collaboration

The Strategic Design Process and Guiding Assessment

Creating and improving collaborative work systems requires an ongoing strategic approach to design and implementation. A strategic approach to design provides a framework for intelligent decision making on a large scale and sets the stage for effective implementation. The workbook provides a map and a process so the adventure will be more manageable and result in more successes.

What Is the Strategic Design Process?

The strategic design process is a way of systematically looking at both the process and the content of the change required for a successful CWS initiative. In this workbook, we provide a framework for you to think about the strategic design process in the form of critical success factors for CWSs. These critical success factors were identified through years of research and experience by the authors. There are two parts of the strategic design process:

Part I: Create a foundation for change. This section examines the "process" of organizational change. We believe that the process of change is just as or more important than the content of change. Any change effort, the CWS initiative in particular, must have a strong foundation.

Part II: Align the organization for collaboration. This section examines the "content" of the organizational change. Redesigning the framework of the organization to support collaboration should improve both business and people results.

The Guiding Assessment

- Measures the two parts of the strategic design process
- Allows you to assess the critical success factors in your organization
- Looks at the gap between the organization's current state and ideal level of collaboration
- Identifies areas that need improvement
- Is a tailored, not prescriptive, approach; you decide how much of each CSF you need

Part I: Create a Foundation for Change

Figure 3.1, part of our organizing model (see Figure 1.1), illustrates the first part of the strategic design process, create a foundation for change.

Each of the critical success factors acts as a brick in the foundation. If any brick is weak, the foundation will crumble and sacrifice the integrity of the entire structure. Each of the critical success factor (CSF) "bricks" in Part I is reviewed in Table 3.1.

The Guiding Assessment: Part I

Time Requirement: For steps 1 through 3, time depends on your method of completion (see Table 3.2); 30 minutes per round for step 4; 1 hour for step 5

Supplies: Assessment 3.1, flip chart, and markers

Overview: Use the Guiding Assessment to rate your current and ideal organization on the critical success factors that comprise the CWS design model. The results should be a better understanding of CWS concepts, a baseline measurement of your current organization, a target for the ideal level of CWS, and awareness of improvement needs to meet that target. Later in this chapter, the Guiding Assessment will be further analyzed, resulting in greater understanding and a prioritized list of chapters to address in this workbook.

Instructions

1. Choose the appropriate method for completing the Guiding Assessment. Methods and pros and cons for each are listed in Table 3.2.

2. Complete Part I of the Guiding Assessment (Assessment 3.1). To complete the tool and compile the data online, go to www.workteams.unt.edu/assessment.htm.

   - For each item, assess the extent to which that item is true in your organization. Use a circle to indicate where your organization is now. Be as honest in your rating as possible, as this establishes a measure of your current organization and will help identify areas where change is needed. Especially if you are just starting or early in your CWS initiative, you may have low ratings.

   - Review the items again. This time, use a square to indicate where your organization would like to be at the highest level of CWS. Rate these items carefully. You may have an urge to select "5" each time, which is fine, as the gap between the two ratings is the most important indicator, but really think through whether you need a "5" in that item in your organization.

3. Compile the data. This can be done by an outside facilitator if one is involved. Otherwise, one of the CLT members can serve in this role.

   - This step is best completed ahead of time, if possible. You can compile individual results, group results, or both, as determined by your method selection in step 1.

   - Tally subscores for each symbol under each CSF.

   - Complete the gap score column (column 4) of Assessment 3.1.

Figure 3.1.   Create a Foundation for Change

Apply Effective Change Principles	Build the Business Case	Identify Needs and Assess Progress
Launch the Change Leadership Team	Charter the Change Leadership Team	Think Strategically About Change

Table 3.1.   Critical Success Factors for Part I: Create a Foundation for Change

#	Critical Success Factor	Overview	Chapter
1	*Launch the change leadership team (CLT)*	The change leadership team is a representative group of individuals responsible for planning and leading the CWS initiative. The CWS initiative is so big that it needs a team to provide adequate range of perspectives and resources for getting it done.	4
2	*Charter the change leadership team*	The charter documents the CLT's guidelines for working together and interfacing with the rest of the organization. The process of chartering builds the team's maturity, which significantly influences the effectiveness of the CWS initiative.	5
3	*Think strategically about change*	A well-planned CWS initiative covers extensive change activities and a long time frame. The planning for such large-scope work requires a strategic framework for framing tactical action, so all aspects of the initiative are aligned with each other and with the business strategy. This chapter provides guidelines and tools for such planning.	6
4	*Apply effective change principles*	Effective change principles represent tested methods of change. Success of the CWS initiative is relative to the extent that effective change principles are applied.	7
5	*Build the business case*	The business case articulates the rationale for the investment in the CWS initiative in terms of business results. Building the business case, including defining what success looks like and putting it in the organization's language, is essential for gaining the commitment of stakeholders in the CWS initiative.	8
6	*Identify needs and assess progress*	Integrate the results of observation, interviews, surveys, and so forth, into an ongoing system of assessment to support the CWS initiative. Assessment builds momentum across the organization for the CWS initiative, gives feedback that helps provide focus on the CWS goal state, renews top management support, identifies when milestones are achieved so short-term successes can be celebrated, and provides an organization-wide perspective needed for creating and implementing the CWS initiative.	9

Table 3.2. Methods for Completing Guiding Assessments

Method	Pros	Cons
Each person completes the Guiding Assessment	• Each person creates their own snapshot of the organization • Very quick and easy	• Results are biased to the viewpoint of the one person completing it • Results are only meaningful to the person completing it
Group members complete the tool individually, then average the results of the group	• Produces an estimate of the group's perception of the situation • Reveals individual differences in member perceptions	• Little discussion as a group to come up with one consensus answer
Work as a group to develop consensus on each item	• If handled correctly, thoughtful discussion creates deeper understanding than averaging results of individuals	• Developing consensus takes considerable time • Individual differences from members who are less vocal or less willing to share in a group setting may be lost
Give the Guiding Assessment to others in the organization (for example, different levels such as managers, workers, different functions) and compile results to look at differences between perceptions of groups	• Better understanding of the perceptions of others in the organization leads to richer data for the process • Can compare and contrast perceptions of different groups for better understanding of specific change needs	• Items may not be clear to those not working on the CWS initiative • If used, education and explanation of items is warranted • Time and effort are needed to coordinate implementation of assessment with others • Time needed from everyone to complete the assessment may be difficult to obtain

4. Assign small groups to discuss each CSF. Use Worksheet 3.1.

   • Assign one or more CSFs to each small group. Have each small group complete Worksheet 3.1 for the assigned CSF(s).

   • For more information on each item, see the section of this workbook indicated in the rightmost column of Assessment 3.1.

   • Ensure that each group assigns a scribe to capture the discussion. Ask each small group to record its findings on a flip chart to facilitate the whole-group discussion.

5. Review small-group results with the whole group. Each small group should take a turn reviewing its results. Reproduce Worksheet 3.1 on a flip chart to capture the discussion. Encourage the entire group to take notes during the discussion. Encourage clarifying questions.

Assessment 3.1. Guiding Assessment: Create a Foundation for Change

CSF #1: Launch the Change Leadership Team

Mark current state with a circle and desired state with a square.

#	Item	Low　　　　　High	□ – ○	Workbook Pages
1-1	Key decision makers, key constituents, and members of the areas undergoing change are represented in the membership of the CLT.	1　2　3　4　5		62, 63, 65
1-2	CLT members understand their roles and responsibilities in the CWS effort.	1　2　3　4　5		62, 65, 73
1-3	The CLT exhibits the team attributes that are expected from other teams in the organization.	1　2　3　4　5		62, 67, 68, 71, 73, 75
1-4	The CLT membership has the knowledge, skills, and abilities needed to effectively lead the CWS effort (for example, knowledge of the business, knowledge of CWSs, ability to coach and mentor).	1　2　3　4　5		63, 73, 75
1-5	The CLT improves its capability through developmental opportunities and by supplementing with outside resources.	1　2　3　4　5		73, 75
1-6	The CLT works with others in the organization to implement plans instead of relying solely on its membership to make it happen.	1　2　3　4　5		81, 98
1-7	The CLT has effective meetings.	1　2　3　4　5		78, 79, 81
1-8	The CLT uses facilitators to help keep meetings on track or provide advice.	1　2　3　4　5		81

○ Raw Subscore CSF #1 =　　　　　　　　□ Raw Subscore CSF #1 =

CSF #2: Charter the Change Leadership Team

Mark current state with a circle and desired state with a square.

#	Item	Low　　　　　High	□ – ○	Workbook Pages
2-1	The CLT has a charter that guides its efforts and is supported by all members.	1　2　3　4　5		89, 117
2-2	The CLT has an explicit set of values and a code of conduct to guide its functioning.	1　2　3　4　5		94, 98, 99, 100
2-3	The CLT charter is periodically reviewed and modified as needed.	1　2　3　4　5		113, 117
2-4	The CLT has a clear, shared vision and mission.	1　2　3　4　5		90, 107, 108
2-5	The CLT has clear goals, measures of those goals, and action plans for achieving those goals, which are reviewed frequently.	1　2　3　4　5		110, 111, 113, 117

Assessment 3.1. (continued)

#	Item	Low High	☐ – ◯	Workbook Pages
2-6	The CLT has an effective relationship with the top management team and a strong sponsor.	1 2 3 4 5		90, 100, 101
2-7	The CLT has a clear decision-making process and a method for escalating decisions that are beyond its control to the appropriate decision maker.	1 2 3 4 5		96, 117
2-8	The CLT understands the expectations of the stakeholders in the CWS initiative (top management, employees, customers, suppliers, regulators, and so on).	1 2 3 4 5		101, 105

◯ Raw Subscore CSF #2 = ☐ Raw Subscore CSF #2 =

CSF #3: Think Strategically About Change

Mark current state with a circle and desired state with a square.

#	Item	Low High	☐ – ◯	Workbook Pages
3-1	The CLT finds and manages the resources needed to support the CWS initiative.	1 2 3 4 5		126
3-2	The CLT has a big picture, long-term view of the CWS initiative but manages milestone to milestone.	1 2 3 4 5		125, 129, 134, 135, 137
3-3	The CLT identifies and manages the scope of the CWS initiative.	1 2 3 4 5		126
3-4	The CWS initiative is aligned with the business strategy of the organization.	1 2 3 4 5		125, 126, 133
3-5	The CLT uses its diversity to create a comprehensive framework for CWS implementation.	1 2 3 4 5		128, 138
3-6	CLT members understand the reasons for the change and communicate them to all stakeholders.	1 2 3 4 5		90, 107, 108, 126
3-7	The CLT communicates to all stakeholders its vision of how the organization will look when the CWS initiative is successful.	1 2 3 4 5		90, 107, 108, 126, 134, 135, 137
3-8	The CLT takes a deliberate and disciplined approach to planning the CWS initiative.	1 2 3 4 5		127, 138

◯ Raw Subscore CSF #3 = ☐ Raw Subscore CSF #3 =

(continued)

Assessment 3.1.   Guiding Assessment: Create a Foundation for Change (continued)

CSF #4: Apply Effective Change Principles

Mark current state with a circle and desired state with a square.

#	Item	Low High	□ – ○	Workbook Pages
4-1	The CWS change plan is designed to minimally interfere with daily operations.	1 2 3 4 5		151, 161
4-2	CLT members have change management skills and experiences.	1 2 3 4 5		147, 148
4-3	The effort to increase collaboration is integrated with other change initiatives.	1 2 3 4 5		151, 159, 161
4-4	The CLT conducted a readiness assessment to gauge the organization's initial collaboration level.	1 2 3 4 5		150, 151, Chapters 3 and 9
4-5	The CLT involves the people who will be affected by the change in the planning of the CWS effort.	1 2 3 4 5		151
4-6	The CLT plans for and deals with resistance to change.	1 2 3 4 5		151, 157, 159
4-7	The CLT takes a "big picture" approach to planning and avoids overspecifying the details.	1 2 3 4 5		151, 157
4-8	The CLT generates short-term successes and builds on them for future success.	1 2 3 4 5		151, 153, 154

○ Raw Subscore CSF #4 =   □ Raw Subscore CSF #4 =

CSF #5: Build the Business Case

Mark current state with a circle and desired state with a square.

#	Item	Low High	□ – ○	Workbook Pages
5-1	The CLT builds the business case for change.	1 2 3 4 5		170
5-2	The scope of the business case for change matches the scope of the change initiative.	1 2 3 4 5		171, 177
5-3	The CWS initiative makes business sense.	1 2 3 4 5		170, 173, 177
5-4	The CLT works closely with its sponsor to ensure support of the CWS initiative.	1 2 3 4 5		170, 179
5-5	The CLT periodically presents the business case and plan to the top management team to gain approval for the CWS initiative and commitment of the necessary resources.	1 2 3 4 5		170, 179, 180

Assessment 3.1. (continued)

#	Item	Low High	□ – ○	Workbook Pages
5-6	The business case presents a compelling reason for the CWS change effort that appeals to all levels of the organization.	1 2 3 4 5		173, 177
5-7	The business case for the CWS initiative provides a cost/benefit analysis that includes intangible benefits.	1 2 3 4 5		174, 177
5-8	The business case for the CWS initiative identifies alternatives for improving the organization other than a CWS.	1 2 3 4 5		174, 177

○ Raw Subscore CSF #5 =   □ Raw Subscore CSF #5 =

CSF #6: Identify Needs and Assess Progress

Mark current state with a circle and desired state with a square.

#	Item	Low High	□ – ○	Workbook Pages
6-1	The CLT has clear and measurable expected outcomes for the CWS initiative.	1 2 3 4 5		186
6-2	The CLT tracks the progress of the CWS initiative and identifies further needs for change.	1 2 3 4 5		186
6-3	The CLT uses ethical assessment principles (voluntary participation, anonymity) to ensure trust and accuracy of information.	1 2 3 4 5		200
6-4	The CLT works to make sure that assessment results are accurate before using them.	1 2 3 4 5		188
6-5	Collaboration is assessed at the team/group level.	1 2 3 4 5		193, 196
6-6	Collaboration is assessed at the organization level.	1 2 3 4 5		190, 193, 196
6-7	Within-team and between-team assessments are combined to get a picture of the whole organization's collaborative capability.	1 2 3 4 5		191, 193, 196, 198
6-8	The results of assessment are shared with the people who were assessed.	1 2 3 4 5		201

○ Raw Subscore CSF #6 =   □ Raw Subscore CSF #6 =

Worksheet 3.1.   Guiding Assessment Small-Group Discussion Sheet

Critical Success Factor Being Discussed: _____

What are the two or three items you should address first? List them in the table below.
(Look at the gap scores and use your own knowledge to decide.)

In your small group, discuss the items you have chosen. Fill in the boxes below.

Item #	Why Is It Important?	Ideas for Addressing It

Part II: Align the Organization for Collaboration
What Is Alignment?

- Alignment is the foundation for successful CWSs.

- Alignment is the process of adjusting parts so that they are in proper relative position. Different parts of organizations may seem to go in different directions, but should be aligned for organizational success.

- Like an ecosystem (for example, the rainforest), in the organization there is interdependence between systems and levels. Alignment is a measure of how well those parts coordinate with each other.

- When all the parts are cooperating instead of conflicting, people in the organization receive consistent messages about what they are supposed to do.

- Alignment is the way strategy is put into motion, through aligning all the parts to support the strategy and by aligning all parts with each other to maximize effectiveness.

Figure 3.2 depicts the second part of our organizing model (see Figure 1.1), Align the Organization for Collaboration.

The work is in the center of the model, inside the building, because ultimately the goal of the organization is to do business, and business reasons should be the "anchor" of the CWS initiative. The environment (like the weather) is on the outside of the organization, but is vital to the success of the organization. The work and the environment are the parts of the model that are the least influenced by organizations. While the organization has

Figure 3.2. Align the Organization for Collaboration

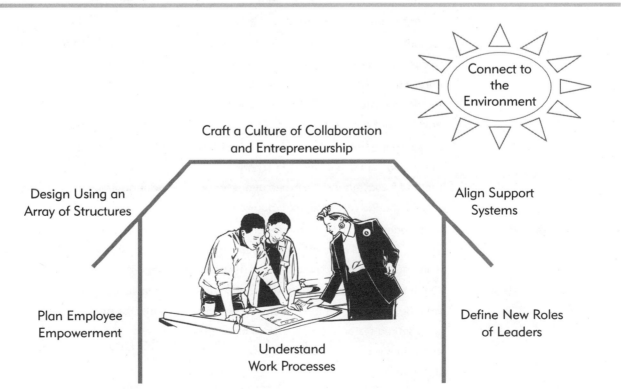

Connect to the Environment

Craft a Culture of Collaboration and Entrepreneurship

Design Using an Array of Structures

Align Support Systems

Plan Employee Empowerment

Define New Roles of Leaders

Understand Work Processes

some impact on them through work redesign and attempts to shape the environment, these pieces are somewhat given, and the organization has to deal with them.

The pieces of the organization that create the framework of the building are culture, structure, employee empowerment, leader roles, and systems. The building framework must be constructed to meet the needs of the work being done inside it and must be able to adjust to the changing demands of the weather (the environment). Each critical success factor in the model is summarized in Table 3.3.

Table 3.3. Critical Success Factors for Part II: Align the Organization for Collaboration

#	Critical Success Factor	Overview	Chapter
7	*Connect to the environment*	The environment includes the forces outside the organization, such as government regulators, competitors, customers, suppliers, and even the corporate level of the business unit or group. No matter how well the organization appears to work internally, if the environment shifts and organization does not move accordingly, success will be threatened.	10
8	*Craft a culture of collaboration and entrepreneurship*	Culture represents the way work really gets done in the organization, the shared values and assumptions of employees. Culture change is difficult and slow, but can be accomplished through changing the more tangible parts of the organization (structure, systems, employee and leader behavior). Until "the way work really gets done" supports collaboration, the CWS initiative is not a full success.	11
9	*Understand work processes*	The work encompasses the tasks, processes, and performance goals that must be achieved to accomplish the business of the organization. The work is the core of the organization; without it, the organization has no reason to exist.	12
10	*Design using an array of structures*	Organizational structure includes the way people are formally organized to carry out the work, including functional and program segments and connections. Different types of work structures (such as individuals, work teams, and project teams) are needed because the work and the environment demand it.	13
11	*Plan employee empowerment*	If you want employee behavior to change, you must lay out a plan for describing your expectations for change. An empowerment plan is a method for laying out the expectations for how behavior and tasks should change as a result of empowerment.	14
12	*Define new roles of leaders*	The leaders of the organization set the tone through their actions and words. They make important decisions that will affect the CWS initiative. Their new roles must be considered if successful change is to occur.	15
13	*Align support systems*	Organizational systems are the infrastructure created to support the work and the people doing the work in the organization. Rewards systems, goal-setting systems, and feedback mechanisms are some of the components of the infrastructure. Systems must support collaboration if true collaboration is desired.	16

The Guiding Assessment: Part II

Time Requirement: For steps 1 through 3, time depends on your method of completion (see Table 3.2); 30 minutes per round for step 4; 1 hour for step 5

Supplies: Assessment 3.2, flip charts, and markers

Overview: Use the Guiding Assessment to rate your current and ideal organization on the critical success factors that comprise the CWS design model. The results should be a better understanding of CWS concepts, a baseline measurement of your current organization, a target for the ideal level of CWS, and awareness of improvement needs to meet that target. Later in this chapter, the Guiding Assessment will be further analyzed, resulting in greater understanding and a prioritized list of chapters to address in this workbook.

Instructions

1. Choose the appropriate method for completing the Guiding Assessment. Methods and pros and cons for each are listed in Table 3.2.

2. Complete Part II of the Guiding Assessment (Assessment 3.2). To complete the tool and compile the data online, go to www.workteams.unt.edu/assessment.htm.

    *   For each item, assess the extent to which that item is true in your organization. Use a circle to indicate where your organization is now. Be as honest in your rating as possible, as this establishes a measure of your current organization and will help identify areas where change is needed. Especially if you are just starting or early in your CWS initiative, you may have low ratings.

    *   Review the items again. This time, use a square to indicate where your organization would like to be at the highest level of CWS. Rate these items carefully. You may have an urge to select "5" each time, which is fine, as the gap between the two ratings is the most important indicator, but really think through whether you need a "5" in that item in your organization.

3. Compile the data. This can be done by an outside facilitator if one is involved. Otherwise, one of the CLT members can serve in this role.

    *   This step is best done ahead of time, if possible. You can compile individual results, group results, or both, as determined by your method selection in step 1.

    *   Tally subscores for each symbol under each CSF.

    *   Complete the gap score column (column 4) of Assessment 3.2.

4. Assign small groups to discuss each CSF. Use Worksheet 3.2.

    *   Assign one or more CSFs to each small group. Have each small group complete Worksheet 3.2 for the assigned CSF(s).

    *   For more information on each item, see the section of this workbook indicated in the rightmost column of Assessment 3.1.

Assessment 3.2.   Guiding Assessment: Align the Organization for Collaboration

CSF #7: Connect the Organization to the Environment

Mark current state with a circle and desired state with a square.

#	Item	Low High	☐ – ○	Workbook Pages
7-1	Information about the organization's environment (for example, the economy, customers, new technology) is distributed to the right people to act on it.	1 2 3 4 5		214
7-2	Methods are in place to create awareness of the organization's outside environment.	1 2 3 4 5		210, 211
7-3	All members, not just top management, contribute to understanding and acting on information about the organization's environment.	1 2 3 4 5		217
7-4	The organization has processes in place to review and take necessary action on information from its environment.	1 2 3 4 5		214
7-5	Employees have open lines of communication with customers and suppliers.	1 2 3 4 5		210
7-6	Members of the organization try to anticipate changes in the organization's environment and respond proactively.	1 2 3 4 5		208, 210, 214, 218
7-7	All levels of the organization rapidly respond to work, supplier, and customer issues.	1 2 3 4 5		214
7-8	The organization quickly makes changes in response to changes in its environment.	1 2 3 4 5		208, 210, 214, 217

○ Raw Subscore CSF #7 =   ☐ Raw Subscore CSF #7 =

CSF #8: Craft a Culture of Collaboration and Entrepreneurship

Mark current state with a circle and desired state with a square.

#	Item	Low High	☐ – ○	Workbook Pages
8-1	The organization has a culture that enhances collaboration and cooperation.	1 2 3 4 5		227
8-2	Different job functions work together without disruptive conflict.	1 2 3 4 5		229
8-3	Employees feel as though they are partners in the business.	1 2 3 4 5		227, 232, 233
8-4	People in the organization want to work together to solve problems.	1 2 3 4 5		227

Assessment 3.2. (continued)

#	Item	Low — High	□ – ○	Workbook Pages
8-5	Anticipating and meeting customer needs are priorities for all employees.	1 2 3 4 5		232, 233
8-6	The culture of the organization is periodically reviewed to evaluate needs for change.	1 2 3 4 5		224, 226
8-7	A vision of the ideal culture is communicated and understood by all employees.	1 2 3 4 5		224, 233, 236, 238
8-8	The ideal organizational culture is represented in a set of values that are used to guide decision making.	1 2 3 4 5		224, 238

○ Raw Subscore CSF #8 =   □ Raw Subscore CSF #8 =

CSF #9: Understand Work Processes

Mark current state with a circle and desired state with a square.

#	Item	Low — High	□ – ○	Workbook Pages
9-1	Key work processes of the organization (tasks necessary for the business to thrive) are identified and understood.	1 2 3 4 5		246, 247
9-2	Work processes are periodically reviewed and improved.	1 2 3 4 5		248, 249, 251
9-3	Organization structure is based on an understanding of work processes and the skills and abilities needed to perform them.	1 2 3 4 5		246, 248, 249, 251, 253, 265
9-4	Teams and groups are established around interdependent work processes.	1 2 3 4 5		248, 249, 251, 253
9-5	Members are organized around whole pieces of work (processes, products, or customers) instead of segmented work with many transitions between groups or departments.	1 2 3 4 5		248, 249, 251, 253
9-6	Change initiatives have business reasons and result in improving the business.	1 2 3 4 5		246
9-7	Customer, supplier, and regulator requirements are evaluated when analyzing work processes.	1 2 3 4 5		256
9-8	Work processes are redesigned to enhance collaboration when possible.	1 2 3 4 5		252, 253

○ Raw Subscore CSF #9 =   □ Raw Subscore CSF #9 =

Assessment 3.2.   Guiding Assessment: Align the Organization for Collaboration (continued)

CSF #10: Design Using an Array of Structures

Mark current state with a circle and desired state with a square.

#	Item	Low High	□ – ○	Workbook Pages
10-1	The organization design (for example, bureaucracy, organization using teams, collaborative organization) is appropriate for the organization's situation.	1 2 3 4 5		264, 269, 270
10-2	Organization structures (for example, departments, teams, individuals, different sites) facilitate, rather than hinder, the work.	1 2 3 4 5		246, 251, 264, 265, 275
10-3	The organization uses a combination of formal collaborative structures (for example, work teams, project teams, quality improvement teams) and informal collaborative structures (for example, informal learning networks).	1 2 3 4 5		264, 269, 273, 275
10-4	Different parts of the organization are integrated to enhance communication and cooperation and limit competition.	1 2 3 4 5		269, 273, 275
10-5	The organization structure uses individuals for individual work and groups or teams for work requiring collaboration.	1 2 3 4 5		269, 273, 275
10-6	Organization structure is periodically reviewed to identify strengths and weaknesses.	1 2 3 4 5		265
10-7	Organizational realities (for example, corporate policies, union contracts, and government regulations) are taken into account when attempting to change organizational structure.	1 2 3 4 5		265, 273, 275
10-8	Well-thought-out plans are created when implementing changes in organization structure.	1 2 3 4 5		275, 279

○ Raw Subscore CSF #10 =   □ Raw Subscore CSF #10 =

Assessment 3.2.   (continued)

CSF #11: Plan Employee Empowerment

Mark current state with a circle and desired state with a square.

#	Item	Low High	□ – ○	Workbook Pages
11-1	Decisions are made at the lowest level of the organization possible.	1 2 3 4 5		288, 292
11-2	Employees have the power and freedom to manage tasks and make relevant decisions.	1 2 3 4 5		288, 292
11-3	Individuals and groups are answerable for accomplishing assigned tasks.	1 2 3 4 5		288, 292
11-4	Members have the information and skills needed for effective decisions and task completion.	1 2 3 4 5		288, 292
11-5	Leader behavior (sharing power, information, decision making) supports employee empowerment.	1 2 3 4 5		288, 292
11-6	Different groups and individuals have empowerment levels that match their skills, authority, and experience.	1 2 3 4 5		292, 294, 299
11-7	Limits on empowerment are identified, communicated, and understood.	1 2 3 4 5		292, 294, 299
11-8	Employee empowerment expectations are planned systematically and communicated so that everyone understands them.	1 2 3 4 5		294, 299

○ Raw Subscore CSF #11 =   □ Raw Subscore CSF #11 =

CSF #12: Define New Roles of Leaders

Mark current state with a circle and desired state with a square.

#	Item	Low High	□ – ○	Workbook Pages
12-1	Leaders are collaborative coaches rather than command-and-control directors.	1 2 3 4 5		308, 310
12-2	Leadership is spread to all parts of the organization, including those who are not in formal positions of power.	1 2 3 4 5		308, 313, 314
12-3	Two-way communication occurs between all levels of leadership.	1 2 3 4 5		313
12-4	Leaders understand how their roles will change over time as employees are empowered.	1 2 3 4 5		308, 313, 332, 333

(continued)

Assessment 3.2. Guiding Assessment: Align the Organization for Collaboration (continued)

#	Item	Low High	☐ – ◯	Workbook Pages
12-5	New leadership roles (such as coaches, sponsors, facilitators) are created to correspond with the empowerment of employees.	1 2 3 4 5		313, 314, 318, 328, 332, 333
12-6	The organization consciously considers how to divide up leadership responsibilities among different leadership roles.	1 2 3 4 5		318, 328, 332, 333
12-7	Roles and responsibilities of leaders are clearly defined and understood at each level of leadership.	1 2 3 4 5		314, 328
12-8	Employees have formal leadership roles (team leaders) and informal leadership roles (leading projects, making decisions).	1 2 3 4 5		313, 314, 332, 333

◯ Raw Subscore CSF #12 =   ☐ Raw Subscore CSF #12 =

CSF #13: Align Systems to Support Collaboration

Mark current state with a circle and desired state with a square.

#	Item	Low High	☐ – ◯	Workbook Pages
13-1	Organizational systems (for example, accounting, rewards, leadership, training) support collaboration and cooperation.	1 2 3 4 5		341, 349, 352, 357
13-2	The organization uses a variety of systems to support collaborative practices.	1 2 3 4 5		349, 352
13-3	Organizational systems support and reinforce employee and leader empowerment.	1 2 3 4 5		341, 355, 357
13-4	Organizational support systems do not contradict one another.	1 2 3 4 5		357, 359
13-5	Organizational support systems are continually assessed and adjusted as needed.	1 2 3 4 5		354, 360
13-6	The organization makes the most of both formal aspects (annual performance reviews) and informal aspects ("how are we doing" meetings) of support systems.	1 2 3 4 5		349
13-7	Organizational systems have appropriate individual, team/group, and organization components.	1 2 3 4 5		349
13-8	Efforts are made to change organizational systems to support collaborative practices.	1 2 3 4 5		357, 359, 360

◯ Raw Subscore CSF #13 =   ☐ Raw Subscore CSF #13 =

- Ensure that each group assigns a scribe to capture the discussion. Ask each small group to record its findings on a flip chart to facilitate the whole group discussion.

5. Review small-group results with the whole group. Each small group should take a turn reviewing its results. The facilitator may want to reproduce Worksheet 3.2 on a flip chart to capture the discussion. Encourage the entire group to take notes during the discussion. Encourage clarifying questions.

Guiding Assessment: Further Analyze Your Results

Time Requirement: Approximately 1 hour

Supplies: Compiled results of Assessments 3.1 and 3.2, Worksheet 3.3, Worksheet 3.4, Worksheet 3.5, flip chart, and markers

Overview: Further analyze Guiding Assessment results to create a big picture view of all critical success factors in the CWS design model. Use that understanding to create an ordered list of chapters to address in this workbook.

Instructions

1. Transfer the circle raw scores and square raw scores from your previous Assessments 3.1 and 3.2 to Worksheet 3.3.

2. Convert raw subscores to adjusted subscores using the chart. Divide the Raw Subscore column by the Number of Items column to determine the adjusted subscore.

3. Plot adjusted subscores on the graph in Worksheet 3.4. Use circles to plot the "where organization is now" adjusted subscores on the graph. Connect the circles with a solid line. Then use squares to plot the "where organization would like to be at highest level of CWS" adjusted subscores. Connect squares with a dotted line.

4. Discuss the graph, using the following questions.

   - Looking at your now completed Worksheet 3.4, what are the biggest gaps between where you are now and where you want to be? Why? What are your preliminary ideas for addressing those gaps?

   - What are the smallest gaps? Why? What successful ideas can you transfer from these smaller gaps and apply to the larger ones?

   - Do you agree with the results? Why or why not?

   - What can you do immediately to close the gaps?

5. Use what you have learned through the analysis to develop a plan for completing the rest of the workbook.

   - Using Worksheet 3.5, review each CSF (each of which corresponds to a workbook chapter) and determine whether that CSF/chapter needs to be addressed. Indicate yes or no in the Need to Review column.

Worksheet 3.2.   Guiding Assessment Small-Group Discussion Sheet

Critical Success Factor Being Discussed: _____

What are the two or three items you should address first? List them in the table below. (Look at the gap scores and use your own knowledge to decide.)

In your small group, discuss the items you have chosen. Fill in the boxes below.

Item #	Why Is It Important?	Ideas for Addressing It

Worksheet 3.3. Guiding Assessment Scoring Summary

CSF #	⭕ Raw Subscore	Number of Items		⭕ Adjusted Subscore	☐ Raw Subscore	Number of Items		☐ Adjusted Subscore
1		÷ 8	=			÷ 8	=	
2		÷ 8	=			÷ 8	=	
3		÷ 8	=			÷ 8	=	
4		÷ 8	=			÷ 8	=	
5		÷ 8	=			÷ 8	=	
6		÷ 8	=			÷ 8	=	
7		÷ 8	=			÷ 8	=	
8		÷ 8	=			÷ 8	=	
9		÷ 8	=			÷ 8	=	
10		÷ 8	=			÷ 8	=	
11		÷ 8	=			÷ 8	=	
12		÷ 8	=			÷ 8	=	
13		÷ 8	=			÷ 8	=	

Worksheet 3.4. Critical Success Factors Graph

○ Where Organization Is Now ☐ Where Organization Would Like to Be

Part I

Part II

Adjusted Subscore

5

4

3

2

1

#1 #2 #3 #4 #5 #6 #7 #8 #9 #10 #11 #12 #13

Critical Success Factors

Worksheet 3.5.   Chapters to Review

Critical Success Factor/Chapter	Need to Review?	Review Order
Launch the Change Leadership Team		
Charter the Change Leadership Team		
Think Strategically About Change		
Apply Effective Change Principles		
Build the Business Case		
Identify Needs and Assess Progress		
Connect to the Environment		
Craft a Culture of Collaboration and Entrepreneurship		
Understand Work Processes		
Design Using an Array of Structures		
Plan Employee Empowerment		
Define New Roles of Leaders		
Align Support Systems		

- Identify the order in which to address the chapters by ranking them in the Review Order column. Determine the order by considering the largest gaps in your Guiding Assessment, priorities that have already been determined in your discussions, and sequencing issues. Does one chapter have to come before another? The workbook order was developed to ensure flow from one chapter to the next, but it can be modified to meet the needs of your organization.

- Review Worksheet 3.5 after completing each chapter to determine where to go next and adjust the workbook plan accordingly.

Summarize the Pressures For and Against Change

What is Force-Field Analysis?

- Force-Field Analysis is a useful technique for looking at all the forces for and against a plan or decision. In effect, it is a specialized method of weighing pros and cons.

- After identifying the forces for the plan or decision, you can create a way to enhance these.

- After identifying the forces against the plan or decision, you can generate ways to reduce them to increase your chances of overall success.

Figure 3.3 shows a sample Force-Field Analysis diagram.

Figure 3.3. Force-Field Analysis

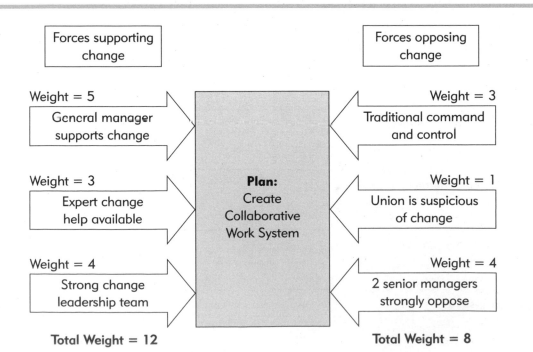

Planning: Summarize the Pressures For and Against Change

Time Requirement: Approximately 1 hour

Supplies: Flip chart, markers, masking tape

Overview: Now that you have an understanding of some of the issues involved in your CWS initiative, it is helpful to summarize these in one place so you can update it periodically and use it as a communication tool. The Force-Field Analysis will help you do this.

Instructions

1. As a group, brainstorm two lists: forces supporting change and forces against change. Go back to the notes you created previously in this chapter for ideas.

2. Create themes. Select either forces supporting or against change to do first, then repeat these steps for the other category when you are finished.

   - Number points on the brainstorming flip chart.
   - On another flip chart, brainstorm themes.
   - Go through numbered points one-by-one and put them into themes. Cross the point off when you have it listed with a theme. Add themes as appropriate.

3. Create force-field diagram. Place the supporting forces on the left side and opposing forces on the right. You may want to color code these (supporting = green, opposing = red). Follow the example in Figure 3.3.

4. Assign weights.

   - Assign a score to each force, from 1 (weak) to 5 (strong).
   - Add supporting force weights and total at the bottom. Do the same for opposing force weights. These weights provide a rough indicator of the likelihood of success of your CWS initiative.

5. Generate discussion. Use the discussion questions to get you started.

   - How can you increase positive forces?
   - How can you decrease negative forces?
   - How will you prioritize your actions to address positive and negative forces?
     - It may be easier to reduce negative than increase positive.
     - It may make sense to attack the forces with the highest ratings first.
     - Don't forget to have some small, quick successes to build momentum.
   - How will you use the force-field diagram to communicate with others?
   - How often will you revisit the force-field diagram to assess your results?

Conclusion

The key question for this chapter is, "How we learn about the strategic design process and apply it to our organization?" Users of the Guiding Assessment develop better conceptual understanding through taking the Guiding Assessment and discussing the results. Looking at the "where is your organization now" ratings provides a checkpoint in your CWS initiative and can be used later as a baseline to show your progress. The ideal level of collaboration ratings sets a target for how far you want the CWS initiative to go and provides material to share with decision makers in the organization to develop common understanding of the goals of the CWS initiative. The gap between current and ideal helps identify change needs and the order in which to address remaining chapters in this workbook. Refer back to this chapter periodically to review your progress.

Keys to the Chapter

- The strategic design process, further defined through critical success factors, is a way of systematically looking at both the process and the content of the change required for a successful CWS initiative.

- The two main sections of the strategic design process are (I) create a foundation for change and (II) align the organization for collaboration.

- The Guiding Assessment provides a way for the organization to look at its current state and envision its ideal state and then start a conversation on how to close the gap.

- The Guiding Assessment allows the organization to tailor the CWS initiative to meet its own needs.

- The Force-Field Analysis provides a summary of forces supporting and hindering the CWS initiative and can be used to communicate these.

Chapter Wrap-Up

- What ideas did this chapter trigger for you and your group? List them in the action planning worksheet at the end of this chapter.

- Review the ideas list. Which of these do you want to implement? List the action item, person or group responsible, and target due dates in the action planning worksheet.

- Were any significant decisions made? Include them at the bottom of the action planning worksheet.

- How can you communicate the pertinent material generated by your work on this chapter to different audiences? Discuss and consider adding action items based on your discussion.

- How can you use the resources list for additional help?

- What chapter should you go through next? Refer back to Guiding Assessment results for suggestions of next steps.

- What can you do tomorrow or within the next week based on what you learned in this chapter? Have each person share what he or she will do, and be sure to follow up.

- What is your biggest learning from this chapter? Ask each person to share. This is a nice way to end the session. Include any resulting ideas or action items in the action planning worksheet.

Resources

Beyerlein, M., Freedman, S., McGee, C., & Moran, L. (Eds.). (2002). *Beyond teams: Building the collaborative organization.* San Francisco: Jossey-Bass/Pfeiffer.

Beyerlein, M., & Harris, C. (2003). Critical success factors in team-based organizing: A top ten list. In M. Beyerlein, C. McGee, G. Klein, J. Nemiro, & L. Broedling (Eds.), *The collaborative work systems fieldbook: Strategies, tools, and techniques* (pp. 19–42). San Francisco: Jossey-Bass/Pfeiffer.

Beyerlein, M., McGee, C., Klein, G., Nemiro, J., & Broedling, L. (Eds.). (2003). *The collaborative work systems fieldbook: Strategies, tools, and techniques.* San Francisco: Jossey-Bass/Pfeiffer.

Forrester, R., & Drexler, A. B. (1999). A model for team-based organizational performance. *Academy of Management Executive, 13*(3), 36–49.

Gerard, R. J. (1995). Teaming up: Making the transition to a self-directed, team-based organization. *Academy of Management Executive, 9*(3), 91–93.

Harris, C., & Beyerlein, M. (2003). Navigating the team-based organizing journey. In M. Beyerlein, D. Johnson, & S. Beyerlein (Eds.), *Advances in interdisciplinary studies of work teams: Vol. 9. Team-based organizing.* (pp. 1–29). Oxford, England: Elsevier Science.

Harris, C., & Beyerlein, M. (2003). Team-based organization: Creating an environment for team success. In M. A. West, K. Smith, & D. Tjosvold (Eds.), *International handbook of organisational teamwork and cooperative working* (pp. 187–209). West Sussex, England: Wiley.

Hitchcock, D. E., & Willard, M. (1995). *Why teams fail and what you can do about it: Essential tools for anyone implementing self-directed work teams.* Chicago: Irwin Professional Publishing.

Lytle, W. O. (1998). *Designing a high-performance organization: A guide to the whole-systems approach.* Clark, NJ: Block Petrella Weisbord.

Mohrman, S. A., & Mohrman, A. M., Jr. (1997). *Designing and leading team-based organizations: A workbook for organizational self-design.* San Francisco: Jossey-Bass.

Mohrman, S. A., & Quam, K. (2000). Consulting to team-based organizations: An organizational design and learning approach. *Consulting Psychology Journal: Practice and Research, 52*(1), 20–35.

Sundstrom, E., & Associates. (1999). *Supporting work team effectiveness: Best management practices for fostering high performance.* San Francisco: Jossey-Bass.

Wageman, R. (1997). Critical success factors for creating superb self-managing teams. *Organizational Dynamics, 26*(1), 49–61.

Action Planning and Summary Sheet

Ideas Generated from This Chapter

#	
1	
2	
3	
4	
5	

#	Action Item	Target Date	Person/Group Responsible
1			
2			
3			
4			
5			
6			

Significant Decisions Made

#	
1	
2	
3	
4	

PART I

Create a Foundation for Change

IN PART I, we concentrate on creating a foundation for the collaborative work system initiative. Constructing the foundation starts with developing the change leadership team (Chapters 4 and 5), then thinking strategically about change and applying effective change principles (Chapters 6 and 7). Building the business case (Chapter 8) ensures approval from top leaders, which makes it easier to align the organization for collaboration (Part II of this workbook). Finally, using assessment to identify needs and measure progress (Chapter 9) provides the tools necessary to understand whether the goals of the CWS initiative are being met.

Key Questions in Each Chapter

Chapter	Key Question
4 Launch the Change Leadership Team	How do we organize our group so we can effectively manage the strategic change process?
5 Charter the Change Leadership Team	How will we work well together?
6 Think Strategically About Change	How should the CLT think about the CWS initiative?
7 Apply Effective Change Principles	What enables a change plan to work?
8 Build the Business Case	How can we use the business case to create support for the CWS initiative?
9 Identify Needs and Assess Progress	How can we track our progress toward the CWS initiative vision?

## CHAPTER 4

Launch the Change Leadership Team

Where Are We in the Strategic Design Process?

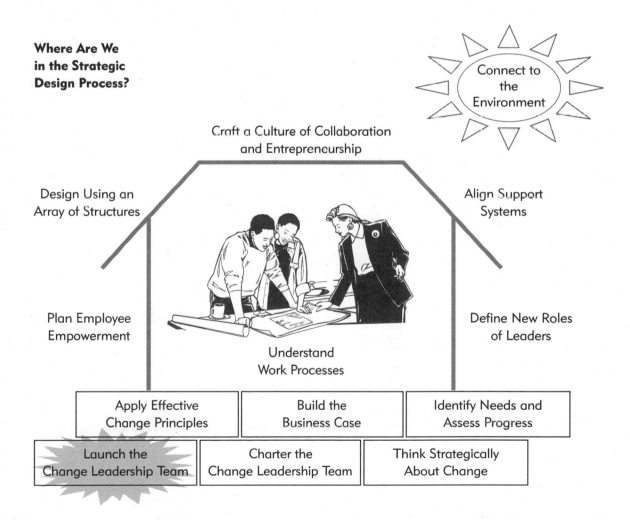

Connect to the Environment

Craft a Culture of Collaboration and Entrepreneurship

Design Using an Array of Structures

Align Support Systems

Plan Employee Empowerment

Understand Work Processes

Define New Roles of Leaders

| Apply Effective Change Principles | Build the Business Case | Identify Needs and Assess Progress |
| Launch the Change Leadership Team | Charter the Change Leadership Team | Think Strategically About Change |

Key Question of This Chapter

How do we organize our group so we can effectively manage the strategic change process?

Quick Look

Overview

The change leadership team (CLT) is the center of planning and action for the change work involved in transforming the organization to a collaborative work system. As the center of action, the CLT forms one of the cornerstones for the success of the CWS initiative. The CLT process, teamwork, and products set the stage for the initiative. The content and exercises in this chapter will aid the members of the CLT to form and develop an effective team with the unity and diversity required for changing a complex system. Setting the boundaries around the team, selecting members, building shared understanding, managing decision making, and meeting effectively are team competencies that will build an effective team process. Outcomes of the chapter include a role audit of CLT members, desirable characteristics of the CLT, team boundary management plan, competency assessment and plan, and meeting quality gap analysis.

Chapter Plan

Topic				
Launch the Change Leadership Team	✓			
Select CLT Members	✓		✓	
Build Common Understanding	✓		✓	
Manage Team Boundaries	✓			✓
Invest in Team Competencies	✓		✓	✓
Manage the Meeting Process for Productivity	✓		✓	✓

Principles of Collaborative Work Systems Series

Exploit the rhythm of divergence and convergence

Create higher standards for discussion, dialogue, and sharing of information

Treat collaboration as a disciplined process

Launch the Change Leadership Team

What Is a Real Team?

A team is a group of people who depend on each other to accomplish a goal. The complexity of a major organizational change requires a team approach. An individual cannot do it alone because of the need for broad knowledge of the organization and a wide range of competencies. A traditionally led group cannot do it well, because the group is typically dominated by the leader and a single point of view limits quality of solutions. In contrast, members of a real team interact as equals and provide mutual support to each other. Their diverse views and ideas are heard and used as input in building shared understanding, planning, and decision making. They are committed to the growth of the group and the achievement of the goal. Working effectively together, they can accomplish more and make smarter decisions.

Each exchange between team members either enables or inhibits more exchanges. For ongoing dialogue, the quality of the exchange must include listening, trust, respect, and honesty. To the extent that those are missing, caution, defensiveness, and hoarding of information reduce the richness of exchange. Openness diminishes and quality of decisions declines. It takes time for a group to establish the conditions that support high-quality exchanges.

What Is a Change Leadership Team (CLT)?

A change leadership team is a group of people coming together to lead a major change initiative:

- The membership ranges from exclusively top management to a representative mix of managers and employees to all employees.

- The mission ranges from oversight of design or project teams where the actual execution of the initiative is carried out and tailored for that local area to the CLT doing that work itself.

- The CLT oversees subgroups of the CLT and special teams of other people, such as design teams, project teams, or task teams.

The responsibilities of the CLT include:

- Functioning as a model team
- Continual learning
- Creating and implementing an appropriate strategic change plan
- Developing and utilizing a communication plan
- Determining the gap between where the organization is now and where it needs to be
- Developing an effective meeting process
- Practicing the principles of good project management and good change management
- Committing to team ownership of the CWS initiative

Select CLT Members

The members of the CLT should represent the whole organization, be able to work together, be able to learn, and be able to take some intelligent risks. Team functioning is enhanced when there is a balance of personalities, qualities, skills, positions, and expertise. The diversity of membership provides better representation of the organization and enables a more complete understanding of the challenges and resources. Moderate diversity is a balance that provides rich input but allows consensus to be reached in a timely manner. At a site with union representation, the union *must* be involved. Otherwise, the initiative is viewed as management's program being imposed on everyone else and a unified effort becomes impossible.

The characteristics of the members make a difference, but the scope of the initiative is so large that there is room for contribution from many different types of people. The talents can include social skills, self-awareness, empathy, motivation, self-control, innovation, adaptability, openness to new experiences, and optimism, as well as business and technical knowledge. Each member has many responsibilities:

- Act as a champion for developing collaborative ways of working. Walk the talk! Model the values of the initiative; use words when necessary.

- Express the enthusiasm and articulate the ideas to the people around them.

- Follow a formal socialization and education process for new team members— don't let it become haphazard.

- Involve those responsible for making the changes—the stakeholders—through either CLT membership or communications.

- Commit to the CLT and its effectiveness.

- Believe in the vision and values of the CWS initiative.

Members selected for the CLT should have the following characteristics:

- Ability to get people to listen to them, and good at listening to people

- Ability to influence their peers

- Capable of collaborating to jointly create solutions

- Open-minded enough to learn

- Hard-working

- Some sense of objectivity and of humor

Avoid selecting the following types of members:

- Know-it-alls who show off their expertise at the cost of the group's discussion

- Silent people who will not be able to learn to speak frequently and effectively about what is important in the initiative

- Fearful people who spend most of their time defending their opinions, decisions, and jobs

- Substitutes for the managers who won't commit the time to participate but want decision-making authority anyway

- Experts who believe they know all there is to know and therefore do not have to listen to the advice and counsel of others (Expertise is almost always discipline-specific, and collaborative work system development requires input from a dozen disciplines; no individual can be expert in so many.)

Author Gary Hamel (1996) stated, "Perspective is worth fifty IQ points." Seeing things in a new way has the effect of making people smarter. Hamel was writing about individuals when he said this. We believe it is even truer of teams. The team gets smarter about the organization as it learns to integrate the multiple perspectives of its members. Each member brings a different point of view to the table. Value that difference. Use it.

The points in this section may lead you to want a large team, but size can be a handicap when it is too large, as well as when it is too small. The size of the CLT should be big enough to be representative and small enough to be manageable. A maximum is probably twelve (fewer for smaller organizations) with a 50–50 mix of managers and front-line workers.

Assessment: Role Audit

Time Requirement: Approximately 1 hour

Supplies: Worksheet 4.1, flip chart, masking tape, and markers

Overview: This assessment enables the CLT to determine how well the organization is represented by its current members and what resources those members bring to the team. It will also allow CLT members to identify people who should be special targets of communication efforts.

Instructions

1. Following the model in Table 4.1, work as a team to fill in the blanks in Worksheet 4.1. Begin with column 1 and work across the table. The fourth column (asking how this person would contribute to the CLT or the CWS initiative) may be the most important.

Table 4.1. Role Audit: Partial Example

Team Member Name	Position	Department/Program	Why an Appropriate Member
RJ	Middle manager	Operations	Oversees a large number of work groups and teams and their leaders
BD	Assembly worker, day shift	Front line; VP of union local	Represents both front-line workers and the union
JF	Director	HR	Responsible for many people issues
	Support—accountant	Finance	Represents a support group but also brings expertise useful in capturing the dollar value of the CWS initiative
		Engineering	Represents a support group
(HA)	Director	Marketing	Brings expert knowledge on how to publicize the initiative and build enthusiasm for it

Worksheet 4.1.   Role Audit Worksheet

Team Member Name	Position	Department/Program	Why an Appropriate Member

2. When all of the CLT's current members are listed, shift your focus to positions and departments that are not yet represented (note the fourth and fifth entries of Table 4.1 as an example). Look for holes, to see whether another member may be required for a key connection to the organization. Add those names and circle them, to indicate that a recruiting effort is required. CLT membership now represents all key stakeholder groups.

3. Next, consider which people outside the CLT will be critical to the CWS initiative. Continue adding names until contact people in all key positions and departments have been identified. Put parentheses around those names to show that special efforts to communicate are necessary.

4. If relationships are needed with more people, create mechanisms for involving those people in other aspects of the CWS initiative, such as design teams, integration teams, liaison roles with departments and programs, and so forth, so the key people are involved but not core members of the CLT.

Build Common Understanding

Effective teams have shared understanding of what they must accomplish, how they will work together, and how they will make decisions. Time, work, and discipline go into developing the shared understanding. Without it, members work at cross-purposes—without a shared language, you will struggle to achieve a shared understanding.

As a simple experiment, silently count the number of words in this paragraph, from the first word of this sentence through the end of the word "correct" at the end of this paragraph. Write down your count. Record each team member's count on the board. Note the differences. What is the correct number of words? There are probably a number of different answers. The differences represent errors in measurement. How will you decide which of the four or five different answers is correct?

Now imagine tackling a much more difficult question, such as ranking the team leaders in the organization by competencies. Won't the results be more varied and the implications of the variance more significant than counting words? Effective use of differences demands a process that all members understand. A key issue is arriving at a common understanding of the CLT's vision and mission. Equally key mental models are the shared belief that the team is capable of doing the job—a shared faith in the team—and the shared belief that the team has an environment where it is safe to take risks. To work toward shared understanding, use activities like the following:

- *Discussion:* Talk through member roles, expectations, and team goals and how they relate to the rest of the organization until a sense of shared understanding emerges and all the members of the team can present the same story to the organization. This discussion will continue on intermittently for some weeks as the understanding of all grows.

- *Rehearsals:* Talk about situations you have run into at the worksite (such as your direct supervisor confronting you about all the time you are spending in CLT meetings and away from the job or a union member arguing with you that the CWS initiative is just another management device to get more work for less pay) and about alternate responses that might apply, then actually practice those responses so the next incident will go better. Everyone can role-play to some extent, and it gets easier with practice.

- *Learning group:* Make space in the meetings to talk about your efforts to champion the initiative. Share ideas on how to be effective as a representative of the CLT and the initiative.

Assessment: Effective Teams

Time Requirement: Approximately 90 minutes

Supplies: Worksheet 4.2, flip chart, masking tape, and markers

Overview: This exercise allows participants to identify the characteristics of the team they want to build and the commonality of their preferences. Reviewing experience in team-like settings provides a knowledge base for the team about what the members believe about team effectiveness. That base then serves as a model toward which the members can strive.

Instructions

1. Think back. You undoubtedly have been a member of a number of teams, committees, or groups over the years in such situations as work, school, community, church, volunteering, or sports. Remember the *most effective* one you belonged to. As an individual, write three phrases on Worksheet 4.2 that made that team a standout.

2. Now think back and remember the *worst team* you belonged to. As an individual, write three phrases on Worksheet 4.2 that describe why it did not function well.

3. Now compile the answers on the flip charts from all members of the CLT. On the left, write a heading for "Best" and on the right for "Worst," then list the phrases each member wrote. (This can be done anonymously by asking people to hand pieces of paper forward for the scribe to copy from, or members can take turns reading their phrases.) When a phrase is redundant, put a check mark next to it to save rewriting it.

4. Now, as a team, cluster together the phrases or ideas that fit with each other to form categories of team qualities. For example, cluster "no clear agendas" and "little participation in meetings" under the topic category "Meetings."

5. As a team, select the clusters and statements that stand out for this group as descriptions of the kind of team you want to create. Write the top eight or so on a flip chart and record them on Worksheet 4.2.

Worksheet 4.2.   Defining an Effective Team

Best Team's Characteristics

1.

2.

3.

Worst Team's Characteristics

1.

2.

3.

Our Team's Characteristics

1.

2.

3.

4.

5.

6.

7.

8.

6. Check to see if the following key points have been included and add the ones that apply:

- The right people on the team for achieving the mission
- Clarity of mission and priorities
- A habit of developing alternative courses of action
- A method for tracking progress and using the data for changes in direction
- A habit of assessing team process and making adjustments
- Members working to help each other succeed
- Effective coordination of activities
- A process that maintains and builds the confidence of the team
- Courage and skill to allow conflict around ideas and minimize it around personalities
- A careful record of decisions made and their rationale
- Voluntary participation (You can't mandate high performance! CLT members should be invited to participate.)

Table 4.2 shows an example of some possible responses for this activity.

Table 4.2. Characteristics of Teams

Best Team's Characteristics

1. Everyone feels like he or she has a voice
2. Conflict leads to better ideas rather than alienating members
3. Meetings start on time and end on time

Worst Team's Characteristics

1. Meetings are dominated by one member; others don't have a voice
2. Lack of trust means people are clammed up—no useful sharing
3. No one comes prepared to meetings

Our Team's Characteristics

1. Everyone has an equal say
2. We trust each other enough to take some risks with our ideas and opinions
3. We listen to each other
4. We have a shared understanding of our mission
5. We aren't afraid to speak up when a member violates our agreed-on norms
6. We keep our commitments to get stuff done on time
7. None of us has hidden agendas that undermine the team's process
8. We learn from each other

7. When the descriptions are complete, conduct a discussion using the following questions:

   - What does the pattern of results mean?

   - How can our team use these categories to assess our own performance? (Design a checklist or scale for periodically assessing your team using the categories.)

   - What standards will we set for ourselves based on this discussion?

Manage Team Boundaries

As the CLT evolves from being just a group of people coming together to tackle a big project toward being a real team, it becomes a self-contained system with its own processes, structure, and boundary. Managing the boundary is a key to the success of the team. The boundary determines what and who is inside the team system and who and what is outside. It contributes to the identity of the team. For example, the boundary sets limits on who can sit in meetings, so work can be done without excessive backtracking or distraction. The guidelines for that boundary maintenance activity could include a description of the process and limits on inviting guests to meetings.

Boundary Maintenance Issues

- People with position power may encroach on the team and derail its focus.
- Decisions by nonmembers may contradict or undermine the work of the team.
- Authority and empowerment from the top can clarify the boundary.
- Members of support groups, such as training and design teams that report to the CLT, may push to become CLT members, so they need clear expectations from the beginning.
- Some CLT team work should remain confidential, such as rating of team leaders or trouble between members.

Planning: Boundary Management

Time Requirement: Approximately 1 hour

Supplies: Worksheet 4.3, flip chart, masking tape, and markers

Overview: This exercise is designed to enable the team to build a plan for managing its boundary transactions. Identifying the appropriate and inappropriate flow of people, information, and demands across the team boundary can help the team cope with challenges from the environment and issues around the implementation of the CWS initiative plan.

Worksheet 4.3. Defining Team Boundaries

Boundary Issue	Action Planning
Mapping: Who supports us and who does not?	
Molding: How can we shape the beliefs and behaviors of outsiders about our team and mission?	
Coordinating and negotiating: Whose work is interdependent with ours? How can we find a balance with them?	
Filtering and buffering: When we are overwhelmed with information, especially negative information, how can we keep our team from feeling overwhelmed and losing momentum?	
Respect: How can we educate others so that they support, rather than interfere with, our work?	
Credit: How can we make our progress visible?	
Alignment: How can we coordinate activities and changes with other groups?	
In-the-know: How can we gather important information from the organization's members so that we are informed about what is needed and how things are going?	
Linking: How can we connect to the power structure without being consumed by it?	
Integrating: How can we link across the organization so that we have the big picture and address the needs of the whole organization?	
Membership: How can we take care of our members so that they remain committed to the team for the long term?	
Load: How can we limit the number of teams our members participate on, so their concentration and energy are not too diluted?	

Instructions

1. Work together as a team to answer the questions in Worksheet 4.3. Each answer should lead to concerted action by team members to maintain a boundary around the team that allows the most useful inputs and outputs.

2. Capture the key points of the discussion as six to twelve boundary management guidelines and capture the action plans that emerge in the action planning sheet at the end of this chapter.

Invest in Team Competencies

The interpersonal competencies of team members provide a foundation for effective group process. Below is a brief list of the key competencies for effective team functioning assembled from an extensive, unpublished analysis done by the Center for the Study of Work Teams:

- Communication skills
- Conflict-management skills
- Group dynamics skills (for example, understands group norms, values diversity, is self-aware)
- Group decision-making skills
- Meeting effectiveness skills
- Metrics and goal-setting skills
- General knowledge and theory of teams (and, for the CLT, knowledge of organization design and change)
- Self-leadership skills (for example, self-monitoring, self-reward, stress management)

Every member of the CLT has some capabilities in these categories, but all can learn enough to reach a higher level of expertise. The competencies needed for team leaders and for change leaders, such as the CLT members, include the above list but go beyond it. Chapter 15 includes more material on the leadership system. Leadership occurs whenever any member of the organization encourages or guides another member's behavior toward achieving strategic goals.

Assessment: Team Competency Audit

Time Requirement: Approximately 30 minutes to take and score the assessment and 30 minutes for discussion

Supplies: Worksheet 4.4, Worksheet 4.5, flip chart, masking tape, and markers

Overview: This exercise is intended to aid the team and its members in identifying where the strengths of the team lie and where special efforts at education should be made. Bundles of knowledge, skills, abilities, and attitudes are called competencies. Each of us has a large array of skills and competencies, and we vary in the

Worksheet 4.4.   Rating Sports Expertise

	Average Level for the CLT				
	Novice	**Beginner**	**Competent**	**Proficient**	**Expert**
Bowling					
Tennis					
Basketball					
Golf					
Skating					

level of expertise we have built in each. The checklist in Worksheet 4.5 asks you to rate the team on overall team competencies. There are five levels of expertise here ranging from "novice," which means that even awareness of the need to build a competency is missing, to "expert," which means true mastery and the ability to teach others. Expert level is rarely attained; it often involves many years of experience. A team with expert-level competencies in all the content and process areas would be extraordinary in its accomplishments. Most teams have a scattering of expert levels across multiple areas. No individual is expert in all areas, but some people are blind to that. Coming together as a team makes it possible to combine and leverage expertise of members across areas.

Instructions

1. To practice rating the team by levels of expertise, have participants use Worksheet 4.4 to rate athletic ability in five different sports. There should be enough diversity of expertise to illustrate that the team has a range of talent in the room. Use the following meanings for the five levels:

   - Novice: no experience, little awareness, amateurish

   - Beginner: aware, partially informed, relatively unskilled

   - Competent: deeper understanding, narrowly skilled, able to perform a few tasks without supervision, like an apprentice

   - Proficient: broadly skilled, knowledgeable in some areas, experienced and reliable, like a journeyman

   - Expert: highly proficient in a particular area and generally knowledgeable; provides leadership and crucial expert insights; mastery of a particular subject (adapted from Wiig, 1994)

2. Ask members to raise their hands to indicate what level of expertise they have for each sport and record the number of people in each box on the table. Note the pattern of skill diversity.

3. Break into small groups of three or four members. Read the list of team competencies in Worksheet 4.5. Have each group arrive at a consensus rating for each item on the worksheet and record the rating by putting an X in the appropriate box (for example, if a group thinks the team as a whole has a fair level of knowledge of the business processes, financial situation, goals, and so forth, they should check the "Competent" box in the first row).

4. Tell them to add any competencies the group thinks should be considered to the list and rate them.

5. Have each group report out to the whole team on each item. Reproduce Worksheet 4.5 on a flip chart and capture the ratings of each subgroup on the flip chart.

6. Examine and discuss the resulting profile for the team.

7. Celebrate any strong points and begin to plan for improving the team's expertise where ratings are low. Tell people not to be too concerned if individual scores are low on any of these factors. Everyone can contribute to the team. For example, a novice can ask "dumb questions" that require the team to return to fundamentals and more clearly define what is important. An expert may have a lot to contribute but become noncollaborative or learning-handicapped because of a lack of humbleness. If everyone is a novice or beginner on a team, the person with the proficient level of expertise has a lot to contribute. It's all relative. This assessment shows the team profile, the pooled expertise of the team. A half-dozen beginners effectively pooling their knowledge and expertise on content or process can boost the team level to competent or proficient. Teaming is about effective pooling—processes that enable the expertise, knowledge, and perspective of a number of individuals to be combined into a new whole.

Planning: Improving Team Competencies

Time Requirement: 45 minutes

Supplies: Completed Worksheet 4.5, Worksheet 4.6, flip chart, marking pens

Overview: This exercise builds on work done by the CLT on Worksheet 4.5, where a pattern of strengths and weaknesses for the team should have become clear. In this activity, you'll identify the weaknesses and begin to plan ways of strengthening them. When the team's competencies on one of these effectiveness factors is less than "competent," there are two options:

1. Build the competencies of the CLT through education or membership changes

2. Supplement the CLT with outside resources (for example, in-house experts, consultants, facilitators)

Instructions

1. As a team, identify the areas in Worksheet 4.5 requiring development and record them in Worksheet 4.6.

Worksheet 4.5.   Competencies Checklist

Competencies	Average Level for Team				
	Novice	Beginner	Competent	Proficient	Expert
Knowledge of the business					
Knowledge of change management					
Knowledge of group dynamics					
Knowledge of collaborative work systems					
Knowledge of organization design and change					
Group decision-making tools and processes					
Meeting effectiveness: logistics and philosophy					
Metrics and goal setting					
Knowledge of top management's goals and expectations for the collaborative work system initiative					
Knowledge of the relationship of the CWS initiative and customer needs and desires					
Self-leadership: individual and team levels					
Coaching, mentoring, and collaboration skills					
Knowledge of team chartering					
Networking capability: who you talk to about what					
Awareness of resource needs					
Skill at accessing resources					
Time management: understanding and managing time needs for a complex initiative					
Maintaining sponsorship of top management					
Integrating the voices of all stakeholders into one view of the organization and the vision					
Skill at presenting charter and progress reports to top management					
Ability to increase level of autonomy and authority so that empowerment is high enough to do the job					
Generating and managing the energy of the group for moving ahead and the belief that the team has what it takes					
Other:					
Other:					

Worksheet 4.6.   Improving Team Competencies

Competencies Needing Improvement	Action Plan for Improving	Rank

2. Create an action plan for solving the problem: either learning opportunities for the members of the CLT or inclusion of outside resources in CLT processes.

3. Work as a team to identify whether learning or inclusion will be the source of the increased expertise. Then rank-order the action plan steps, identifying where to start by putting numbers in the third column.

Note that there are trade-offs between these two types of solutions (learning or inclusion) to consider. For example, consultants cost money, sometimes a lot, but errors in planning and execution of the initiative may cost far more. It takes time to educate the CLT members, especially on so many factors, but that development pays off in every meeting and outside of meetings. The education must be ongoing, but assume it is one of the top priorities for the first eighteen months of the life of the CLT and commit the resources (time, money, study, travel, and so forth) to make it happen or settle for a mediocre plan and execution. Completion of this workbook will build many of the competencies on the list.

Manage the Meeting Process for Productivity

The mechanics of meeting management make a difference in meeting productivity. Meetings benefit from (1) established norms for meetings, (2) required attendance, (3) an agenda, (4) using mechanisms for staying on task, (5) taking minutes and sharing them, and (6) ending the meeting with a list of action steps and a brief review of the meeting process.

However, meeting process depends more on process and purpose than on mechanics. The use of formal meeting management methods like *Robert's Rules of Order* stifle process. Such methods may prevent poor performance, but they do not enable excellence. A meeting philosophy that focuses on achieving goals, giving everyone a voice, open sharing, and respect for each other sets the stage for high performance. This approach is especially true when creativity and innovation are essential for achieving goals. The ambiguity and complexity of a change project demand that the CLT use the talents and expertise of all the members. In fact, when the process enables the team to consider all relevant inputs before forging a decision, the quality of the decision is higher than any individual in the team could have made.

The First Meeting

A good portion of the first team meeting should be devoted to ensuring that members understand their charge and the standards for working together. The first meeting's agenda should follow this format:

1. Introduce team members, clarify each member's role on the team (why they are there and what they think they can contribute to the process) and explain the facilitator's and team leader's roles. If members do not understand why they are there and what roles they can play on the team, they will be reluctant to participate.

2. Develop team guidelines (also known as standards of behavior or ground rules). A team's guidelines should outline the following:

   - The team's decision-making model (that is, under what conditions to use consensus, plurality, majority vote, or other methods)

   - Behaviors encouraged by the team (for example, respect and good listening skills)

   - Team etiquette (for example, starting and finishing meetings on time). Be sure that ground rules are adhered to and that members know it's okay to "call someone on it" (politely, of course) if that person is disregarding a ground rule.

   These guidelines can move the individuals in a group from thinking in terms of "me" to "we." Guidelines also help keep the team on track, get everyone involved in the team's work, and strengthen the team's ability to discuss issues openly and develop effective solutions. The guidelines are captured in a charter, which is described in Chapter 5.

3. Ensure that everyone understands the problem-solving model being used to keep the group on track with its work. Several members may have different models to suggest.

4. Work through the exercises in this chapter together and use the results to help plan the next meeting and what happens between meetings—the action plan.

5. End the meeting with creation of an action plan; record it on the action planning sheet at the end of the chapter. Begin the next meeting with a review of the sheet to determine what has been accomplished.

Assessment: Meeting Practices

Time Requirement: 90 minutes

Supplies: Assessment 4.1, flip chart, markers

Overview: In this activity, you'll determine what, if any, weaknesses exist in the team's meeting processes.

Instructions

1. Work as individuals to complete Assessment 4.1. Have everyone use a circle to indicate where they think your team is now.

2. Now work as individuals again to assess the team on where people would like it to be. This time, have everyone use a square to indicate where the team should be on each item.

3. Capture the ratings of the whole group on the flip chart or overhead.

4. Answer the following questions:

   - Were there any differences between scores of individuals? Why?

   - What are the biggest gaps between where you are now and where you want to be? Use these gaps to identify priority of addressing issues (bigger gaps probably indicate a higher priority).

Assessment 4.1.   Meeting Practices Gap Analysis

	Rating				
	Low				High
1. Practice active listening—for example, summarizing, encouragements, paraphrasing.	1	2	3	4	5
2. Ask questions: What about . . . ? What if . . . ? Imagine. . . .	1	2	3	4	5
3. Build common understanding.	1	2	3	4	5
4. Work until you arrive at consensus. Don't resort to voting on anything more important than refreshments.	1	2	3	4	5
5. Everyone is treated equally.	1	2	3	4	5
6. Attend all meetings. (When upper-level managers begin missing CLT meetings for other meetings, question their commitment.)	1	2	3	4	5
7. Carry out responsibilities on schedule.	1	2	3	4	5
8. Do not allow side conversations.	1	2	3	4	5
9. Share all relevant information.	1	2	3	4	5
10. Continue a discussion until all understand it; be patient.	1	2	3	4	5
11. Make decisions based on data. (Ask, "Where's the data?" often.)	1	2	3	4	5
12. Stay on task; use a "parking lot" (a separate flip chart for ideas to return to later) for capturing ideas that would otherwise sidetrack the discussion.	1	2	3	4	5
13. Start and end meetings on time. (This helps attendance.)	1	2	3	4	5
14. Manage the talkative members and draw out the quiet members who reflect on ideas.	1	2	3	4	5
15. Challenge ideas.	1	2	3	4	5
16. Attack ideas, not people; constructive conflict focuses on ideas and avoids personal attacks.	1	2	3	4	5
17. Turn ideas into action. End each meeting with an action list including who will do what by when.	1	2	3	4	5
18. Prevent interruptions from the outside, including visitors and phones.	1	2	3	4	5
19. Use breaks to refresh, provide thinking time, and manage emotion.	1	2	3	4	5
20. Respect differing viewpoints and experiences.	1	2	3	4	5
21. Capture the key points. Check with all members to be sure that has happened.	1	2	3	4	5
22. Use graphic tools, not just words. (For example, use concept mapping, sketches, cartoons, diagrams, matrices, timelines, fishbone diagrams.)	1	2	3	4	5
23. Tolerate some emotional stretch; work a little distance outside your comfort zone.	1	2	3	4	5
24. Value silent periods; ten or fifteen seconds of silence may be uncomfortable, but it can lead to a higher level of discussion.	1	2	3	4	5

- Think of the gaps in terms of sequential order of implementation. Do some of them need to be addressed before others? Think about this when creating a prioritized list.

- What can you do to close those gaps? Look for action items in this discussion and capture them in the action planning sheet at the end of this chapter.

Planning: Create a Meeting Agenda Form

Time Requirement: 90 minutes

Supplies: Table 4.3, Worksheet 4.7, flip chart, marking pens

Overview: Table 4.3 shows a sample Meeting Agenda and Outcomes form that provides one way to capture process, decisions, and follow-up actions during a meeting. The meeting form provides several benefits: (1) a written record of the meeting, (2) a discipline for attending to various facets of the meeting process, and (3) a method of tracking follow-up actions by identifying who was responsible for what by when.

Instructions

1. Have everyone identify the parts of Table 4.3 they want to use in the team's meeting process and list them in the left column of Worksheet 4.7.

2. Then, in the right column, have them determine additional elements that your team will use. Determine the final form as a group.

3. Have everyone keep and use the form you settle on regularly. It will provide a useful record of the team's decisions and accomplishments that can be referred back to in a week or in a year. The archive of records can also be used to help bring new members up-to-speed.

Meeting Facilitators

Both content and process facilitation may be of value to the CLT. Content facilitation comes from having someone with organization development expertise help the CLT think through the issues. The organization development (OD) expert can share stories of how a decision worked out in another organization or suggest tools and alternatives the CLT has not yet discovered. Selecting from a set of existing options is much more efficient than inventing from scratch.

The process facilitator can help the members feel safer, communicate more fully and clearly, and keep the meeting on track. Sometimes both content and process skills are available in the same person or persons. Considering the difficulty of creating a CWS initiative and implementing it, we recommend the CLT utilize both types of experts during the first several years and carefully choose whether or not to continue the practice in later years. The members of the CLT can and should develop these competencies, but that takes time. Meanwhile, the team's process and decision making will be much more effective with facilitator support. Most meetings without facilitators only achieve mediocre levels of resource use, such as the time, knowledge, and talent of the members.

Table 4.3.   Sample Meeting Agenda Form

MEETING AGENDA AND OUTCOMES

Purpose: Brainstorm list of training modules and schedule their development

---

Location: Conference Room B   **Date/Time:** June 6, 2 pm

Attendees: KT, CH, KB, LG, HG, HP, FV, CM

Prework or Materials to Bring: Each member brings a list of ideas to share about key competencies we should provide training for to build collaborative capacity

---

Previous Decisions Related to Topics in This Meeting: Decision to use modules already available in the Training Department as much as possible to reduce development time for new modules

---

Previous Action Items

Due	Person	Action Assigned
7/1	KT	Clean up the resource list, including voting and elimination of items with no votes
7/12	CH	Add evolving practices to possible actions list
done	KB	Bring module 2 materials to next meeting

Process Observations for This Meeting

Process improved over last meeting. Better attendance. More people contributing. Use of the flip chart to capture suggestions worked well when discussing how to get the word out. Listening to each other can still improve.

Decisions from This Meeting

• Clean up resource list

• Send three members to workshop on conflict

• Subgroup of KT, HP, DT, and ES will outline module on meeting management

---

AGENDA

Item #	Person	Time	Type	Topic	Outcome Goals	Disposition
1	All	5 min.	Review	Action items	Review status of action items	Done
2	FK	30 min.	Decision	Module topic	Identify topic for next module to be developed	Done
3	JN	15 min.	Update	Business case	Present latest work by task group on building the business case	Later
4	HH	5 min.	Suggestion	Team design	Reconsider how teams choose their own design	Parking lot

Worksheet 4.7.   Form for Creating a Meeting Agenda

Parts You Want to Use from Example	Additional Elements Needed

Conclusion

The CLT is the planning and activity hub of the CWS initiative. The activities that comprise the change initiative depend on how well the CLT members work together, the expertise available, and the boundaries that protect or enhance the work. If there are problems with the initiative, look first at the CLT process to see how that can be improved. Change there will ripple outward through the whole change system.

Keys to the Chapter

- Representative membership in the CLT provides a rich network for communications and a diverse set of perspectives for effective decision making.

- Responsibility for the success of the initiative rests with all members of the organization. Responsibility for creating a plan and environment for supporting that success rests with the CLT.

- Create a network throughout the organization through selection of members and key points of communication.

- Build the CLT's team competencies through member selection and development.

- Establish an effective meeting process to avoid waste of CLT resources.

- Supplement the expertise of the CLT with content and process facilitators, especially the first year or two as member skills grow.

Chapter Wrap-Up

- What ideas did this chapter trigger for you and your group? List them in the action planning worksheet at the end of this chapter.

- Review the ideas list. Which of these do you want to implement? List the action item, person or group responsible, and target due dates in the action planning worksheet.

- Were any significant decisions made? Include them at the bottom of the action planning worksheet.

- How can you communicate the pertinent material generated by your work on this chapter to different audiences? Discuss and consider adding action items based on your discussion.

- How can you use the resources list for additional help?

- What chapter should you go through next? Refer back to Guiding Assessment results in Chapter 3 for suggestions of next steps.

- What can you do tomorrow or within the next week based on what you learned in this chapter? Have each person share what he or she will do, and remember to follow up.

- What is your biggest learning from this chapter? Ask each person to share. This is a nice way to end the session. Include any resulting ideas or action items in the action planning worksheet.

Resources

Ancona, D., & Caldwell, D. (1992). Bridging the boundary: External activity and performance in organizational teams. *Administrative Science Quarterly, 37,* 634–666.

Aslinger, G., & Whipple, G. (1998). How to jump start your task team. *Journal for Quality & Participation, 21*(3), 42–46.

Beyerlein, M. (2003). A tool approach to forgotten team competencies. In M. Beyerlein, C. McGee, G. Klein, J. Nemiro, & L. Broedling (Eds.), *The collaborative work systems fieldbook* (pp. 581–592). San Francisco. Jossey-Bass/Pfeiffer.

Hamel, G. (1996). Strategy as revolution. *Harvard Business Review, 74*(4), 69–83.

Harrington-Mackin, D. (1996). *Keeping the team going: A tool kit to renew & refuel your workplace teams.* New York: New Directions Management Services.

Inspiration Software, Inc. The leader in visual thinking and learning™. http://www.inspiration.com/home.cfm

Keen, T., & Keen, C. (1998). Conducting a team audit. *Training & Development, 52*(2) 13–16.

Klein, G. (2003). Increasing collaboration success through new meeting behavior. In M. Beyerlein, C. McGee, G. Klein, J. Nemiro, & L. Broedling (Eds.), *The collaborative work systems fieldbook* (pp. 573–579). San Francisco: Jossey-Bass/Pfeiffer.

Lytle, W. O., & others. (1993). *Visiting innovative work sites: A guide for successful planning.* Clark, NJ: Block Petrella Weisbord.

Marks, M. A., Mathieu, J. E., & Zaccaro, S. J. (2001). A temporally based framework and taxonomy of team processes. *Academy of Management Review, 26*(3), 356–377.

May, D. R., & Schwoerer, C. E. (1994). Developing effective work teams: Guidelines for fostering work team efficacy. *Organization Development Journal, 12,* 29–39.

Mind Tools (1995–2002). *Mind Maps™—A powerful approach to note taking.* Retrieved May 31, 2003, from http://www.mindtools.com/pages/article/newISS_01.htm

Schwarz, R. (2002). *The skilled facilitator: A comprehensive resource for consultants, facilitators, managers, trainers, and coaches* (2nd ed.). San Francisco: Jossey-Bass.

Sterling Insights (2001). *Graphic facilitation.* Retrieved May 31, 2003, from http://www.sterlinginsights.com/gf.html

Townsley, C., & Larkin, S. (2003). Team member selection: "Tell us about a time when . . . ." In M. Beyerlein, C. McGee, G. Klein, J. Nemiro, & L. Broedling (Eds.), *The collaborative work systems fieldbook* (pp. 411–429). San Francisco: Jossey-Bass/Pfeiffer.

Wiig, K. M. (1994). *Knowledge management: The central focus for intelligent-acting organizations.* Arlington, TX: Schema Press.

Action Planning and Summary Sheet

Ideas Generated from This Chapter

1	
2	
3	
4	
5	

#	Action Item	Target Date	Person/Group Responsible
1			
2			
3			
4			
5			
6			

Significant Decisions Made

1	
2	
3	
4	

## CHAPTER 5

Charter the Change Leadership Team

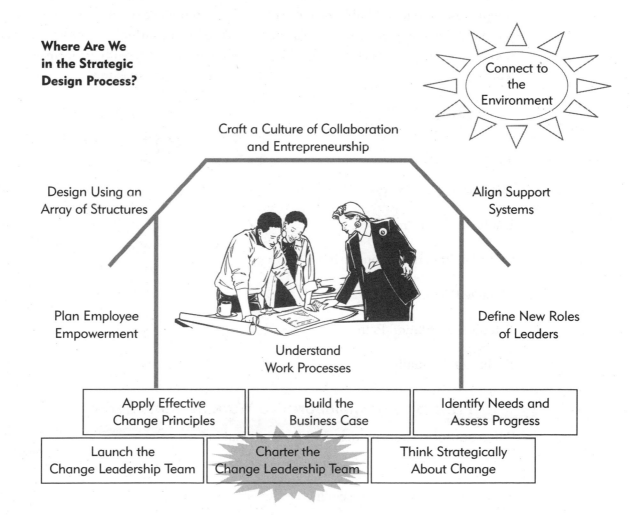

Connect to the Environment

Craft a Culture of Collaboration and Entrepreneurship

Design Using an Array of Structures

Align Support Systems

Plan Employee Empowerment

Understand Work Processes

Define New Roles of Leaders

Apply Effective Change Principles	Build the Business Case	Identify Needs and Assess Progress
Launch the Change Leadership Team	Charter the Change Leadership Team	Think Strategically About Change

Key Question of This Chapter

How will we work well together?

Quick Look

Overview

A charter is like a contract that members make with each other. It specifies agreed-on goals, measures, roles, norms, values, and expectations, including how the team will be accountable to its stakeholders and the members to each other. The goal is to reach agreement on the principles and procedures the CLT will follow during its life and capture in writing those agreements that can be updated as needed.

The process of creating the charter is as important for the CLT as is the charter itself, since it involves reaching shared understanding and therefore creates a common language for talking with other members of the organization. Some top managers prefer to create the charter and hand it down to the team; however, we recommend the team do its own chartering work as much as possible and have top management ratify it. Although the CLT might be able to build a charter on its own, the process would probably be more effective with the use of an experienced facilitator. The primary outcome of this chapter is the team charter. It includes clarification of stakeholder expectations, clarification of the relationship with the team sponsor, team vision and mission, team values, and team goals and measures.

Chapter Plan

Topic				
The Chartering Process	✓	✓		✓
Establish Team Processes	✓			✓
Establish Effective Sponsorship	✓			✓
Manage Performance	✓		✓	✓
Establish Escalation Path	✓			
Recharter Annually	✓			✓

Principles of Collaborative Work Systems Series

Align authority, information, and decision making

Treat collaboration as a disciplined process

The Chartering Process
What Is a Charter?

- A document that outlines agreements the team has made for how it will be accountable to its stakeholders and to each other

- A set of agreements that clearly states:

  - What the team wants to accomplish

  - Why those particular accomplishments are important

  - How the team will work together for results

- A reminder to keep the team focused on its agreements and the end results as pressures build and difficulties arise

- Documentation of the common understanding of authority and responsibility of the team

- One of the most important ongoing parts of the group development process

To begin considering the chartering process, team members should discuss the following questions. While this preliminary discussion will provide a starting point, the remainder of this chapter will help the team to flesh out its ideas about these issues.

Discussion

1. What does our team already know about chartering?

2. Where do we use charters in our organization now?

3. What do those examples look like?

4. What should we borrow from those examples and processes for enhancing our chartering process?

Initiate Chartering

The team sponsors or the top management group usually initiates chartering of a CLT for introducing a major change initiative in the organization. They identify the initiative, define its purpose, and select initial team members. Those team members then identify the additional members who are likely to go through the rest of the chartering steps.

Initiating the charter process may primarily be the responsibility of the sponsor, but the CLT members should ask for clarification until they feel they understand the goals of the change program, the resources available, the expected results, and the process for communicating with the sponsor.

Planning: Define the Relationship with the Top Management Team

Time Requirement: Approximately 90 minutes

Supplies: Worksheet 5.1, flip chart, masking tape, and markers

Overview: The effectiveness of the CLT will be greatly enhanced or restricted by the top management team (TMT). Articulating the CLT's understanding of that relationship at the beginning and updating it often will help with managing it for more effectiveness.

Instructions

1. Using Worksheet 5.1, discuss the six questions one at a time.

2. Capture the essence of the discussion under the Comments column.

3. Identify areas where action may be required.

These foundation questions should be revisited periodically to update and clarify them as necessary.

Clarify Statement of Work

The purpose of the CLT is to carry out the work assignment. The team needs to know "Why are we here?" The clarity of the answer is a key to the team's ability to make progress. The answer should be captured in the charter document and be easily described when CLT members talk with others in the organization. A brief description of the CWS initiative should answer questions from Worksheet 5.2.

Planning: Statement of Work

Time Requirement: Approximately 90 minutes

Supplies: Worksheet 5.2, Worksheet 5.3, flip chart, masking tape, and markers

Overview: To develop a statement of work that will guide the CLT's decision making and enable clear communications with other members of the organization. The process of developing a clear and complete statement of work for the CLT will build a common understanding among team members that will facilitate communication and action.

Worksheet 5.1.   Communicating with the Top Management Team

Question	Comments
1. Who is on the top management team (TMT)?	
2. What does the TMT expect? (Strive for clarity and completeness here.)	
3. How will the TMT show support for the CLT?	
4. When will the CLT meet with the TMT?	
5. What policies, rules, or other constraints limit the CLT's activities?	
6. What level of empowerment or authority is the TMT granting the team?	

Worksheet 5.2.   Elements of the Statement of Work

Focus Question	Initial Ideas
1. What does the team want to accomplish?	
2. Why does the CWS initiative need to be implemented?	
3. What is the scope of the initiative?	

Worksheet 5.2. (continued)

Focus Question	Initial Ideas
4. How will the team demonstrate that the CWS initiative's goals have been achieved (including measurement methods and soft and hard program results)?	
5. What is the timeline for the CWS initiative? (Keep it loose; include frequent minor and major milestones; make it an ongoing process of continual development over five years.)	
6. What are the expected outcomes? (Clarity here is most important.)	

Instructions

1. Complete Worksheet 5.2 as a team to brainstorm tasks to be performed, beginning at the top and working down to lower levels of details and tasks.

2. Be sure to capture all deliverables, including implied requirements, in the project statement of work. Note that, in brainstorming, the most important rule is that there are no evaluative comments allowed and that ideas that seem crazy or out of the box are as welcome as those that do not.

3. When Worksheet 5.2 is complete, work as a team to write a one-paragraph statement of work that summarizes the worksheet's contents. Record the result in the top of Worksheet 5.3.

4. Prepare an "elevator speech" that summarizes the statement of work in three or fewer sentences that can be delivered to anyone in one minute or less—no technical terms allowed. Record the speech in the second half of Worksheet 5.3.

5. Incorporate the group's responses to the questions on Worksheet 5.2 in the charter. Rehearse answering them with each other so you can talk about the CWS initiative program with other members of the organization intelligently.

Establish Team Processes

Team processes significantly affect team results. Some processes deserve special attention. In this section guidelines for the following processes are presented: identifying the team's values, decision making, regrouping members into subgroups and other configurations for work, and establishing a code of conduct. Other important processes such as meeting management and building common understanding were covered in Chapter 4. Identifying the processes is only the first step; following them as a discipline for high performance is the key.

Identify Team Values

What does your team stand for? What are the standards of behavior for team members with each other and with nonmembers? Acceptable behavior is based on values. The CLT should take the time to articulate its value set.

Planning: Core Values

Time Requirement: Approximately 90 minutes

Supplies: Worksheet 5.4, flip chart, masking tape, and markers

Overview: The core values of the CLT serve as the benchmark for all the behaviors, decisions, and activities the team and its members engage in. Because of the central role of these values for the CLT, the same values play a central role in the CWS initiative. Selecting them carefully, committing to them, and looking for ways to express these values lays a foundation for a successful initiative.

Worksheet 5.3.   Statement of Work: Formal and Elevator Versions

Statement of the Work

Elevator Speech

Instructions

1. Review the list of values in Worksheet 5.4.

2. Decide as a group which of these are appropriate for your team.

3. Reword those that need it.

4. Add to the list any value statements that you can reach agreement on.

5. Print the final list of values on a poster and hang it in your meeting room. Refer to it when meeting. Say things like, "I like what Ralph said; I think it reflects the value on . . ." or "I can't go along with what Cindy said; it seems to contradict the value on. . . ." Recognize when a member sets a good example while acting on the basis of one of the values.

Decision-Making Process

Perhaps the most critical process is the decision-making process, for example, choosing long-term versus short-term focus, selecting consensus versus majority vote, inviting outside input or not, determining when a decision by a subgroup can be overturned by the team, and deciding when the team should escalate a decision (delegate upward) to its sponsor.

An effective decision-making process is shown by four outcomes:

- A decision that is timely, relevant, and appropriate (for example, requires reasonable resources)

- Commitment of the decision makers

- An action plan

- Enough satisfaction with the process to return to it at the next meeting

Discussion, information gathering, conflict, debate, and consensus take time. However, the use of time in arriving at a decision is not the most critical value for assessing the effectiveness of the decision-making process. Successful execution is the key value: *Does the decision get carried out by the members in a way that generates the expected results?* Ask this question frequently.

Good-quality decisions depend on having necessary and sufficient information as input into the decision-making process. Having representatives from each part of the organization in the room facilitates access to that information. It also facilitates coordination of the actions necessary to execute the decision.

Important decisions will be accompanied by vested interests that may generate conflict. Conflict can be constructive or destructive. Emotional conflict includes anger, personal friction, personality clash, and tension. Fear of this type of conflict stifles communication. In contrast, cognitive conflict involves disagreements over different ideas and differences about the content of the decision. Such general differences of opinion add a rich diversity to the perspective of the group on any issue and should be encouraged.

When conflict arises, try to keep the focus on differences about the content of the decision, not on personal attacks.

Worksheet 5.4.   Values List

Appropriate for Team?	Need to Reword?	Value
		Honesty and open sharing of information
		Confidentiality to protect members of the team and sources of information
		Equality of members during any and all CLT activities
		Continuous improvement and learning and unlearning
		Long-range view to frame short-range action
		Management by fact—data-based decision making
		Decision making by consensus—"all of us are smarter than any of us"
		Win-win methods, so no one is consciously sacrificed or hurt for the sake of others' gains during the change process
		Commitment to the success of the CWS initiative
		Commitment to the success of fellow CLT members
		Active involvement in the CLT process and the change initiative
		Own and commit to the vision with enthusiasm
		Maintain a focus on business results—improving company competitiveness, performance, and capabilities
		Ethical behavior

Additional Values:

When decisions are made, capture those decisions on the Action Planning and Summary Sheet that ends each chapter in this workbook. The summary sheet works as a tool for committing the group to an action and as a group memory that can be revisited for checking on progress. Add additional columns as your team sees the need, such as who needs to be informed about a decision or give formal permission, resources needed, backup plans, and so forth.

Work Groupings

All CLT members should be able to work both collaboratively and individually, depending on the situation. The CLT has the flexibility to work in four modes: whole team, subgroups, individual members, and members partnering with nonmembers. For example, major decisions should involve the whole group; development of training modules or information gathering can be done by small groups; contact with specific members of the organization can be handled by individuals. Using these alternative work designs for the team creates efficiencies.

Following is a guide for when to collaborate and when to work alone. Collaborate when:

- Broader skills, knowledge, and expertise are needed
- Meetings take less time than developing individual members' skills and knowledge so they can work solo
- People must depend on each other to accomplish the task—that is, it cannot be done in isolation
- The work takes less time with more people working together
- Sharing ideas and challenging ideas is valued
- Successful implementation depends on everyone's commitment
- Alignment and coordination across teams requires their sharing of resources
- Solutions depend on a shared understanding of the problem

Do not work collaboratively when:

- Stakeholders do not need complex solutions that require inputs from multiple contributors
- Management is unwilling to share the necessary information and resources or empower the contributors
- One individual is capable of the creativity needed
- Tasks are simple and routine (Every organization has some of these tasks and needs to emphasize efficiency in their processes. The risk is categorizing tasks as simple and routine when they are not, and vice versa.)
- Competition prevents people from sharing openly and honestly (A culture that pushes members of the same organization to compete with each other will have to be changed to make it possible to leverage collaborative opportunities.)

- The reward system focuses entirely on individual contribution (The self-centered behaviors that emerge in this situation will undermine attempts to introduce collaborative work practices. Change the reward system first and reward individual and team in proportion to how much each contributes.)

- The political environment will make the collaborative outcome worthless (If the politics emphasize self-promotion and blame, collaboration will be very difficult.)

- Time and resources are limited (list adapted from Beyerlein, Freedman, McGee, & Moran, 2003)

A key issue in working with subgroups is clarifying when the group is empowered to make a decision and when it is only empowered to make a recommendation to the CLT as a whole. If a subgroup believes it is supposed to make a decision and works hard to do it well, the members become quite demoralized when the CLT overturns the decision. Define the task and its limits clearly ahead of time to avoid such problems.

Create Code of Conduct

What is a "code of conduct"? A code of conduct is a list of guidelines or set of standards or norms that describe appropriate personal behavior in a meeting and in the work setting. Examples of items that teams might consider including in their codes include the following:

- Regardless of status within the organization, CLT members must agree to treat each other as equals with respect to the CLT's work.

- Each team member must be committed to the team's work and should not be out to advance a personal agenda.

- Members need to feel safe enough to express opinions that are controversial, share ideas that are half-baked, make errors, and take stands without being attacked; part of the secret for making this work is the agreement to *attack ideas, not people.*

- All members commit to participate in all tasks.

- All relevant information is shared with the CLT.

- Focus on contributions that move the CWS initiative ahead, rather than defending or justifying one's own position as, for example, union steward or member of the top management group.

- Confront one another's unproductive behaviors, but do it supportively and with respect.

- Work to minimize distractions, including off-task remarks, interruptions, and catching up of people who missed the prior meeting.

- Take the time to understand each other, including how each key word is used.

It takes time, agreements, and discipline to build the trust that a high-performing team depends on; it only takes one violation to create a serious setback. The quality of innovation for the CLT depends on members feeling safe enough to take chances with each other and with ideas. Otherwise, the resources of the team will be underutilized, some members will languish, and the solutions to problems will be sterile and uncreative. The guidelines play a key role in establishing the kind of work environment that will enable the CLT to excel.

Why is a code of conduct important?

- To create common expectations and understanding among team members

- To define and reinforce desirable behavior for individual team members

- To support the self-management of the team

- To create a safe enough environment so that members will voice their opinions

Planning: Developing the Code of Conduct

Time Requirement: Approximately 90 minutes

Supplies: Flip chart, masking tape, and markers

Overview: The effectiveness of the CLT depends on the behavior of its members. Setting norms for the behavior creates a target of conduct to shoot for and a standard for determining when behavior should be praised and emulated and when it should be censored and altered.

Instructions

1. Create a list of the principles of behavior in your organization.

2. Supplement that list with any other principles team members believe will achieve the four purposes listed above for a code of conduct.

3. Eliminate the redundant principles and the less important to arrive at a final set of six to ten.

4. Refine the code of conduct using the following questions:

   - How will violations of the principles be dealt with—minor, intermediate, and serious violations?

   - How will your new code of conduct be implemented?

   - How will the code be publicized outside of CLT for building the credibility of the team and the initiative?

   - Identify any aspects of the code that seem to conflict with organizational policies and practices. How will you deal with those conflicts?

   - How and when will your code be reviewed and revised?

Establish Effective Sponsorship

The CLT must have high-level support, be protected, and have resources. This is the job of the team sponsor. The sponsor is usually a top-level manager who firmly believes in the value of the initiative and will work at the top level to protect it and the CLT. The sponsor is an agent for change, a team advocate, and a mentor. The sponsor also understands that the CLT must be empowered and that micromanaging would undermine it and the change initiative. Other top-level people know who the sponsor is; part of the performance appraisal of the sponsor should depend directly on the success of the CLT.

Planning: Managing the Sponsor

Time Requirement: Approximately 2 hours

Supplies: Worksheet 5.5, flip chart, masking tape, and markers

Overview: Some executives have the skills to be an effective sponsor and an understanding of what the role involves. Other executives need some development. The CLT can influence that development through clarification and communication. It is part of the team's role in managing its environment.

Instructions

1. As a group, discuss the questions on Worksheet 5.5. The discussion should begin with clarification and move toward action planning.

2. Develop an action plan for each item as necessary.

Manage Performance

The performance level of the CLT sets an upper limit on the quality of the CWS initiative. A number of performance dimensions need to be considered in striving for high performance. This section provides guidelines for the following dimensions: stakeholder expectations, mission, vision, team name, goal definition and planning, measuring CLT performance, and conducting reviews of performance. To respond well to the challenge of a large-scope change project and to hold up well under the spotlight that others will shine on the CLT, performance must be intelligently managed.

Capture Stakeholder Expectations

Ask, "Who is affected by the change process?" Stakeholder expectations are the "wants" of all the team's stakeholders, including inside and outside customers, suppliers, team members, and regulators—anyone affected by the outputs of the CLT. By understanding stakeholder expectations, the team can make decisions in their best interests, which in turn allows for the growth of the business.

Many different groups have a stake in the CWS initiative. Some of the groups include:

- *Customers:* people, internal or external, who receive your outputs (products and/or services)
- *Suppliers:* people, internal or external, who provide your inputs (raw materials)
- *Change leadership team members:* members of the group leading the CWS initiative
- *Employees:* co-workers who depend on each other to get the job done
- *Regulators:* federal, state, and local regulatory agencies who affect aspects of your work
- *Corporate office:* people to whom your business or division reports
- *Community:* families of employees, area economy, and community citizenship

Worksheet 5.5.   Managing Sponsorship

- Who is our sponsor(s)? How can we pinpoint where solid sponsorship will come from?

- What level of buy-in does our sponsor have? How can we determine that level and boost it?

- Does our sponsor understand the scope of the initiative? Some sponsors will underestimate the scope, so how can we check to see if the CLT and sponsor visions align?

- What do we need from our sponsor? Specify what form support should take and plan how to pursue it.

Worksheet 5.5.　(continued)

- How can we communicate our needs, progress, and issues to our sponsor? Consider as examples: invite the sponsor to occasional meetings, meet to do periodic updates.

- Do we have clear understanding of the decisions that the team is allowed to make and not make? Create a list of the areas in which the CLT is empowered to make decisions and a list of the areas where it can only make recommendations to the sponsor and clarify the lists with the sponsor. Push to expand the empowered areas, if the CWS initiative will benefit.

- Do we have a clear understanding of when team decisions can be overturned by the sponsor or the top management team? List the situations when this might happen. Anticipate them and increase communication and involvement of top management ahead of time in these cases.

(continued)

Worksheet 5.5.   Managing Sponsorship (continued)

- Has our sponsor provided us with the time, space, resources, and access to information to get the work done (space = freedom from some regular job duties so the work can be done without grief from supervisors focused only on production)?

- Does our sponsor support us having easy access to information, to education, and to CWS initiative expertise?

- Do we have a budget of our own? Whose budget is it? (If the budget is part of a department budget, such as HR or Operations, conflict over use of funds is likely to emerge.) How can we increase control of the budgetary resources?

- *Shareholders:* the shareholders or owners of your company
- *Other business units:* other business units in your organization that may have to work with you and may learn from your example
- *Sponsors of the CWS initiative:* the individuals who have initiated the change or who are "change champions" or advocates of the change

Each of these groups wants different things from the CWS initiative. It is important that the CLT think of these stakeholders and their different needs.

Assessment: CWS Initiative Stakeholder Expectations

Time Requirement: Approximately 90 minutes

Supplies: Worksheet 5.6, flip chart, masking tape, and markers

Overview: Work as a team and in subgroups to profile the stakeholders that will be involved in and affected by the CWS initiative. Use the list above as a starting point in identifying the stakeholder groups. Then capture the expectations each group is likely to have about the CWS initiative. This information will help in planning, communications, and implementation.

Instructions

1. As a group, brainstorm the stakeholders for your CWS initiative and record the results on a flip chart. Eliminate redundancies and create categories (if needed). Then prioritize to come to a number amenable to a small-group activity.

2. Form small groups of three or four members. Assign one or more stakeholders to each small group. Try to assign stakeholders to groups in a way that makes sense—make sure (if possible) that subgroup members have some knowledge of the stakeholder (for example, managers deal with corporate office, employees deal with employees, and so on).

3. Within each group, assign a scribe to capture the discussion about likely stakeholder expectations on a flip chart. Individual group members can take notes on Worksheet 5.6.

4. Once all subgroup discussions are concluded, each small group should take a turn reviewing its results with the whole group. Suggestions from the whole group can then be added to improve the description of expectations for each stakeholder group.

5. Discuss the following questions:

   - How can you communicate to the different stakeholders? Think about communication methods and different ways to craft the messages.
   - What links to the stakeholders can you create that will help you keep in touch with their needs?
   - What measures of success can be developed based on the expectations of stakeholders?

Worksheet 5.6.   Stakeholder Analysis

Stakeholder	Their Expectations for CWS Initiative

6. Update the description of stakeholder expectation at least once a year. Use the results as a guide in decision making and communication.

State Vision and Mission; Name Team

Vision statements are used together with the mission statement to express how the world will be different as a result of the CLT's work. The vision paints an image of how the organization will look at the conclusion of the CWS initiative. A vision statement emphasizes a future goal or achievement, while a mission statement guides strategic decision making in the present.

A vision statement should be a simple, engaging statement that can:

- Create clear and positive mental images of "what it should be like around here"

- Give meaning to the work expected from people

- Create pride, energy, and a sense of accomplishment

- Link the CWS initiative with results

The vision statement can evolve over time as understanding and direction upgrade it.

A mission statement guides decision making. The mission statement reminds your team and the world about your purpose and what it is that makes you special. By understanding your team's mission, you have a better idea of what direction to take when confronted with decisions. Mission statements are formal statements that provide direction for the CLT and communicate the team's identity and purpose to the broader organization, stating:

- What we are

- Who we are

- What we do

- Who we serve

- What we offer

- How we serve

- Why we exist

- What we want to accomplish

Effective mission statements help focus everyone to work together in a defined manner to achieve the group's purpose.

Here are two examples of mission statements:

A. Our CLT objective is to provide three things to our stakeholders:

1. The most useful plan for the CWS initiative
2. The most reliable, efficient, quality implementation available
3. Balanced improvement in both quality of work life and business results

Our goal is to provide these things to our stakeholders while maintaining a commitment to business growth in our organization.

B. The CLT is committed to building an environment that enables people to work well together whenever collaboration adds value to the enterprise by providing the highest quality CWS initiative possible and the most professional support of that initiative.

Related vision statements might read as follows:

Create a workplace where collaboration achieves maximum value

Achieve world-class excellence at working well together

The team name provides a symbol of what the team stands for. The team name is part of the identity of the team; it should capture the essence of what the team stands for. The clearest name might be "The Change Leadership Team."

Planning: Vision, Mission, and Name

Time Requirement: 2 hours

Supplies: Worksheet 5.7, flip chart, masking tape, and markers

Overview: As a team, go through the steps provided to develop a team vision, mission, and name. When finalized, all of these elements will be part of your team's charter.

Instructions

1. *Vision.* A good vision statement generates energy and enthusiasm by clarifying the desired outcomes of the work for the team and for the stakeholders.

   To begin crafting your team's vision, ask, "What will the organization look like in five years if the CLT is highly successful with the change initiative?" Speculate freely on this and build in some detail, for example, "Turnover will drop below 5 percent," "Our market share will increase by 5 percent," "People will look forward to coming to work," "Accidents will drop to one in a million hours," "People will feel respected by top management," or "Ideas for innovation will triple." A sample vision statement is: "Our organization will be recognized for excellence in utilizing collaboration to leverage resources that lead to world-class products and services." Record your vision on Worksheet 5.7.

2. *Mission.* As a team, craft a mission statement by considering the responses to the following questions:

   - What is our business as a CLT?
   - How can we make the stakeholders more successful? (The stakeholders consist of the stakeholder groups identified earlier.)
   - How will the CWS initiative add value to the organization?
   - What is the best way to create that value?

   Record the team mission on Worksheet 5.7.

3. *Team name.* Begin by brainstorming some possible names for your team. After all ideas have been listed, have the team come to consensus on the final name. Consensus among CLT members is important in resolving any of the identity issues, including the team name. When you compile the charter in a binder, put the name of the team on the cover. Record the team name on Worksheet 5.7.

Worksheet 5.7.   Team Vision, Mission, and Name

Vision

Mission

Team Name

Lay Out Goals and Action Plans

Having defined a problem, a vision, and a mission statement, the group is ready to get to work. To achieve its vision there must be a *clear and measurable set of goals*. A goal is the purpose toward which effort is directed. Effective goals encourage decision making, motivate people, focus the energy and resources of the group, and make it possible to measure progress. Examples of goals include the following:

- Reduce grievances by 10 percent in three years

- Restore our organization to the list of 100 Best Companies to Work For by 2010

- Establish a pattern of growth in quality by reducing rework by 50 percent over five years

A recommended model for defining goals is the SMART goal-setting process: make goals specific, measurable, achievable, realistic, and time-based.

An effective goal statement does four things:

1. Describes an end result or a statement of intent

2. Gives a clear picture of what is expected

3. Keeps all members on the same page to coordinate efforts

4. Sets expectations that can be observed and measured

Goals also must be flexible, since information gathered later in the planning process may cause the group to add or modify goals.

Goals come in three "sizes"—short term, medium term, and long term. On any complex project, the three types of goals must be aligned. That is achieved by starting with defining your long-term goals and then working backward to the short-term ones. For example, one long-term goal of the CLT may focus on increased innovation. Using the SMART model, the CLT would craft a goal statement like this one: "The number of process innovations generated by work teams will double and the value of the innovations will double within two years." This statement becomes the long-term goal. A medium-term goal statement that aligns would be something like this, "A tracking system will be implemented within twelve months, so the value of team innovations can be tracked and appropriate rewards given to the team." The aligned short-term goal might be, "Key managers, such as those in finance, accounting, and HR, will be interviewed to determine how team innovations are now tracked and rewarded."

Planning: Goal Setting

Time Requirement: 90 minutes

Supplies: Worksheet 5.8, flip chart, masking tape, Post-it® Notes, and markers

Overview: In this activity, you'll create an initial list of goals for turning the mission statement into action. Using the critical success factors and the keys to success in this workbook as input, work as a team to identify the goals of the CWS initiative.

Instructions

1. Start by brainstorming goals for the CLT.

2. Simplify the list by eliminating duplicates and trivial or impossible goals.

3. Group together any related goals and label them with an overall purpose.

4. Then categorize the goals as short-term, medium-term, or long-term.

5. Capture the list on a flip chart modeled after Worksheet 5.8.

6. The long-term goals should be included in the team's charter.

7. The rest of the goals will probably be too detailed and change too often for inclusion in the charter, but should be captured in a team log, such as the one shown in Worksheet 5.8.

Goals are worthless unless they are achieved or redefined into something that is achieved. That means that, once the team selects its goals, it should create an action plan of specific steps needed to reach each goal.

Select Team Measures of Performance

Teams should be judged by shared results, not by measures of team cohesion or individual performance. A measure of team performance is an indicator of how the team is progressing toward its key goals. The measures provide the team with the information it needs to track its performance and solve problems. Ultimately, what gets measured gets done!

The measures chosen by the CLT need to be practical and relevant—that is, tracking of progress on the measure should be moderately easy and the measure should be obviously linked to the goal. Worksheet 5.9 provides examples. Create a worksheet like this for the CWS initiative.

Planning: Identifying Measures for the CLT

Time Requirement: Approximately 90 minutes

Supplies: Filled-in Worksheet 5.8, Worksheet 5.9, flip chart, masking tape, and markers

Overview: Measures provide an indication of progress on the CWS initiative. To be effective, the measures must fit into the strategic context of CLT's plan. The initiative is complex, so it is possible to feel overwhelmed by measures and their tracking. Select the set that aids progress, rather than focusing on measurement in lieu of progress.

Instructions

1. Refer back to the long-term goals from Worksheet 5.8 to select items for the first column of Worksheet 5.9. The goals represent the "what" or purpose of the initiative.

2. Identify action steps or the "how" for reaching each goal and record them in the second column.

Worksheet 5.8.   Determining Goals

Purpose of Goal	Short-Term Goals	Medium-Term Goals	Long-Term Goals
Communicating	Share draft of CLT charter with sponsor	Present final CLT charter to top management team	Use the example of the CLT living by its charter to educate the rest of the organization about the possibilities of the CWS initiative
Culture	Hold a town hall meeting to discuss the values of the new culture	Provide bonuses for outstanding teamwork	Craft a culture of collaboration
Planning			
Training			
Assessing			

3. Select measures that are specific, measurable, and observable that will indicate movement toward or away from the goal and record them in the third column.

4. Set targets that represent the desired level the CLT wants to achieve on each measure and record. Note that a 100-percent target is not always necessary; meaningful progress may be broken into smaller steps that finally add up to something near 100 percent.

5. If work has begun on the goal, show how much has been accomplished or comment on why it has fallen short.

6. Make this a living document by recording the current date and then updating the entries and also by editing the material to show progress in understanding and redirection.

7. Share the worksheet with the CLT sponsor to obtain input about aligning the material with the business strategy. (Table 5.1 shows a partially filled-in worksheet as a sample.)

As with all team assignments, individuals should be held accountable by the team. When assignments are clear and deadlines reasonable, the team should confront members who fail to deliver decent work on time. The confrontation should be constructive—that is, aimed at solving any problems that prevented delivery. Keep a problem-solving focus. If this approach fails to change the performance of the member, a change in membership may be necessary.

Conduct Team Review

A team review is a check on progress toward team goals. Assessment of progress for the CLT should be continual and both formal and informal. By reviewing team performance in a formal manner periodically (for example, quarterly), the team can identify areas for improvement and see how its efforts are resulting in progress. Formal reviews are scheduled at regular intervals. That is not enough to keep the CLT on track. Informal assessment is continual. It occurs every time a CLT member raises an issue in a meeting that deals with CLT performance and CWS initiative progress.

Categories for review can include team development, team meetings, and achievement of the team's business goals (progress on the CWS initiative in terms of its contribution to the organization's strategic goals). These categories can be assessed using the metrics from Worksheet 5.9, from progress on the CLT charter, from analysis of themes in the stories team members gather, from action plans completed, and so on. The review is for the team's use in introducing changes in its progress, but also for communicating with top management. Demonstrating progress to the top management team is most effective when the metrics are used, but stories and testimonials from members of the organization can also build strong cases for continued support from the top.

Worksheet 5.10 is a form for recording team reviews at the completion of each phase of the CWS initiative or at milestones. Reviews of CLT work can be done weekly, monthly, quarterly, annually, or when important changes occur, such as adding or losing a team member.

Table 5.1. Sample Measuring Goals Worksheet

Long-Term Goals	Action Steps	Measure(s) Indicating Progress Toward Goal (more than one is okay)	Targets	Current Level of Success and Comments	Date
Craft a culture of collaboration	Hold a town hall meeting	Number of people attending meeting	95 percent of all employees at the site	88 percent	Sept. 6
Craft a culture of collaboration	Hold a town hall meeting	Number of questions for the CLT from the town hall meeting participants	One question for every five people	One for every seven; need to create a greater sense of trust for people to speak up	Sept. 6
Build the CLT into a model team	Complete the team charter	Completed checklist for charter	90% consensus on 90% of the checklist items	75% of checklist complete; 66% consensus on 75% of items	Aug. 5
Build top management support for the CWS initiative	Present CWS business plan to top management team	Assess buy-in through informal conversations during the following week	80% express buy-in	45% express buy-in	Oct. 20
Educate members of the organization about the CWS initiative	Communicate the essence of the CWS initiative to all members of the organization via newsletter, bulletin board, Web site, and so on	Number of people who can describe the initiative	80% of organizational members can describe the initiative with an 80% accuracy on key points	55%	Oct. 15
Complete each phase of the CWS initiative ahead of schedule and under budget	Track and review progress for each phase	Milestones are set for completion of each phase	Completion occurs one week before milestone	Ran over by two weeks on last milestone	Nov. 2

Worksheet 5.9. Measuring Goals

Long-Term Goals	Action Steps	Measure(s) Indicating Progress Toward Goal (more than one is okay)	Targets	Current Level of Success and Comments	Date

(continued)

Worksheet 5.9.   Measuring Goals (continued)

Long-Term Goals	Action Steps	Measure(s) Indicating Progress Toward Goal (more than one is okay)	Targets	Current Level of Success and Comments	Date

Planning: Team Review

Time Requirement: Approximately 1 hour

Supplies: Worksheet 5.10, flip chart, masking tape, and markers

Overview: This activity is designed to help the CLT summarize information about progress on the CWS initiative from multiple sources.

Instructions

1. Work as a team to answer the questions in all of Worksheet 5.10 except the last line.

2. Meet with the CLT sponsor to review the form and then complete the last line.

3. Repeat this activity once a month to track progress.

Establish Escalation Path

An escalation path is how you and your team deal with problems you cannot resolve. It represents a special communication problem. By identifying the escalation path up front, the team and its members know what to do when confronted with a decision they cannot make. This avoids some painful "spinning the wheels" time that may occur when the team is at a dead end. An effective escalation process includes knowing when to take a problem "upstairs" and to whom and how to ask for help. If a top manager makes the decision for your team, rather than helping you make the decision, the follow-up action will be less successful than when the CLT makes the decision. Escalate when the team is truly stuck, but be aware of the possible cost in time and loss of control over the outcome. For example, when conflict in the CLT threatens to disrupt work, look for solutions within the team as much as possible. Only take it to the sponsor for intervention if the internal options have been exhausted. On the other hand, if a top manager is obviously working to undermine the CWS initiative (this happens when people are scared of the results, fail to see personal benefits, believe they will lose power or control, and so forth) and the CLT has tried appropriate solutions without success, ask the sponsor to talk with the manager and then to take the issue to the top management team, if necessary. Some issues are outside the scope of the CLT's authority.

Recharter Annually

Rechartering is a process that is done at least annually or possibly semi-annually, in which your team revises your charter as needed. The review acts as a reminder and reconfirmation of the team's charter. As the organization continues to grow and change, the team may need to revise its charter to reflect that change. The rechartering is both an editing process and a commitment process, so renewal of the charter is the vital center of the CLT's work.

Worksheet 5.10.   Review Form for Team Milestones

Date:	CWS Initiative Phase Start Date:
Team Name:	Proposed Completion Date:
Location:	Revised Completion Date:
Team Members:	Session Facilitator:

Percentage of Project Phase Completed:

Problem Owners:

Current Month's Accomplishments/Current Status:

Next Goal(s):

Proposed Benefit(s) to be Achieved:

Actual Benefit(s) to Date:

Critical Factor Needed for Sponsor Review:

Sponsor Comments:

Planning: Assess Completeness of Charter

Time Requirement: Approximately 90 minutes

Supplies: Worksheet 5.11, flip chart, masking tape, and markers

Overview: This activity is designed to help the CLT determine whether or not the chartering process is complete.

Instructions

1. Work through Worksheet 5.11 as a team to determine what holes you have left to fill in the construction of your team charter. Note that the order in the worksheet is roughly the same as in this chapter. Some chapter items are omitted, since their results are more for internal use of the CLT and do not need to be reported to the TMT.

2. Plan the steps necessary to achieve completion.

Conclusion

This chapter was long and thorough because chartering is such a core competency for the team and the process of chartering is a team-building experience that creates a common understanding of the CLT's mission and vision and how the members will work together to achieve them. The charter tells the rest of the organization what the CLT stands for. Adapt this material for use in chartering the rest of the teams in the organization, starting with the top management team. Streamline it where necessary to make it practical.

Keys to the Chapter

- Involve the entire team in creating the team charter.
- Take the time to develop a solid charter.
- Make sure all members, especially new members, understand the expectations spelled out in the charter.
- Present your team charter to the top management team to build support; plan how to do the presentation and practice it.
- Regularly review the charter and recharter any or all of the facets of the charter when it does not fit what the team needs to do to succeed.
- Use the CLT charter experience as a guide for facilitating the chartering process of other teams in the organization.

Chapter Wrap-Up

- What ideas did this chapter trigger for you and your group? List them in the action planning worksheet at the end of this chapter.

Worksheet 5.11.   Assessing Progress on the Charter

Charter Step	Captured in the Charter?	Supported by the Team?	Supported by the Sponsor(s)?	Action Items
Team name				
Statement of work				
Vision				
Mission				
Values				
Processes: a. Decision making b. Meeting c. Discussion d. Work groupings				
Code of conduct				
Stakeholder expectations				
Goals				
Measures				
Action plans for goals				
Review schedule				
Resource needs				
Other (identify here):				

- Review the ideas list. Which of these do you want to implement? List the action item, person or group responsible, and target due dates on the action planning worksheet.

- Were any significant decisions made? Include them at the bottom of the action planning worksheet.

- How can you communicate the pertinent material generated by your work on this chapter to different audiences? Discuss and consider adding action items based on your discussion.

- How can you use the resources list for additional help?

- What chapter should you go through next? Refer back to Guiding Assessment results in Chapter 3 for suggestions of next steps.

- What can you do tomorrow or within the next week based on what you learned in this chapter? Have each person share what he or she will do, and then follow up.

- What is your biggest learning from this chapter? Ask each person to share. This is a nice way to end the session. Include any resulting ideas or action items in the action planning worksheet.

Resources

Beyerlein, M. (2003). A tool approach to forgotten team competencies. In M. Beyerlein, C. McGee, G. Klein, J. Nemiro, & L. Broedling (Eds.), *The collaborative work systems fieldbook* (pp. 581–593). San Francisco: Jossey-Bass/Pfeiffer.

Bisson, B., & Folk, V. (2000). Case study: How to do a business process improvement. *Journal for Quality & Participation, 23*(1), 58–64.

Dowling, K. (2003). Chartering your team for peak performance. In M. Beyerlein, C. McGee, G. Klein, J. Nemiro, & L. Broedling (Eds.), *The collaborative work systems fieldbook* (pp. 77–87). San Francisco: Jossey-Bass/Pfeiffer.

Eisenstat, R. A., & Cohen, S. G. (1990). Summary: Top management groups. In J. R. Hackman (Ed.), *Groups that work (and those that don't): Creating conditions for effective teamwork* (pp. 78–86). San Francisco: Jossey-Bass.

May, D. R., & Schwoerer, C. E. (1994). Developing effective work teams: Guidelines for fostering work team efficacy. *Organization Development Journal, 12,* 29–39.

Mohrman, S. A., Cohen, S. G., & Mohrman, A. M., Jr. (1995). *Designing team-based organizations: New forms for knowledge work.* San Francisco: Jossey-Bass.

Pope, S. (1996). The power of guidelines, structure, and clear goals. *Journal for Quality & Participation, 19*(7), 56–61.

Sims, H. P., Jr., & Manz, C. C. (1994). The leadership of self-managing work teams. In M. M. Beyerlein & D. Johnson (Eds.), *Advances in interdisciplinary studies of work teams: Vol. 1. Theories of self-managing work teams* (pp. 188–221). Greenwich, CT: JAI Press.

Sundstrom, E. (Ed.) (1998). *Supporting work team effectiveness: Best management practices for fostering high performance.* San Francisco: Jossey-Bass.

Zobal, C. (1998). The "ideal" team compensation system, part I. *Team Performance Management Journal, 4*(5), 235–249. Also available: http://www.emerald-library.com

Zobal, C. (1999). The "ideal" team compensation system—an overview, part II. *Team Performance Management Journal, 5*(1), 23–45. Also available: http://ernesto.emeraldinsight.com/vl=1446460/cl=71/nw=1/rpsv/~1089/v5n1/s3/p23

Action Planning and Summary Sheet

Ideas Generated from This Chapter

1	
2	
3	
4	
5	

#	Action Item	Target Date	Person/Group Responsible
1			
2			
3			
4			
5			
6			

Significant Decisions Made

1	
2	
3	
4	

## CHAPTER 6

Think Strategically About Change

Where Are We in the Strategic Design Process?

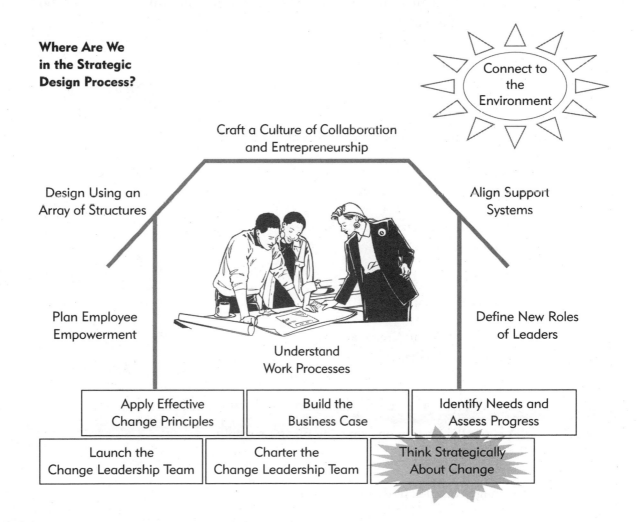

Connect to the Environment

Craft a Culture of Collaboration and Entrepreneurship

Design Using an Array of Structures

Align Support Systems

Plan Employee Empowerment

Understand Work Processes

Define New Roles of Leaders

| Apply Effective Change Principles | Build the Business Case | Identify Needs and Assess Progress |
| Launch the Change Leadership Team | Charter the Change Leadership Team | Think Strategically About Change |

? Key Question of This Chapter

How should the CLT think about the CWS initiative?

Quick Look

Overview

Planning the transformation to a collaborative work system requires an ongoing strategic approach to design and implementation of the change initiative. A strategic approach to design provides a framework for intelligent decision making on a large scale and sets the stage for effective implementation. The implementation of a CWS, whether in the form of teams, lateral organization, team-based organization, or collaborative organization, consists of a journey that is full of challenges and learning moments for the CLT and for the organization. A strategic approach maps the terrain, so the adventure will be more manageable and result in more successes. This chapter provides a view of how to think about the creation of that map or implementation plan—the strategic design process. The chapter outcomes include fitting tactical plans into the strategic framework, aligning with other initiatives, and identifying the sources of pain in the organization.

Chapter Plan

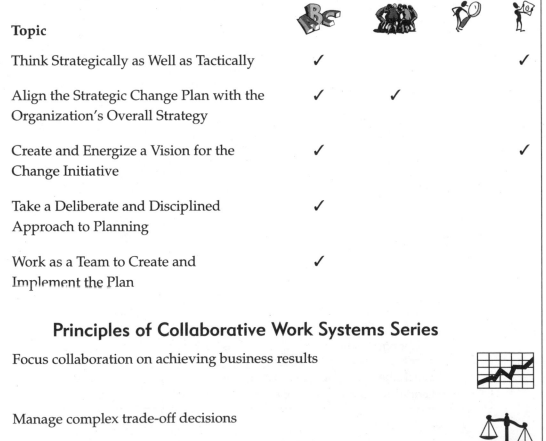

Topic				
Think Strategically as Well as Tactically	✓			✓
Align the Strategic Change Plan with the Organization's Overall Strategy	✓	✓		
Create and Energize a Vision for the Change Initiative	✓			✓
Take a Deliberate and Disciplined Approach to Planning	✓			
Work as a Team to Create and Implement the Plan	✓			

Principles of Collaborative Work Systems Series

Focus collaboration on achieving business results

Manage complex trade-off decisions

Treat collaboration as a disciplined process

Think Strategically as Well as Tactically

Major change initiatives require a big picture, long-term view of the organization. They are long-term strategic investments for building resources and markets that will sustain the organization into the future. Organizations that do not use this perspective go out of business. A short-term, tactical focus in change work tends to be reactionary, without continuity, and lacking in the ability to build on prior successes.

Strategic change is not an event but a process of continual adaptation and change within a carefully designed framework. Planning for such large initiatives requires a different kind of thinking than does short-term, action-oriented planning. Strategic thinking creates a framework for making tactical decisions intelligently—the smaller steps are integrated by being pieces of a larger plan. Both strategic and tactical planning are essential activities of members trying to create a more viable organization.

Most change initiatives fail. Total quality management (TQM), business process re-engineering (BPR), mergers and acquisitions (M&A), enterprise resource planning systems (ERP), and team-based organization (TBO) initiatives fail to achieve expected results well over half the time (Spector & Beer, 1993). Analysis of the failures shows several common causes, including failure to involve the people affected by the change, failure to provide the necessary resources, lack of commitment by top managers, and inadequate preparation and planning.

Common pitfalls of TQM, BPR, and similar initiatives include the following (Cicmil, 1999):

- Nothing new
- Nothing tangible
- Nothing strategic
- Nothing happens
- No profound learning

Strategic thinking provides the process for preparing a change plan that is more likely to succeed in two ways: (1) aligning the initiative with the business strategy and (2) planning for the long haul. Strategy is viewed by experts as the starting point: "What do we want to achieve?" followed by "How will we get there?" Remind each other to think long-term, to think outside the box.

Three approaches to planning combine the tactical and the strategic: (1) make the strategic improvement activities tactically attractive, (2) start a small tactical effort and gradually build it into a strategic improvement program (Humphrey, 2000), or (3) combine O-change and E-change, where O-change focuses on long-term development of organization resources and E-change is economic value-driven change that focuses on short-term technical changes (Beer, 2001). The combination of the two is more effective than either alone.

Table 6.1 provides an overview of key dimensions of strategic work on change. Some of the dimensions are described in greater detail later in the chapter, accompanied by assessment and planning activities to aid the CLT in creating a

Table 6.1.　Key Ideas for Thinking Both Strategically and Tactically

Dimension	Suggestions
Think Strategically as Well as Tactically	• Take a long-term, strategic approach to planning the CWS initiative • Align the CWS initiative strategy with the business strategy; misalignment will result in cancellation • Understand the big picture but manage from milestone to milestone • Align action steps (the tactical) with the big picture (the strategic) • Tailor the CWS initiative to your site. But do it within the corporate framework to avoid the immune system terminating your program
Align the Strategic Change Plan with the Organization's Overall Strategy	• The purpose of the CWS initiative is to create new capability that will enable the organization to execute the business strategy • Building the internal capabilities or core competencies of the organization means increasing resources, creating new ones, or leveraging existing ones for business results • The strategic decision makers provide the support for the CWS initiative when it clearly contributes to the business strategy • Business results in the broadest sense provide the benchmark for the success of the CWS initiative
Create and Energize a Vision for the Change Initiative	• Articulate a vision of what the organization will look like in five years if the CWS initiative is highly successful • Working together to create the vision leads to a shared understanding and commitment—"our vision" (see Chapter 5 for more on this) • The vision should represent the values of CWS, including consensus decision making, innovation, entrepreneurship, empowerment, and customer relations • Think outside the box. Do not assume the new organization will look like the current one. • Create a variety of ways to communicate the vision and the "why" of the CWS initiative to all stakeholder groups in the organization
Identify and Manage the Scope of the Initiative	• Decide on a realistic but worthwhile scope • Use only the best ideas to alter scope—the 20 percent that generate 80 percent of the value • Identify competing initiatives and seek ways to coordinate and collaborate with them (see Chapter 2 for more on this)
Find and Manage the Resources to Support the Initiative	• Remember that major change requires major investment of resources • The most critical resources are now people's time and attention • There will be competition for resources, so plan to manage it through collaboration with other initiatives

Table 6.1. (continued)

Dimension	Suggestions
	• The size of the investment increases with the size of the organization and the size of the gaps between current reality and vision
	• Extreme conditions, such as significant layoffs, severe downturns in the market, catastrophes such as fire or hurricanes, and mergers greatly increase both the difficulty of the CWS initiative and the value of collaboration
	• Extreme conditions create significant stress for people and drains on resources, so change work is seen as an overload and lower priority
	• The first resource needed is the change leadership team; the second is the support of the top management team
Take a Deliberate and Disciplined Approach to Planning	• Discipline produces results because it is based on carefully selecting a process and consistently following it
	• The principles of project management and quality management help with the disciplined process of the CWS initiative
	• The members of the CLT bring some of the tools for disciplined planning with them, such as project management skills, understanding of the business, and experience with other change initiatives
	• There are two challenges with discipline—sticking with it and not letting it stifle creativity—it is a means to an end, so be flexible when circumstances warrant it
Anchor the New Approaches in the Culture	• Culture represents the shared assumptions, values, and beliefs of the organization's members and is expressed in the daily routines and practices
	• If the organizational culture does not align with the CWS initiative, the CLT's work will fail
	• Assessment of culture alignment is essential and will probably lead to significant change work (see Chapter 11 for ways to do this)
	• Shared values may include a healthier workplace, a more competitive organization, respect for each other, and so forth, but opinions may differ about how to live by these values
	• The CWS initiative and vision rest on a foundation of values that should influence the organizational culture (see Chapter 5 for CLT work on vision and values)
	• The goal is creation of a collaborative culture
	• It is easier to change a strong, homogeneous culture than a weak one where there are a lot of subcultures
Beware of the Dark Side of Collaboration	• The "dark side" emerges when the self-interest of a few members of the organization leads to sacrificing others for their own gain
	• If the CLT is being created for political purposes rather than improving the organization as a whole, it will fail and members may become scapegoats

(continued)

Table 6.1.   Key Ideas for Thinking Both Strategically and Tactically (continued)

Dimension	Suggestions
Beware of the Dark Side of Collaboration (*continued*)	• If the CWS initiative is intended to be an excuse for such activities as downsizing or influencing a union vote, instead of building the collaborative capability of the organization as a whole, it will fail
	• When top management acts as if the CWS initiative is just for everybody else in the organization and not for them, it will fail; the principles of collaborative organization must be applied universally
	• Use of the power of collaboration for individual and subgroup gain costs the rest of the organization and undermines its viability; strategic change work builds in safeguards against this
	• When the team slips into "groupthink" where the value of diverse and dissenting views is lost in conformity, errors in judgment increase in frequency and scope
Work as a Team to Create and Implement the Plan	• A team that represents the organization's stakeholder groups will have immediate access to most of the perspectives that determine how members make sense of the CWS initiative
	• Integration of diverse viewpoints will enable the team to act wisely
	• A diverse team is better networked with the rest of the organization than any individual or any group representing a single stakeholder group (see Chapter 4 for more on the CLT as a team)
Gain Perspective	• Strategic thinking creates a broad perspective, so short-term urgencies are managed better
	• Urgencies disrupt the change work as well as other activities in the organization; they distract attention from what is important
	• The team's perspective is wiser than the individual members' on most occasions, so consensus makes team decisions smarter
	• Good team process improves CLT perspective
	• The opposite of a broad and integrated perspective is called "silo mentality"
	• Symptoms of silo mentality include:
	• Believing one's point of view is the only right one
	• Believing everyone else sees things the same way we do
	• Assuming others will automatically agree with us
	• Seeing the problem as simple
	• Feeling pride that one's own idea won over everyone else's
	• Always being ready to set other people straight
	• Knowledge is interpreted data; the interpretation depends on the perspective
	• How you look determines what you see, which determines what you do; perspective leads to actions, so smart implementation depends on an integrated point of view

strategic framework. After reviewing the ideas in Table 6.1, complete the planning exercise that follows, where the distinction between strategic and tactical steps will become more clear.

Planning: Combine Strategic and Tactical Planning

Time Requirement: Approximately 1 hour

Supplies: Table 6.1, Worksheet 6.1, flip chart, masking tape, and markers

Overview: Strategic thinking is difficult. Most of us do not naturally have a long-term perspective for our thinking, although it is important for successful change efforts. Most people have a short-term perspective, so it takes work to develop a long-term, strategic view. Try this brief exercise as a way to assess the balance and integration of your team's viewpoints. Using personal planning as a warm-up, this exercise starts the CLT thinking strategically at the highest level and linking it to action at the tactical level.

Instructions

1. Working individually, in the left column of Worksheet 6.1, list the personal areas where the group is doing some decision making. In the right two columns, list the short-term (up to six months) and long-term (longer than six months) activities related to that area. There are several examples to get you started.

2. Note the difference in tactical and strategic time frames and plans.

3. Also note the links between the tactical and the strategic.

4. As a group, share the insights that came from this exercise.

5. Still working as a group and using Table 6.1, think about how the CLT can use this approach for beginning the planning of the CWS initiative.

Planning: Tactical and Strategic Planning for the CWS Initiative

Time Requirement: Approximately 90 minutes

Supplies: Worksheet 6.2, flip chart, masking tape, and markers

Overview: Imagine how your organization will look in five years if your team is wildly successful in its work on the CWS initiative. That image is your vision.

Instructions

1. Work as a team or, if the team is more than seven people, as subgroups, to complete Worksheet 6.2.

2. First, review the examples on the worksheet and decide which of them is relevant enough for the CLT to keep or to modify and keep.

3. Add new items in any of the three columns that will flesh out the planning menu.

Worksheet 6.1.   Tactical and Strategic Planning for Personal Activities

Planning Area	Tactical Activities	Strategic Activities
Education (for example, take a class, work on a certification, earn a degree)	Six months to get certified as a C+ programmer	Over next two years accumulate certifications for promotion to senior programmer
Investments (for example, 401k, IRA, pension, real estate)	Saving $50/month extra on top of Social Security deduction and company contribution to 401k for rest of career of twelve years	Over next twelve years, pay off mortgage and double savings in accounts to supplement pension
Hobby (for example, weaving, fishing, travel, gardening)	Planning to use tiller in the garden next month to get ready for spring planting	Rotate crops and add fertilizer to keep garden plot viable for years to come

Worksheet 6.2.	Tactical and Strategic Planning for CWS Initiative Activities	
Planning Area	**Tactical Activities**	**Strategic Activities**
Educate the CLT	As a CLT, complete one workbook chapter per week; create a timeline today to show this As a team, attend a workshop or conference September 23 Read a book and share the ideas from it on March 12	Systematically increase the knowledge of the CLT over the next two years using a variety of methods
Build the business case for the CWS initiative	Brainstorm the contents of the business case the week of Feb. 1 Refine the business case and prepare the presentation to the top management team (Feb. 7–Feb. 21) Present the business case to the top management team (Feb. 22)	Continually make the business case for the CWS initiative clear to the top management team, and keep them informed of progress to sustain their support
Use assessment as the basis for planning for the CWS initiative	Have the top management team complete the gap analysis questionnaire from Chapter 2 the week of March 4 Analyze the gap data and prepare report the week of March 11 Present results of gap analysis to top management team the week of March 18 Conduct six focus groups with a random sample of employees at all levels the week of March 25	Develop an assessment system using a variety of tools, use it on an ongoing basis to assess needs and track progress, and archive the data for baseline and trend analysis

(continued)

Worksheet 6.2.   Tactical and Strategic Planning for CWS Initiative Activities (continued)

Planning Area	Tactical Activities	Strategic Activities

4. Discuss the way items in column 2 relate to those in column 3. The tactical should lead to the strategic.

5. Work as a group to consider how the CLT will deal with the following issues:

   • Making consistency of purpose possible over the years

   • Preventing loss of focus when short-term issues and detail distract from the long-term and big-picture view needed to keep the initiative strategic

   • Coordinating multiple activities for the CWS initiative

   • Encouraging the rest of the organization to think strategically

6. Revisit these issues several times each year.

Align the Strategic Change Plan with the Organization's Overall Strategy

The overall business strategy of the organization is designed to result in a business plan that will work in the market environment. The relationship between the business and the environment is complex. Strategy is an attempt to align the design of the organization with that environment and to align the parts of the organization with each other. It includes adapting to change and trying to influence the environment (see Chapter 10 on environment and Chapter 16 on alignment). The design of the organization plays a key role in the business strategy, because design determines which aspects of the organization will be emphasized and used to generate the key capabilities that lead to protecting and increasing market share.

The overall strategy cascades down from above to frame the changes within the organization. Alignment is essential between the levels of strategy. Organization design or redesign represents the implementation of the strategy defined by the top management group (Windsor, 2002). In this way, the CWS initiative becomes a strategic change process.

Discussion

1. Does your team know the business strategy? Which of the following does it fit? Discuss the choice and then circle it (there may be multiple answers, but one should stand out).

   • Create and shape the future

   • Anticipate the future and prepare for it

   • React to the future when it has happened

   • Ignore the future

2. Which of the following types does the primary business strategy aim to be? Discuss it as a team and then circle the best answer (there may be multiple answers, but one should stand out).

- Diversifying

- Low-cost provider

- Niche focus

- Market follower

- First to market

The plan to create a more effective collaborative work system should make sense within the business strategy and contribute directly to it. For example, if the strategy is to be first to market with new products, innovation and speed will be key drivers of processes in the organization. Innovation and speed depend on open sharing, excellent learning, streamlined decision making, and other factors. Collaborative work is essential in this environment. However, being the low-cost provider of knockoffs typically means narrow margins, so collaboration may be an effective means of finding efficiencies in processes and making the best use of resources. These business strategies differ, so the change initiative must be adapted in each to achieve alignment. Without alignment between the change strategy and the business strategy, benefits of the investment in change will be reduced and the initiative is likely to be abandoned before it is complete.

Create and Energize a Vision for the Change Initiative

If you don't know where you are going, you can't get there. That is the basic argument for starting strategic planning with articulation of a vision. The process of jointly determining the vision makes it a shared vision, so the actions of the group's members become aligned. Instructions for the development of a CWS initiative vision statement are in Chapter 5. The vision describes the kind of organization you want to become. Dominant features should include consensus decision making, innovation, entrepreneurship, working smarter, empowered teams or groups, world-class products and services, emphasis on ability and contribution in place of status, rewarding real contributions, and customer-focus.

Think outside the box. Do not assume that the future organization will look like the current one. Organizations grow in five ways: (1) increased size, (2) more copies of the same kinds of units (McDonald's), (3) increased variety of products and services, (4) transformation—that is, a change to something really new, and (5) death. Adding similar units to increase size, as McDonald's does, is simpler than diversifying products or businesses, and that is simpler than full transformation. Collaboration can help with all of these, but especially the latter. Organizations that do not change die. Look around at other organizations to get some ideas of the possibilities. Many aspects of an organization that do not seem changeable are. But also look inward at where the pain and the possibilities are to see what you want to change. To identify the "pain" in your organization that may be indicative of a need to change, work as a team to complete Worksheet 6.3.

Planning: Identify the Pain in the Organization

Time Requirement: Approximately 30 minutes

Supplies: Worksheet 6.3, flip chart, masking tape, and markers

Overview: Change is either subtle or blatant. The latter is usually resisted unless there is enough pain to take the leap. The feeling of pain creates a sense of urgency that then drives the effort to change. The danger is that when the pain drops, comfort increases to the point where the effort to make the change is dropped and gains are lost as people revert back to the old ways of doing things. Sources of pain may be an undiscussable topic in your organization's culture, but this activity will help you to begin that process.

Instructions

1. In small groups of three or four CLT members, brainstorm causes of individual and organizational pain. Capture the ideas on Worksheet 6.3. Examples of individual pain include stress, fear, layoffs, accidents, illness, loss of pride, feeling too controlled, boredom, and so on. Examples of organizational pain include reduced sales and market share, projects that don't pay off in the market, loss of talent, technological changes that make tools or products obsolete, and so forth. The left column of Worksheet 6.3 shows some additional examples.

2. Reconvene the whole team and compile a joint list from all the small groups on flip-chart paper and post it so all can see.

3. Individually, using Worksheet 6.3, rate the pain level of each item on a scale from 1 (low) to 6 (high).

4. Compile the ratings of the group on the flip chart.

5. Discuss the range of ratings and what they mean.

6. Circle the five highest rated sources of pain as possible targets of the CWS initiative.

Although pain may be a primary motivator for change, a shared vision can be another motivator with a more positive emphasis.

Energize Your Vision

Chapter 5 helped the CLT to create a shared vision for the CWS initiative. However, it's not enough to just have a vision; the team must be enthused about it and must communicate it to the rest of the organization in a way that builds energy and momentum.

Worksheet 6.3.   Sources of Pain

Location of Pain and Possibilities Within the Organization	Level of Pain					
	Low					**High**
Error rates	1	2	3	4	5	6
Quality of new hires	1	2	3	4	5	6
Number of new product development projects is overwhelming the developers	1	2	3	4	5	6
Customer satisfaction	1	2	3	4	5	6
Rework	1	2	3	4	5	6
Amount of blaming	1	2	3	4	5	6
Number of orders	1	2	3	4	5	6
Budget	1	2	3	4	5	6
	1	2	3	4	5	6
	1	2	3	4	5	6
	1	2	3	4	5	6
	1	2	3	4	5	6
	1	2	3	4	5	6
	1	2	3	4	5	6
	1	2	3	4	5	6
	1	2	3	4	5	6
	1	2	3	4	5	6
	1	2	3	4	5	6

The following steps can be taken to help build energy for the vision:

- Co-create the vision. If someone in authority creates the vision and hands it down, ownership by the change leadership team will be minimal and energy will be diluted.

- Remove the hurdles to progress on the CWS initiative. Identify and manage your allies, adversaries, and fence sitters (Block, 1999).

- Describe the present state of the organization and compare it to the vision. (See the assessments in Chapter 3 to review the team's previous work on this topic.) Think about both the current and future states *at the same time*. Notice the tension of thinking about that gap. That is the creative tension that generates the energy for achieving the vision (Fritz, 1989).

- Celebrate each milestone on the journey toward the vision.

- Make the vision and the progress public. Share it up and down the line so others will be aware of what is happening and why and provide feedback.

- Take an Appreciative Inquiry approach where the focus is on how far you have already come, what resources you have, and what you want to achieve, rather than on problems that need fixing.

- Be bold.

Planning: Develop a Vision for Change

Time Requirement: Approximately 30 minutes

Supplies: Flip chart, masking tape, and markers

Overview: In this activity, you'll imagine how your organization will look in five years if your team is wildly successful in its work on the CWS initiative. Then the team will compare that ideal to the vision previously created and update the vision if necessary.

Instructions

1. Sit quietly for two minutes thinking about the kind of place you would like to work where people work really well together. Jot down some notes to describe that place.

2. Share the notes with the team—ideas, pictures, graphs, and so forth.

3. Capture the ideas shared on flip charts and post them around the room.

4. Notice and discuss the patterns. Which items can be eliminated or combined? Which items can be treated as high-level or more detailed?

5. Now review the vision statement the CLT crafted in Chapter 5 and compare it with what you have on the flip charts. If the vision statement needs to be modified to capture the ideas on the flip chart, do that now.

6. The result of Step 5 is probably a complex paragraph. Boil it down to one or two sentences. That's the vision statement for the CWS initiative.

7. Present it to the CLT sponsor for input and approval.

8. Present the approved version to the top management team to generate their buy-in and check for strategic alignment.

9. Revisit it again every quarter to polish it and to make sure your work is aligned with it.

10. Communicate the final vision statement to the rest of the organization often.

Take a Deliberate and Disciplined Approach to Planning

In sports and fitness training or in changing personal habits, such as quitting smoking or fatty foods or nail biting, discipline is important. It means a careful process is followed without deviation over a long period. Major change initiatives are similar but more complex, since they involve large numbers of people and processes. The planning work is subject to the same quality requirements as any other creative work. The quality of the planning is a big factor in determining the quality of the implementation. Haphazard planning shows in sloppy execution that makes the initiative more vulnerable to cancellation.

The CLT has a number of tools available for managing various kinds of projects that can be applied to the CWS initiative; thinking about the initiative as a broad form of continuous improvement, organizing with project management tools, using design of experiments for pilot testing, and so on, provides a discipline to make the effort effective. However, when and how to use each of these tools must be decided within the overall framework of strategy, change principles, and CWS values. The tools do not drive the initiative; they aid it.

Another discipline is available through the use of this book. It provides a thorough overview of the critical areas. The change is so complex that a guide can aid the CLT in achieving thorough and logical coverage of the planning and implementing processes. This should be done in real time—that is, your planning should parallel your action. You won't necessarily finish the entire planning process before getting started with implementation/communication—in fact, we suggest you do not do that!

A more subtle form of discipline is leaving room for improvisation (Pascale, Millemann, & Gioja, 1997). A good plan is useful, but it is general. Each locale of application will require tailoring—adjustments to scheduling, individualizing training, modifications to procedure, and so forth. In addition, new opportunities will become visible to the CLT, so it can make mid-course changes to more effectively use resources and more rapidly approach milestones on the way to achieving the vision.

Work as a Team to Create and Implement the Plan

Some days you may wish you were a little smarter, made better decisions, or could get more done. Strategic planning depends on intelligence to generate high-quality decisions. The easiest way to increase intelligence, quality of decision making, and accomplishments is to work with a team. When a group of people come together to accomplish a shared goal and they have both the task work skills and the teamwork skills necessary, there is a good chance that the outcomes will be superior to what any one of the members could have accomplished in isolation from the others. The diverse perspectives of an effective team allow it to:

- Generate a clearer view of the reality of the situation
- Utilize the resources in the room and accept, respect, and appreciate the diverse membership
- Create and innovate as demand and opportunity occur, recognizing that creativity is a choice
- Focus on mission and avoid ego-centered conflict
- Work flexibly as a whole group or subgroups or individuals as fits the task
- Maintain a perspective and calm even when the going gets rough, completing the adventure without loss of poise
- Maintain an energy and enthusiasm through commitment, creativity, and celebration
- Create an example of what the overall culture will become and maintain it in the face of pressure from outside the group
- Maintain standards of member behavior that elevate it to a higher level of quality, thoughtfulness, dependability, honesty, and empathy
- Find fun, humor, and excitement to be legitimate parts of the group experience

When a team of people with diverse expertise and perspectives comes together effectively, they may achieve the highest levels of performance. We refer to that as "team genius." A team approach to strategic planning can provide the following:

- Group checks on members' perceptions and judgments that increase accuracy and reduce distortion
- Mutual support around complex, emotional, ambiguous, and risky issues
- Innovation and creativity that go beyond the conventional ways of approaching problems
- More effective intelligence gathering through having many sets of eyes scanning the organization
- Problem-focused work rather than ego-centered work that takes too narrow a view

The change leadership team may be configured in several different ways:

1. The team may consist of a group of top managers or executives who lay out the overall strategy (a guiding coalition) and then delegate to design teams to handle implementation in various sections of a large organization.

2. In a smaller organization the top management group might play both the strategic planning and design and implementation roles (a steering team).

3. Another option is to create a team out of a vertical slice of the organization, with members representing all layers of the hierarchy.

Members may include key decision makers or executives, mid-managers, floor supervisors, line managers, internal or external consultants, change agents, champions, union representatives, team members, and others who have a role in the organization's design. There are pros and cons to each arrangement. Some favor the guiding coalition because it is less likely to conflict with the National Labor Relations Board (NLRB) ruling about line workers making management decisions. We favor the vertical slice, because having members from the top and the bottom and from support systems in the room at the same time provides an opportunity for communication between the levels and for building a more accurate picture of the organization. The term *change leadership team* (CLT) in this workbook is intended to represent all of these designs.

Conclusion

If change is so hard, why is it worth the effort? The potential payoffs are significant. Even organizations that only go partway have generated substantial benefits in tangible and intangible payoffs and increased competitive advantage. (These benefits are detailed in Chapter 7.) A strategic approach to change is vision-driven. Urgent issues are put in perspective rather than emerging to dominate thinking and action. Urgency implies lack of preparation or surprise from environmental changes that were not foreseen. Vision drives the organization that has surplus to invest. Urgency-driven and vision-driven initiatives take resources, but the spending has a different feel to it and often a different outcome. Launch the CWS initiative from a position of strength with forethought, rather than a position of urgency and deficit.

Keys to the Chapter

- Take a long-term, strategic approach to planning the CWS initiative.
- Develop a realistic view of the scope of the change effort (it is always bigger than you think) and of the time and resources required.
- Understand the big picture, but manage from milestone to milestone.
- Align the CWS initiative strategy with the business strategy.
- The CLT members need to thoroughly understand and communicate the strategic "why" for the change.
- The work of designing and implementing a major change initiative is difficult to do well. It takes a team because of the value of multiple perspectives, an effective communication network, varied expertise, and mutual support.

Chapter Wrap-Up

- What action items did this chapter trigger for you and your group? Complete the action planning worksheet at the end of this chapter.

- Were any significant decisions made? Include them at the bottom of the action planning worksheet.

- What can you do tomorrow or within the next week based on what you learned in this chapter?

- How does what you learned in this chapter relate to your business case?

- How can you communicate the pertinent material generated by your work on this chapter to different audiences?

- What chapter should you go through next? Refer back to the Guiding Assessment in Chapter 3 for suggestions of next steps.

Resources

Barney, J. (1991). Firm resources and sustained competitive advantage. *Journal of Management, 17,* 99–120.

Becker, B. E., Huselid, M. A., & Ulrich, D. (2001). *The HR scorecard: Linking people, strategy, and performance.* Boston: Harvard Business School Press.

Beer, M. (2001). How to develop an organization capable of sustained high performance: Embrace the drive for results-capability development paradox. *Organizational Dynamics, 29*(4), 233–248.

Block, P. (1999). *Flawless consulting: A guide to getting your expertise used* (2nd ed.). San Francisco: Jossey-Bass.

Bradshaw, C., Roberts, J., & Cheuy, S. (2003). Real collaboration requires power sharing: The participative design approach. In M. Beyerlein, C. McGee, G. Klein, J. Nemiro, & L. Broedling (Eds.), *The collaborative work system fieldbook* (pp. 259–274). San Francisco: Jossey-Bass/Pfeiffer.

Cicmil, S. (1999). An insight into management of organizational change projects. *Journal of Workplace Learning, 11,* 1.

Collins, J. C., & Porras, J. L. (2002). *Built to last: Successful habits of visionary companies.* New York: HarperBusiness.

Creating a vision. (n.d.) Retrieved May 31, 2003, from National School Boards Association Web site: www.nsba.org/sbot/toolkit/cav.html

de Guerre, D. (2003). The participative design workshop and its variations. In M. Beyerlein, C. McGee, G. Klein, J. Nemiro, & L. Broedling (Eds.), *The collaborative work system fieldbook* (pp. 275–285). San Francisco: Jossey-Bass/Pfeiffer.

Eisenhardt, K. M., & Sull, D. N. (2001). Strategy as simple rules. *Harvard Business Review, 79*(1), 106–117.

Finley, M. (1997, Oct. 21). *"Cadillacs and steak knives": Judith Bardwick on the topic of entitlement, earning, and the borderless economy.* Retrieved May 31, 2003, from www.mastersforum.com/archives/bardwick/bard-r.htm

Fogg, C. D. (1994). *Team-based strategic planning: A complete guide to structuring, facilitating, and implementing the process.* New York: AMACOM.

Fritz, R. (1989). *The path of least resistance: Learning to become the creative force in your own life.* New York: Fawcett Columbine.

GSM Analysis—Thinking about strategy: Nature, purpose, perspectives, process, and economics. Retrieved on May 31, 2003, from University of Strathclyde, Department of Economics Web site: www.economics.strath.ac.uk/PDF/jsmba2.pdf

Hamel, G. (1996). Strategy as revolution. *Harvard Business Review, 74*(4), 69–83.

Huffman, B. (2001). What makes a strategy brilliant? *Business Horizons, 44*(4), 13–21.

Humphrey, W. S. (2000). Making the tactical case for process improvement. *News @ SEI Interactive, 3*(2). Retrieved May 31, 2003, from http://interactive.sei.cmu.edu/news@sei/columns/watts_new/2000/spring/watts-spring00.htm

Liedtka, J. (2000). In defense of strategy as design. *California Management Review, 42*(3), 8–31.

Pacanowsky, M. (1995). Team tools for wicked problems. *Organizational Dynamics, 23*(3), 36–52.

Pascale, R., Millemann, M., & Gioja, L. (1997). Changing the way we change. *Harvard Business Review, 75,* 126–139.

Rankin, T., & Lytle, B. (2001). *Accelerating the design of high-performance work systems.* Presentation at the annual Organizational Design Conference, San Antonio, TX.

Rose, E. (1999). *Self-directed work teams: A trainer's role in the transition.* Alexandria, VA: ASTD Press.

Spector, B., & Beer, M. (1993). Organizational diagnosis: Its role in organizational learning. *Journal of Counseling & Development, 71*(6), 642–651.

Van Gels, J. (2002). *Collaboration for success.* Industry keynote address at the annual International Conference on Work Teams, Dallas, TX.

Ward, A. (2000). Getting strategic value from constellations of communities. *Strategy & Leadership, 28*(2), 4–10.

Windsor, D. (2003). Change management competencies for creating collaborative organizations. In M. Beyerlein, D. Johnson, & S. Beyerlein (Eds.), *Advances in interdisciplinary studies of work teams: Vol. 9. Team-based organizing* (pp. 31–66). Oxford, England: Elsevier Science.

Action Planning and Summary Sheet

Ideas Generated from This Chapter

1	
2	
3	
4	
5	

#	Action Item	Target Date	Person/Group Responsible
1			
2			
3			
4			
5			
6			

Significant Decisions Made

1	
2	
3	
4	

## CHAPTER 7

Apply Effective Change Principles

Where Are We in the Strategic Design Process?

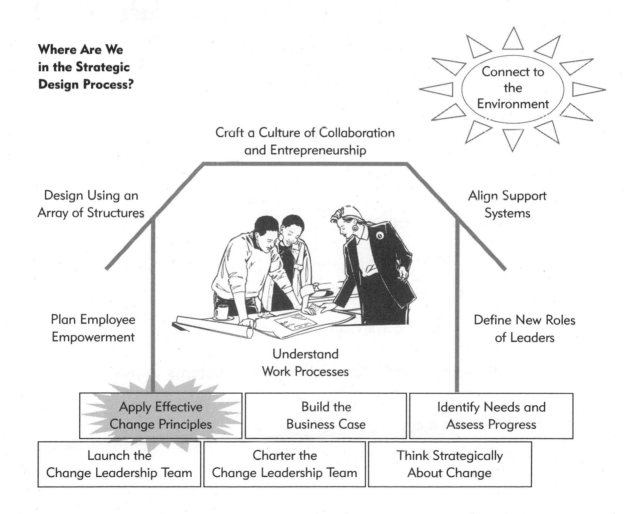

Connect to the Environment

Craft a Culture of Collaboration and Entrepreneurship

Design Using an Array of Structures

Align Support Systems

Plan Employee Empowerment

Define New Roles of Leaders

Understand Work Processes

Apply Effective Change Principles	Build the Business Case	Identify Needs and Assess Progress
Launch the Change Leadership Team	Charter the Change Leadership Team	Think Strategically About Change

Key Question of This Chapter

What enables a change plan to work?

Quick Look

Overview

Principles of change management have been discovered and tested over the years to the point that some are very dependable. Many change initiatives fail to achieve expectations because one or more of these principles has been ignored. This chapter provides overviews of some of those critical principles and exercises to assist the CLT in putting them into practice. This chapter also provides mechanisms to assess readiness for change, sources of resistance, competing initiatives, and other factors. Outcomes from this chapter include an assessment of CLT expertise in change management, a map of major milestones for the CWS initiative, and an assessment of sources of resistance to change.

Chapter Plan

Topic				
Build a Big Picture of Change Management	✓			
Build Expertise in Strategic Change Processes	✓		✓	
Effective Change Principles	✓			
Start from Where You Are	✓			
Generate Short-Term Wins	✓			✓
Minimize Critical Specifications	✓			
Plan for Resistance	✓			✓
Integrate with Other Change Initiatives	✓			✓
Do Not Create the Plan in a Vacuum	✓			

Principles of Collaborative Work Systems Series

Align support systems to promote ownership

Create higher standards for discussion, dialogue, and sharing of information

Align authority, information, and decision making

Design and promote flexible organizations that foster needed collaboration

Build a Big Picture of Change Management

Change happens continually in organizations. It is either planned or unplanned. The change leadership team has responsibility for planning a major change and then making it happen. The effort will take years and cost a great deal of time and some money. Motivation to make such a change comes from either a vision of the future and the desire to close the gap between real and ideal or from an awareness of problems that demand solutions. When a change goal is established—vision or problem fix—the CLT should proceed using the best principles of change management. Before exploring the specific principles, however, team members should gain familiarity with an overall picture of the change management process. One way to think about this process is described below in the Five Phases of Intervention.

Five Phases of Intervention

I. *Defining roles:* defining the roles and responsibilities of the change leadership team, top management group, and design teams; defining the change goal, targets, and problems

II. *Diagnosing and assessing:* identifying the current situation, including process mapping, attitude assessment, leadership audit, and so on (note that people experience assessment as an intervention, so expect a reaction)

III. *Planning:* working out a high-level picture of the change program and the major milestones, including alignment issues, readiness of the organizational systems for change, assessment of change leadership team power and influence, and identification of leverage points for change

IV. *Implementing the intervention:* a continual process based on approximating the plan and continually modifying it from feedback—the period of most failures

V. *Monitoring and feedback:* to achieve stabilization and integration over time; the focus of monitoring is to ensure that post-intervention levels of performance are maintained and to re-implement interventions as necessary (Halfhill, Huff, Johnson, Beyerlein, & Ballentine, 2002)

Figure 7.1 shows the basic links between these five stages of the change process. Note how some boxes have feedback arrows (two-way). This represents a nonlinear

Figure 7.1. Five Phases of the Nonlinear Change Process

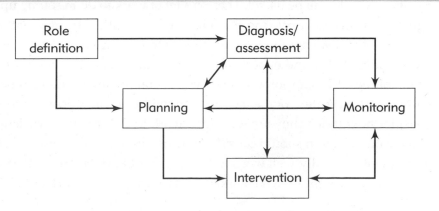

process—an ongoing, dynamic system of steps that allows for guided development of the change initiative.

Build Expertise in Strategic Change Processes

Although this workbook is designed to educate you about the strategic change process necessary for creating a collaborative work system, it is only one of many resources the CLT should tap. The membership of the CLT will likely have a range of expertise on change processes, but will likely not have any experts on the subject. Some CLTs utilize internal or external consultants with organization development and change (ODC) expertise as resources for both the process and the planning of the transformation.

Assessment: Assess the Change Expertise of the CLT

Time Requirement: Approximately 20 minutes

Supplies: Worksheet 7.1, flip chart, masking tape, and markers

Overview: Assess the change management experience of the CLT to get a snapshot of the internal resources the group brings to planning the CWS initiative.

Instructions

1. Have members assess their individual expertise level by answering the questions about experience with change programs in Worksheet 7.1.

2. Have them add up their points and record them at the bottom of their worksheets.

3. Now each person should write his or her scores on a piece of paper and fold it. Have one team member collect the pieces and compile the scores on a board or flip chart.

4. Total the scores and divide by the number of team members to get an average team score.

A CLT with an average team score between sixteen and twenty may not need an organization change and development (OCD) consultant, but a skilled meeting facilitator would still be useful. There is a lot of work to do in setting up meetings, managing the process, capturing the outcomes, and other things that such help could provide. Most teams will average between ten and fifteen points. They bring a basic level of knowledge and experience to the job but need OCD support. Continual education of the CLT is important, but teams averaging fewer than ten points must begin with intense education of the members. Individuals with a score lower than ten should consider how much they are willing to work to build their knowledge, and the CLT and the organization should consider how much they will invest in that education. The investment is usually well worth it. There is a lot to learn! Begin that learning process by having each member who marked a 4 on a question in Worksheet 7.1 tell the story of

---

Worksheet 7.1.   Change Experience

Circle the number next to the answer that best fits your experience.

A.   I have gone through a major change program before in an organization (business, church, club, local government, volunteer organization).

   1.   No

   2.   Yes, as a member of the group that was changed

   3.   Yes, as a leader of the group that was changed

   4.   Yes, as a member of the group that planned the change

B.   I had a leadership role in a major change effort.

   1.   No

   2.   Yes, as a change team member

   3.   Yes, as a change team leader

   4.   Yes, as a change expert

C.   I have had special training in change management.

   1.   No

   2.   Attended a workshop

   3.   Taken a course with over forty hours of meeting time

   4.   Earned a degree

D.   I have knowledge of change processes.

   1.   No

   2.   Experienced a change

   3.   Read extensively about change

   4.   Participated in the strategic planning for a major change program

E.   I have skills in:

   1.   Nothing related to change projects

   2.   Project management

   3.   Implementation of a major initiative not focused on collaboration, such as TQM, BPR, or lean manufacturing

   4.   Implementing a CWS initiative

Add up your points on the five questions and write them here: _____ (maximum possible is 20)

---

their experience on that project to the rest of the CLT. (See Chapter 4 for more on CLT education and skill building.)

Effective Change Principles

In the remainder of this chapter, we will explore the following effective change principles:

- Start from where you are
- Generate short-term wins
- Minimize critical specifications
- Plan for resistance

- Integrate with other change initiatives

- Do not create the plan in a vacuum

Table 7.1 shows how the various principles intersect with the five phases of intervention reviewed earlier. Note that not every principle applies to every phase.

Start from Where You Are

Assessment begins the process. It answers the question, "Where are we now?" which provides a baseline, a picture of current reality. It also acts as an index of readiness for major change—what prerequisites need to be put in place before launching the change initiative. Readiness can be assessed through a number of methods, including questionnaires, interviews, and focus groups. The same methods can be used periodically to capture the changing picture of progress on the CWS initiative. The strengths and weaknesses of various methods are described in Table 7.2.

As broad as the list of options in Table 7.2 seems to be, there are other methods as well. However, unless the CLT has access to assessment experts, some methods will be too difficult. We suggest that the CLT initially rely on the questionnaire in Chapter 3, that they supplement it with observation (walking around with your eyes open), informal interviews (conversations), archival records for establishing trends, and possibly Force-Field Analysis and focus groups. In an organization of modest size that is used to change, a professional facilitator can be used for large-scale change events, but the CLT needs to study that method before choosing it, as there is a large menu of options, each with its own strengths and weaknesses (Holman & Devane, 1999).

A readiness questionnaire provides a convenient method of benchmarking current levels of practice and then, through repeated administrations, of monitoring progress and measuring results. As such it is a diagnostic tool that profiles current reality. Comparing current reality with the CLT vision clarifies the gap that is to be closed and generates the energy for the work. The energy comes from thinking about both the current situation and the vision at the same time. This simultaneous awareness provides a clear experience of the gap and generates motivation to close it (Fritz, 1989). Major initiatives based on a "fix the problem" approach typically run out of energy after a short while. The organization is likely to maintain the status quo rather than achieve new levels of excellence.

A combination of assessment methods is better than a single method. Various methods can be repeated at regular time intervals, but mixing the methods over time can also produce richer results than any single method. Data-based change is superior to change based merely on opinion or mandate from above. Recognize that all the data you have is old data. Things change so fast in organizations and markets that data collection is always behind the pace. But some data is better than no data, and good data is better than poor data.

Whichever methods of assessment are selected to help the CLT acquire data about the organization, some basic principles must be followed:

1. Participation *must be* voluntary. Any participant has the right to skip any or all questions; forced participation will result in garbage for answers and damage the trust employees have in the CLT.

Table 7.1. Using Effective Principles in Various Phases of the Intervention

			Phases of Intervention		
Change Principles	**Defining Roles**	**Diagnosing and Assessing**	**Planning**	**Implementing**	**Monitoring and Feedback**
Start from Where You Are		Use Chapter 2 for gap analysis			
Generate Short-Term Wins			Plan the implementation to create quick payoffs at a steady pace		Identify, publicize, and celebrate small successes
Build Leadership of the Change Initiatives	Who will play what leadership role	How the leadership system is aligned with the CWS initiative		Build shared leadership in the CLT and throughout the organization	
Involve the People Who Will Be Affected	Select representative CLT membership and build a network	Assess attitudes and culture for involvement	Implement so that stakeholders play key roles at the local level	Co-create the CWS initiative implementation instead of imposing the solution	
Minimize Critical Specifications	Provide flexibility in roles		Plan at a high level to allow ground-level tailoring		
Plan for Resistance		Assess resistance levels and sources	Build in steps for reducing resistance	Partner to reduce resistance rather than bulldozing the resisters	Seek feedback from resisters who may have good points to make
Integrate with Other Change Initiatives					
Do Not Create the Plan in a Vacuum					

Table 7.2. Strengths and Limitations of Various Assessment Methods

Assessment Method	Strengths	Limitations
Questionnaires; usually twenty to forty minutes	• Some already exist, such as the one in Chapter 3 • Can be created from scratch and so tailored to the organization • Some have databases for comparing across companies • Some have been well-validated • Efficient—can get input from a large number of people with minimal time investment • Produce quantitative data • Can be done by paper-and-pencil, mail, Web site, e-mail, or telephone, but some methods, such as phone, require use of fewer and simpler questions, and some, such as mail, may be slow	• Trade-off between validated, commercial instruments and tailored or homemade ones may be difficult decision • Require some reading ability from participants; may need versions in several languages
Focus groups; usually two hours	• Tailored questions can be asked and explored in-depth • Participants stimulate each other's thinking • Generate rich material • More efficient use of facilitator than interviews • Questions can range from yes/no questions to open topics that might reveal new ideas	• Fairly skilled facilitator needed, often with a scribe • Supervisors should not be included but then are suspicious of the process • Scheduling so all attend is challenging • Getting a representative sample can be difficult • The group may easily stray off the topic
Force-Field Analysis can be done within the CLT as well as with other groups, such as the top management team; about two hours	• A graphic summary of the forces for and against the change initiative that prioritizes issues (see Chapter 2 for instructions and example)	• Group participating gets much more out of the process than others who review the output
Interviews; usually one hour per person	• Face-to-face allows for probing to get at deeper meanings • Allow for more complex questions • Allow interviewee to ask questions • Generate richly detailed data that can reveal issues the CLT is missing • Can range from yes/no questions to open topics that might reveal new ideas	• Time-consuming • Analysis of massive amounts of qualitative data is difficult • Some skill is required to build rapport and capture notes

(continued)

Table 7.2.   (continued)

Assessment Method	Strengths	Limitations
Observation, a continual process	• Can be based on reflection on own experience, keeping one's eyes open, and casual conversation	• Limited to impressions formed • Nothing is quantifiable • Lack of controlled conditions may create mistrust
Whole systems meetings (Holman & Devane, 1999, provide an excellent overview of such meetings); typically, three days	• The shared experience leads to a shared vision of the changed organization • Produce energy for change, possibly resulting in a critical mass that accelerates the change process • Generate input from all stakeholder perspectives, so the resulting picture of the organization is more accurate • Typically include a day of vision work	• Need expert facilitation • Take more employee time than other methods • Although most methods claim to involve the whole organization, some are limited to twenty-four participants
Review of records in archives, an ongoing process	• Measures of productivity, turnover, sales, error rates, customer complaints, percent of income from new products, and so on, all provide information that can be tracked over time to identify trends. Mapping the CWS initiative milestones over the trends gives an idea of the impact of the CLT's work.	• The information may be too old to provide an accurate picture of current reality • Access to records may be difficult • Key information may not be archived

2. All answers are anonymous. Names are never associated with specific answers; violation of this principle in a *single case* will destroy the credibility of the whole data collection process. The best way to handle "voluntary" and "anonymous" issues is to have it spelled out on the first page of the questionnaire or Web page and/or to read it from a printed script before starting an interview or focus group.

3. Only aggregated results are presented in reports, with the exception of illustrative quotes where identity is carefully concealed.

4. Design the whole process so no one can be harmed.

5. Discussion of results in the CLT is confidential; do not share any details outside the meetings about results that can be connected to the person they came from.

Generate Short-Term Wins

Periodic successes built into the change process provide positive milestones that mark progress and energize the CLT. Small successes can be achieved in two ways. Either work with subunits of the organization, piloting and refining the intervention there before taking it to the larger system, or break the change initiative into phases and milestones. Every major change program takes time. During the two to five years or more that the initiative takes to near a sense of completion, the spirits of CLT members will rise and dip depending on sense of success. Nobel prize-winning scientist Marie Curie wrote, "One never notices what has been done, one can only see what remains to be done." Marking the successes, logging the progress made, and celebrating each milestone achieved will generate energy for the next phase. Publicizing the successes will generate support from members of the organization for the initiative and help sustain it over the long haul. To generate short-term wins:

- Plan for early successes. Identify and harvest the low-hanging fruit during early stages to build support for the initiative.

- Make successes visible by publicizing them through reports, presentations, informal discussion, newsletter stories, bulletin board exhibits, and other means.

- Capture the return on investment (ROI) for the change effort. This is a potentially difficult area but a critical one. The usual approaches to ROI include the use of the balanced scorecard, utility analysis, and ROI analysis. The CLT should work toward one or more of these methods over time but begin by capturing stories of success, records of change, and estimates of the value of improvements.

- Identify the facets of change that will be easier to implement and run them concurrently with those that will be difficult, so energy from the easy will leak over to fuel the difficult.

- Link short-term tactical action to the long-term strategic umbrella, so a sense of accumulating value emerges without having to wait for the long-term outcomes.

Planning: Mapping Milestones

Time Requirement: Approximately 1 hour

Supplies: Worksheet 7.2, flip chart, masking tape, and markers

Overview: The goal of this activity is to create a list of short-term milestones that can then be used as a tracking sheet.

Instructions

1. For each CSF listed in the left-hand column of Worksheet 7.2, brainstorm possible short-term wins or milestones. There are several examples on the top portion of the worksheet.

2. Have someone record the lists on a flip chart.

3. Then, for each CSF, review the ideas and eliminate or combine items as necessary.

4. Record the results on Worksheet 7.2.

5. Regularly review the worksheet to note the date that milestones are achieved.

6. Repeat this activity regularly to add new items as necessary.

Worksheet 7.2.   Planning for Short-Term Wins

Sample

Critical Success Factor (Chapter Title)	Short-Term Wins or Milestones	Date Achieved
Launch the Change Leadership Team	Complete selection of members for CLT Complete worksheets in Chapter 4 Establish meeting process and schedule	June 6 June 20 June 27
Charter the Change Leadership Team	Complete worksheets in Chapter 5 Complete charter Present charter to sponsor(s) Present charter to top management team	July 18 August 2 August 9 August 16
Think Strategically About Change	Complete worksheets	July 2

Worksheet

Critical Success Factor (Chapter Title)	Short-Term Wins or Milestones	Date Achieved
Launch the Change Leadership Team		
Charter the Change Leadership Team		
Think Strategically About Change		
Apply Effective Change Principles		
Build the Business Case		
Identify Needs and Assess Progress		

(*continued*)

Worksheet 7.2.   Planning for Short-Term Wins (continued)

Critical Success Factor (Chapter Title)	Short-Term Wins or Milestones	Date Achieved
Connect to the Environment		
Craft a Culture of Collaboration and Entrepreneurship		
Understand Work Processes		
Design Using an Array of Structures		
Plan Employee Empowerment		
Define New Roles of Leaders		
Align Systems for Collaboration		

Minimize Critical Specifications

Planning can create bottlenecks or stifle action. Just as micromanagement over-controls to reduce sense of risk, micro-level planning can seem to increase the safety of the decisions but, in fact, undermines the initiative because of loss of adaptation to local conditions. Brown and Duguid (2000) found that on the front-line or "where the rubber meets the road" employees had to make adjustments to any policy or procedure and any piece of equipment to enable it to fit the local situation.

The technical term for planning at a high enough level to allow employees to have enough room for adjustments is "minimum critical specifications." It means that only a few essential requirements should be stated; the rest of the specifications within that framework are left to the employee. Each practice situation has idiosyncrasies, so you cannot impose a template. When implementing the initiative at ground level, adaptation has to occur. The CLT should avoid over-specifying the steps and work at a higher level in decision making and implementation.

Plan for Resistance

Resistance to change occurs at all levels of the organization for a variety of reasons and at a variety of levels. The corporate immune system (Pinchot, 1985), like the body's immune system, destroys invaders—seeks out and terminates activities that do not fit with the culture or the assumptions of top management. Resistance may also take the form of indifference at the top level. Middle managers may fear loss of jobs. Everyone may fear appearing inadequate when trying new behaviors. And finally, the inertia of tradition and habit create a comfort with the present that hinders investing in the future.

At the personal level, Fox & Amichai-Hamburger (2001) have identified four categories of resistance:

1. *Uncertainty:* Individuals don't know what is really changing, how it will affect them, what response is available, and the consequences of these reactions. Providing good information in a timely fashion is the best antidote.

2. *Utility focus:* People wonder "What's in it for me?"—money, goods, services, love and social relations, status and power, and information—at personal and organizational levels. If present benefits are perceived as better than future gains, change is seen as not worthwhile. Communication of potential payoffs is the best antidote.

3. *Process focus:* People see the change procedure as faulty or use resistance as a lever for other agendas. They see change as wrong and believe it won't achieve its objective or see it as unfair. Change leaders might be seen as untrustworthy. Information provided might be seen as insufficient. Timing may be seen as wrong. False resistance may appear here as a mask to disguise a person's attempt to use the change as an opportunity.

4. *Value and identity focus:* People are concerned that the change may affect deep-rooted values and harm current self-identity or organization-identity. Change can shake the deep values of a person's personality—central attitudes, values,

aspirations, habits, self-identity, self-image, and so forth. This type of resistance is past-oriented and future-oriented, value-laden, and emotional. Converting such people to the cause will be nearly impossible and usually not worth the effort.

The above four types of resistance have nothing to do with the actual merits of the change. Most of the above reasons for resistance are irrational or nonrational.

Table 7.3 shows some of the questions that may occur to people in different roles that will result in resistance to the CWS initiative.

Steps for Reducing Resistance

- Build trust in the change leaders.

- Communicate, communicate, communicate! Provide as much information as possible about planned changes and how they will affect each position.

- Err in the direction of making too much information available (but in a way that does not bury key points in an avalanche of details), being too honest, and communicating too early. Too little information, too little honesty, and too slow a communication process will undermine the CWS initiative.

- Make procedures and decisions clear and their rationale public.

Table 7.3. Examples of Resistance in Four Categories

Type of Resistance	Top Management	Middle Management	Support Systems (for example, HR or Engineering)	Union(s)
Uncertainty	Will it reduce my power?	Will I fail at this new way?	Will it make my work more difficult?	Is this an attempt to undermine union power?
Utility Focus	What will this cost me in pay or bonuses or status?	Will I be demoted when they flatten the organization?	Will my work be valued less?	Will this result in reduced overtime pay or fewer jobs?
Process Focus	This seems like the wrong approach to me.	This is not a good time for such an initiative. We should wait for a better economy.	How can I piggyback my plan for a knowledge management system onto this initiative?	I will go along with them for now just to see how it can strengthen my position.
Value and Identity Focus	This set of values seems all wrong to me.	What will happen to my opportunities for moving up the ladder?	We were meant to provide services, not get involved.	This could undermine the adversarial nature of our relationship with management and change things in ways that don't fit what we believe.

- Show how the timeline is reasonable.

- Show how members of the organization in different positions will benefit from the CWS initiative; translate the benefits for the organization into individual terms, such as how an increase in quality will increase the market share, which will translate into job security and raises.

- Recognize that each category of resistance is different and that different approaches may be necessary for each.

- Value identity; maintain continuity between the past and present.

- Involve people; participation provides opportunity for input as well as communication.

- Show how the change will help resolve other problems.

There is no change without resistance. Resistance is a source of information to leaders. It is active communication in contrast to compliance. CLT members should welcome this venue of feedback and the opportunity it provides to explain and discuss the value of the CWS initiative.

Planning: Identify Sources of Resistance to the CWS Initiative

Time Requirement: Approximately 90 minutes

Supplies: Worksheet 7.3, flip chart, masking tape, and markers

Overview: In this activity, you'll compile a list of groups that might resist the change and consider what the CLT can do to respond to the resistance.

Instructions

1. As a team, in the left-hand column of Worksheet 7.3 list each of the groups in your organization from whom you might expect to receive some resistance (for example, first-line managers, union, HR, finance, engineering, top management).

2. For each group, identify which of the four types of resistance might be exhibited (uncertainty, utility, process, and value and identity) and note those in column 2.

3. For each group, given the anticipated type of resistance, record in the third column some of the actions the CLT can take to reduce it.

Integrate with Other Change Initiatives

Most business units have multiple change initiatives under way at the same time, such as team-based organizations (TBO), enterprise resource planning (ERP), total quality management (TQM), business process re-engineering (BPR), lean manufacturing, Six Sigma, leadership development, and so on. Each initiative requires resources. Usually, competition builds between the leaders of each initiative for access to seemingly scarce resources. The competition undermines the efforts being made by all. At best, one initiative wins out over the others and resources are wasted or an aura of failure grows

Worksheet 7.3.   Sources of Resistance

Groups	Type of Resistance	Response

around the losing initiatives and people say things like "Well, that kind of program just doesn't fit around here." The competition represents the error of suboptimization—optimizing a subsystem at the cost of the larger system. Change initiatives need to be coordinated, so they can develop leverage off each other—the value of the combined wins will exceed the isolated wins. The CLT must catalog all the change initiatives and then find ways to inform, coordinate, mutually support, and integrate others. A jointly created team with a representative from each initiative should meet on a regular basis to find ways to support the overall change effort.

Planning: Integrating with Other Initiatives

Time Requirement: Approximately 1 hour

Supplies: Worksheet 7.4, flip chart, masking tape, and markers

Overview: Identifying the other initiatives and how they might act as allies or competitors is a first step toward collaborating with them. An integrative effort will leverage resources rather than waste them.

Instructions

1. Using Worksheet 7.4 as a guide, identify as a group all of the change initiatives under way at your site (one organization had seventeen change initiatives under way at the same time!) and record these in column 1.

2. Then, for each initiative, list the best person to contact to discuss ways of working together, opportunities for collaboration, and concerns about competition and conflict over resources. A few examples are provided at the top of the worksheet.

Use this information to begin an integration process. One organization brought representatives from all of the change initiatives together for a one-hour meeting every other week to update each other on what was going on and explore areas of support and conflict. Top management sponsorship of such a group is crucial.

Do Not Create the Plan in a Vacuum

The organization must continue to do business during the planning and implementation phases. The CLT must find ways of implementing the plan that minimally interferes with the daily operations of the business unit. A written plan endorsed from the top can be communicated. Temporary adjustments in scope or schedule can be made to allow for fluctuations in production. Training can sometimes be scheduled during slower production periods. If the initiative interferes substantially with doing business, top management will terminate it. However, if the CLT and its members are not assertive about the need to get things done and use employee time, progress will be so slow that faith in the initiative and energy to make it happen will dry up. Problems to watch out for include the following:

- Important differences in expectations between the top management group and the CLT

Worksheet 7.4.　Aligning Change Initiatives

Sample

Change Initiative	Primary Contact	Collaborative Opportunities	Likely Competition for Resources
CWS	CLT spokesperson		N/A
ERP	BK in IT	People in each department work with ERP planners and technicians to create smooth transition to new computer system	Time used for tuning systems to fit the requirements of the ERP
TQM	SI in Quality		
Lean manufacturing		Use process analysis of work flow to determine where teams should be implemented	

Worksheet

Change Initiative	Primary Contact	Collaborative Opportunities	Likely Competition for Resources

Worksheet 7.4.   (continued)

Change Initiative	Primary Contact	Collaborative Opportunities	Likely Competition for Resources

- Neglecting key areas, such as leadership training at all levels and support system alignment

- Poor coordination of activities across CLT subteams and across change initiatives (for example, two major initiatives having key events that demand lots of employee time during the same week)

- Inadequate communication during handoffs from one team or level to another (We tend to assume that others know what we know and so don't make the extra effort to clarify key assumptions.)

- Inadequate communication to members of the organization whose jobs will be changed by the initiative—too little, too late, too indirect, and lacking in accuracy

- Failure by the top management group to acknowledge the work load and responsibility that CLT members have taken on with change initiative work on top of their regular jobs

Integrating the changes created by the CWS initiative into the systems, policies, and procedures of the organization institutionalizes the work of the CLT. It changes the way things are done on a regular basis so the changes are more resistant to extinction when there are changes in top leadership or the business environment. Fitting the changes with the rest of the organization and making it the *new* "business as usual" sustains the initiative over the long term. The specific steps for this work are presented in Part II of this workbook.

Conclusion

There is no roadmap for simple navigation of the change terrain. The CWS initiative is pioneering work in your organization. But with the proper tools, you can navigate the landscape and reach your desired destination. The process is nonlinear and concurrent; there will be some jumping around and some simultaneous activities. The nonlinear change process requires constant adjustments as the terrain changes. Detours must be made around obstacles and in search of opportunities, but the target of the CWS initiative as captured in the vision statement does not change. Keeping it in sight and applying the tools of change will lead to valuable progress over time. It is high-level, because the flow of attention and action over time will recycle to various topics quickly and often. For example, culture change as covered in Chapter 10 will require continual attention with a large number of interventions over time. Using the principles in this chapter will enable a smoother and more successful implementation of the CWS initiative.

Keys to the Chapter

- Following the principles of good change management increases the chances of success for the CWS initiative.

- Start with a readiness assessment to get a baseline of collaborative capacity in the organization (see the Guiding Assessment in Chapter 3 as a sample).

- Use assessment at the beginning and end of the CWS initiative and at regular intervals in between.

- Use gap analysis to prioritize change targets and track progress; it helps identify short-term successes that build energy and credibility for the CWS initiative.

- Resistance to the CWS initiative takes many forms; most can be dealt with through communication and other prevention tactics.

- Partnering with other initiatives improves the use of resources.

Chapter Wrap-Up

- What ideas did this chapter trigger for you and your group? List them in the action planning worksheet at the end of this chapter.

- Review the ideas list. Which of these do you want to implement? List the action item, person or group responsible, and target due dates in the action planning worksheet.

- Were any significant decisions made? Include them at the bottom of the action planning worksheet.

- How can you communicate the pertinent material generated by your work on this chapter to different audiences? Discuss and consider adding action items based on your discussion.

- How can you use the resources list for additional help?

- What chapter should you go through next? Refer back to Guiding Assessment results in Chapter 3 for suggestions of next steps.

- What can you do tomorrow or within the next week based on what you learned in this chapter? Have each person share what he or she will do, and then follow up.

- What is your biggest learning from this chapter? Ask each person to share. This is a nice way to end the session. Include any resulting ideas or action items on the action planning worksheet.

Resources

Bisson, B., & Folk, V. (2000). Case study: How to do a business process improvement. *Journal for Quality & Participation, 23*(1), 58–64.

Brown, J. S., & Duguid, P. (2000). *The social life of information.* Boston: Harvard Business School Press.

Bryson, J. M., & Anderson, S. R. (2000). Applying large-group interaction methods in the planning and implementation of major change efforts. *Public Administration Review, 60,* 143–163.

Fox, S., & Amichai-Hamburger, Y. (2001). The power of emotional appeals in promoting organizational change programs. *Academy of Management Executive, 15*(4), 84–95.

French, W. L. (1994). A checklist for organizing and implementing an OD effort. In W. L. French, C. H. Bell, Jr., & R. A. Zawacki (Eds.), *Organization development and transformation: Managing effective change* (pp. 522–532). Boston: Irwin/McGraw-Hill.

Fritz, R. (1989). *The path of least resistance: Learning to become the creative force in your own life.* New York: Fawcett Columbine.

Halfhill, T., Huff, J., Johnson, D., Beyerlein, M., & Ballentine, R. (2002). Interventions that work (and some that don't): An executive summary of the organizational change literature. In R. Lowman (Ed.), *The California School of Organizational Studies handbook of organizational consulting psychology: A comprehensive guide to theory, skills, and techniques* (pp. 645–667). San Francisco: Jossey-Bass.

Holman, P., & Devane, T. (Eds.). (1999). *The change handbook: Group methods for shaping the future*. San Francisco: Berrett-Koehler.

Kennedy, F. (2003). Return on teaming initiative (ROTI): Measuring teaming outcomes to optimize their performance. In M. Beyerlein, C. McGee, G. Klein, J. Nemiro, & L. Broedling (Eds.), *The collaborative work systems fieldbook* (pp. 89–101). San Francisco: Jossey-Bass/Pfeiffer.

Levenson, A. R. (2003). ROI and strategy for teams and collaborative work systems. In M. Beyerlein, C. McGee, G. Klein, J. Nemiro, & L. Broedling (Eds.), *The collaborative work systems fieldbook* (pp. 103–115). San Francisco: Jossey-Bass/Pfeiffer.

Lytle, W. O., & others. (1993). *Starting an organization design effort: A planning and preparation guide*. Clark, NJ: Block Petrella Weisbord.

Pinchot, G., III. (1985). *Intrapreneuring: Why you don't have to leave the corporation to become an entrepreneur*. New York: Harper & Row.

Porter, G. (2003). Balancing skills for collaboration with individual development. In M. Beyerlein, C. McGee, G. Klein, J. Nemiro, & L. Broedling (Eds.), *The collaborative work system fieldbook* (pp. 595–608). San Francisco: Jossey-Bass/Pfeiffer.

Warrick, D. D. (1994). What executives, managers, and human resource professionals need to know about managing change. In W. L. French, C. H. Bell, Jr., & R. A. Zawacki (Eds.), *Organization development and transformation: Managing effective change* (pp. 463–472). Boston: Irwin/McGraw-Hill.

Action Planning and Summary Sheet

Ideas Generated from This Chapter

1	
2	
3	
4	
5	

#	Action Item	Target Date	Person/Group Responsible
1			
2			
3			
4			
5			
6			

Significant Decisions Made

1	
2	
3	
4	

Build the Business Case

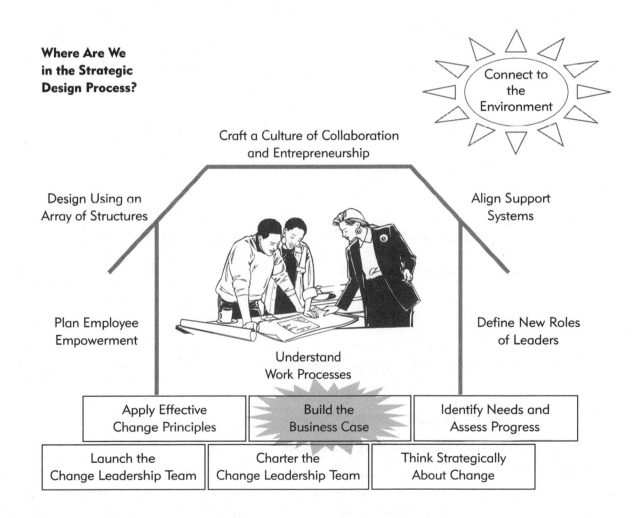

Where Are We in the Strategic Design Process?

Connect to the Environment

Craft a Culture of Collaboration and Entrepreneurship

Design Using an Array of Structures

Align Support Systems

Plan Employee Empowerment

Understand Work Processes

Define New Roles of Leaders

| Apply Effective Change Principles | Build the Business Case | Identify Needs and Assess Progress |

| Launch the Change Leadership Team | Charter the Change Leadership Team | Think Strategically About Change |

? Key Question of This Chapter

How can we use the business case to create support for the CWS initiative?

Quick Look
Overview

This chapter provides a framework and tools for building and presenting the business case for collaborative work systems, for identifying and capturing the value of the investment in the CWS initiative. Maximizing the value depends on careful planning, implementation, and alignment. All of that depends on sustained support from top management. The business case builds that support by succinctly communicating the what, why, where, who, and how of the CWS initiative. The business case is the first step in creating a feedback loop between the CLT and top management and between the CWS initiative and strategic decision-making processes. The primary outcome of this chapter is the business case—ready for presentation to top management.

Chapter Plan

Topic				
What Is the Business Case?	✓			
Contents of the Business Case	✓			✓
Presenting to the Top Management Team	✓			

Principles of Collaborative Work Systems Series

Focus collaboration on achieving business results

Manage complex trade-off decisions

Align authority, information, and decision making

What Is the Business Case?

The business case is a written document presented by the CLT to the top management group to obtain approval for the general plan of the CWS initiative and commitment of the necessary resources. The presentation ought to result in authorization to proceed with the first steps of the initiative. When agreement is reached between the CLT and the top management team, the business case acts as a contract with a statement of the work and the scope of the initiative and with a record of the expectations of the CLT and of the top management group.

The top management group will use the business case to:

- Analyze the rationale for the project
- Assess the economics
- Analyze the impact of the project
- Align these against other factors, such as the major risks and the prevailing political environment
- Prioritize the project with other current initiatives

The business case is an important document for the CLT. It should be carefully and thoroughly prepared. Estimate about 3 percent of the total budget for this work. For example, if the budget calls for one thousand person-days for the entire CWS initiative investment, thirty person-days (one full week for a six-person team) would go into creation of the business case (since the average team-based enterprise spends about one week in training for each employee each year, these estimates are for mid-sized worksites and should be expanded for large sites; one site of two thousand employees invested the equivalent of twelve thousand person-days per year; world-class companies tend to invest considerably more than these figures).

Why such a large investment in creating this document? The investment involved in changing the organization in the ways spelled out in Part II of this workbook is substantial. If part of that investment has already been made, it makes sense to make a statement of that progress in the business case. If little progress has occurred, that too should be noted and a clear statement made about how far the organization has to go—how much work the CLT has to do.

 ## Contents of the Business Case

The scope of the business case should match the scope of the change initiative being proposed. For example, a simple business case is adequate when the initiative does not fundamentally alter the financial assets of the company, is limited to a small part of the company, requires minimal funding, and does not require use of outside specialists in consulting roles. A CWS initiative could be simple, such as "implement training for teams," or complex, such as "build a collaborative culture and align operations to leverage collaborative opportunities."

Medium-scale and large-scale projects such as Six Sigma, business process re-engineering, or team-based organization may radically alter the organization. Such projects can involve the redesign of one or more business processes, affect how the company interacts with its customers and suppliers, and generate new levels of efficiency and effectiveness within and across parts of the organization. Initiatives of this scope are also expensive and must be justified to shareholders. The business case must be carefully prepared and thorough to provide the rationale for a top management decision to commit resources on this scale.

The business case may include some or all of the following sections: cover page, executive summary, table of contents, introduction, background, situational assessment and problem statement, critical assumptions and constraints, identification of options, comparison of options, cost/benefit analysis, recommendation, appendices and glossary. Details on each are provided on the following pages.

The larger the scope of the CWS initiative, the more sections the business case will need to include. The more up-front work the CLT does in preparing the business case, the better. Discuss your ideas with other "experts" to get a broader view of the overall situation. Take pains to be clear and precise in the organization and writing of the document. Include only essential information, so important points are not obscured by excessive detail.

Cover Page

Include team name, CWS initiative name, date, and who the document is written for, such as the sponsor and the top management team.

Executive Summary

This makes the first impression on the reader and maybe the only impression. If the business case is more than one page long, this may be the only part that gets read by some top managers. It must be able to stand alone and be a logical, clear, and brief summary of the important points in the business case. Write it last so that it can cover everything at a high level. Include the business need, summary of options, analysis, costs, benefits, and timeline in a maximum of *one* page. Include why the CWS initiative is being launched, its scope, objectives, resources needed, expected benefits, any special funding requirements, your statement of the vision for the change initiative, and your goal for submitting a business case. That may sound impossible. It will take more work to write this one page than to write most of the rest of the document, but the investment will be worthwhile.

Table of Contents

This page is placed after the executive summary, so no pages have to be turned to get a general idea of the initiative. Include this only if the document is long or has many parts. Regardless of whether or not you include a table of contents, be sure to number the pages of this document.

Introduction

Define the CWS initiative as an element of your organization's business strategy. The change should not be an end in itself, such as implementing it "because a competitor did." This is not about following fads; it is about strengthening the organization's ability to improve its financial or competitive position. The CLT should be clear about how the change will move the organization toward a strategic advantage and how it aligns with the organization's business strategy. Clarity of purpose makes it easier to establish the priority of the CWS initiative in comparison with other organizational initiatives, which in turn determines the allocation of resources and scheduling of project activities.

Background

This section of the business case contains a brief (one or two pages) description of the history that led up to this point in the CWS initiative: Why was the business case prepared? What prompted the formation of the CLT? What has happened in the organization to lead to this initiative? Review previously prepared documents such as the Guiding Assessment in Chapter 3 and the team's vision statement to help prompt thinking for this section.

Situational Assessment and Problem Statement

This section explains why the investment in the CWS initiative should be made. The step involves defining the circumstances that make the CWS initiative worth considering: What problem, or opportunity, or need prompted the search that identified the CWS initiative as the likely solution? The business strategy, goals, and objectives must be taken into account. For example, if the primary strategy is to be first to market with new products, the CWS initiative must be able to contribute to innovation and speed. Clearly define the need for managerial action. Define the problem broadly enough so that you consider the important issues, but not so broadly that you are unable to make concrete action recommendations. Be sure to frame the problem in measurable terms (that is, concrete dollar figures and timetables).

The following questions can be used to help frame this section:

- What evidence is there for a need (for example, sales are dropping, competitors are winning on quality, costs are rising, customers demand the best, or see opportunity to improve)? (Borrow material from Worksheet 6.4 in Chapter 6, which identifies where the pain is.)
- What are the conditions that will support or impede development of the initiative?
- How is the business getting by now without the initiative?
- What is the gap between the current state of the organization and the vision?

Critical Assumptions and Constraints

Identify any assumptions being made or being carried forward from prior initiatives (for example, time and resource assumptions that need to be brought out into the open). For each option, it would be helpful to list any assumptions about the state of technology and the environmental conditions or organizational constraints within which the investment is expected to operate. Assumptions might include:

- Expertise is available on-site with existing personnel or can be developed in a timely manner.
- CLT members can handle the CWS initiative work in addition to their regular jobs.
- Decisions will not be remade without substantial new information becoming available.
- The CLT is the owner of the CWS initiative process.

- The sponsor for the CWS initiative will provide guidance for the CLT's work and support its decisions and recommendations in top management meetings.
- The work will be appropriately documented.

The assumptions need to be discussed to determine whether the top management team and the CLT understand them in the same way.

Identification of Options

For purposes of the business case, identify optional approaches to closing the gaps identified by the questionnaire in Chapter 3. In creating this list, strive to limit the number of options to between three and five, which is about the number that can reasonably be handled during the business case presentation and discussion. Options can be presented that cover a range from doing nothing to doing more than the CLT considers feasible. List the options in order of required investment, as shown in the following list:

1. Do nothing; maintain status quo
2. Option that does less than CLT's preferred option (for example, focusing on solo teams or a subset of support systems as described in Part II of this workbook)
3. Lateral organization, where emphasis is on linking teams with one another
4. Team-based organization, including emphasis on aligning support systems with teams
5. The collaborative organization, including options 2 through 4

Comparison of Options

Compare the options listed in your previous section against the organization's strategic goals. Doing this in table format makes comparison easier. (See Table 8.1 for a sample comparison.)

Other strategic goals not shown in this table include the following: decreased voluntary turnover; increased market share; improved sense of employee ownership; smarter risk taking; better flow of information; better responsiveness to change; increased return on assets; and better risk management.

Cost/Benefit Analysis

A cost/benefit analysis compares the anticipated costs of the initiative against the expected benefits to determine whether or not the investment will be worthwhile. Benefits may be direct or indirect, tangible or intangible. Direct benefits include increased revenue or reduced costs. Indirect benefits affect other things that end up affecting revenue and costs, such as communications, attitudes, and innovation. Tangible benefits are those that can be easily measured and even counted; they may be referred to as "hard" numbers. Intangible benefits are not directly measurable, such as increased expertise, better relationships, and increased sense of ownership.

Table 8.2 provides some examples of both tangible and intangible benefits.

All of these types of benefits are important, but the direct and tangible may build a stronger case with some top management teams. In the long run, however, the

Table 8.1. Sample Comparison of Options

Strategic Goal	Collaborative Organization	Team-Based Organization	Lateral Organization	Teams
Increased sales	Formal and informal collaborative work systems reinforce each other, so sales are enhanced by bringing all relevant expertise to bear	Increased efficiency and effectiveness reduces costs and improves service, increases commitment and innovation	Opportunities for process innovations become more visible to boundary spanners	Sales teams and work teams may have direct contact with customers and so improve relationships
Increased customer satisfaction	All members of the organization focus on the common mission and so align efforts more effectively to quickly meet customer needs	Smooth handoffs between teams upstream and downstream	Better communications across functions through liaison members, integrated product teams, and cross-functional teams, so customer complaints decrease	More ownership, fewer errors, more innovation, possibly more contact with customer through face-to-face, telephone, and survey methods
Decreased costs	Enhanced communication and collaboration within and across groups and teams, inside and outside the organization, improve effectiveness	Waste is reduced as teams implement ideas and plans to make process improvements	Less work-in-process (WIP) due to smoother handoffs	Better communications between management and union representatives reduce number of work stoppages
Faster, better decisions	Groups and teams can operate effectively across boundaries, so their decisions are aligned with the rest of the organization	People closest to the situation have the knowledge, responsibility, and authority for making and implementing decisions	Reduced time to launch new products; fewer design flaws	Consensus decisions improve quality of decisions
Increased quality	Shared understanding of standards and goals enables members to think about quality in broader terms	Teams are connected in a way that promotes establishing and following best practices	Reduced silo mentality, so less balls are dropped in handoffs	Teams can focus on process innovations that reduce rework, scrap, and customer complaints

Note: Benefits tend to accumulate as you move across the table from right to left.

Table 8.2.   Examples of Tangible and Intangible Benefits

Tangible Benefits	Intangible Benefits
• Direct dollar savings	• Intellectual capital (increased learning, sharing knowledge, generating knowledge, expertise, and so on)
• Direct dollar earnings	• Improved concentration (reduced interruption and distraction from important parts of the work)
• Indirect dollar savings	• Increased innovation and creativity
• Indirect dollar earnings	• Better relationships with customers and suppliers
• Improved safety	• Collaborative capital (increased capability to work together well in any arrangement or situation)
• Reduced turnover	• Organizational capital (more effective and adaptive design of the organization)
• Reduced absenteeism	• Increased commitment and sense of ownership among employees

intangible will probably contribute the greater value to the organization. The international consulting firm Cap Gemini Ernst & Young developed a Value Creation Index to assess the value that intangibles added to the bottom line (Low, 2000). Using nonfinancial performance indicators like innovation, employee relations, customer relations, and alliances, the Index showed that 50 percent of a traditional company's value was based on these indicators. For e-commerce companies, 90 percent of their value was determined by intangibles.

Some business cases include the dedication of personnel to the initiative; others do not. If it seems like a good idea to the CLT to include the cost in time for organizational members, completion of a table like the one shown in Table 8.3 can be a handy way to summarize that factor. However, since this inflates the cost of the CWS initiative by adding money that will already be spent, omit this table, if possible, from the business case and merely use it for planning purposes for the CLT.

Recommendation

When you recommend your selected option, describe the choice and the process of arriving at it in a paragraph or two, then present the following:

- A summary of the analysis covered earlier in this chapter with your reasons for choosing this option

- A summary of the key issues that face the project, including business, financial, and technical hurdles that the CLT foresees, such as project costs, slow payback, difficulty in measuring the intangible benefits, and alignment with other change initiatives currently under way

- A brief outline of the steps the CLT will take to move the CWS initiative ahead

Table 8.3. Assessing People Costs

Person	Relationship to CWS Initiative	Role with CLT	Percentage of Work Time Dedicated to the CWS Initiative
FK	Key to CLT process	Process facilitator	20 percent
AA	Key to CLT planning	Content facilitator (OD)	30 percent
FF	CLT member	High-level manager	15 percent
SG	Oversight of CLT and CWS initiative	Sponsor	5 percent
AJ, BK, SS, SG, FK, and JG	Oversight	Top management team	2 percent
HM	CLT member	Union representative	15 percent
JS	CLT member	Director of HR	10 percent
RO	CLT member	Assembly worker	15 percent

- Expected effects on the business, including business process, changes in type or amount of work employees perform, training needs, changes in organizational structure (some of this will be at a high level at this point and details will only become available as the CLT works through the exercises in Part II of this workbook)

- The full cost of the project, the range of potential benefits, and the human issues to consider when implementing it

Appendices and Glossary

Include supporting material here that can be omitted from the business case but may be of interest to some readers, such as a more detailed report of the gap analysis or the financial analysis. Omitting this material from the main text of the case keeps the case more succinct and readable.

Planning: Checklist for the Business Case

Worksheet 8.1 contains a checklist to use while preparing your business case. Adjust the contents of the table to meet your needs. For example, add or drop sections of the business case contents as long as clarity and succinctness are balanced. Add columns to the worksheet to indicate interim steps (for example, when a first draft is due) if desired. Once the contents are determined, fill in who will write each section and when it is due. The CLT should write the executive summary as a group, since it is the most important piece. Expect this page to take four or five hours to write, as the quality of content and style are highly important to the top management team members who read it. Everyone should also be involved in drafting the recommendation section.

Worksheet 8.1. Business Case Planning Checklist

Contents	Writers	Due Date
Cover		
Executive Summary	All	
Table of Contents		
Introduction		
Background		
Gap Analysis		
Situational Assessment and Problem Statement		
Critical Assumptions and Constraints		
Identification of Options		
Comparison of Options		
Cost/Benefit Analysis		
Recommendation	All	
Appendices and Glossary		

Sponsor Signoff

Sponsors must sign off on the business case, attesting to the objectives, risks, and benefits of the plan proposed by the CLT. The sponsor may have suggestions for improving the business case. Listen to them, use the ones that seem to add value, and push back on the ones that seem to miss the point of the CWS initiative. Following signoff, the business case should be presented to the top management team. The sponsor must be available when the top management team meets, to clarify any issues and champion the initiative. Approval of the business case automatically starts the clock on the initiative.

Presenting to the Top Management Team

Now that the CLT has completed the business case and the sponsor has okayed it, the CLT is ready to take it to the top management team. This should be done as a presentation, and the whole CLT should be present and contribute appropriately.

Rehearse the presentation. Check the presentation materials and the business case for completeness, clarity, and errors (typos will reflect poorly on the team and its efforts). Reserve enough time in the top management meeting to give an adequate presentation and answer some questions, perhaps an hour.

Focus the presentation on the business issues and not on the content of the CWS initiative. Don't spend a lot of time talking about what an effective team or team-based organization is. Instead, spend the time talking about how the CWS initiative will affect facets of the business such as communication, increased performance, quality, service, turnover, rework, sales, costs, or innovation.

Top management team members think about strategic investment in terms of a long-term cost/benefit ratio and risk. They want to make smart decisions, so they want good information to base the decisions on. Estimate the cost/benefit ratio of the CWS initiative, plot a timeline to show when the break-even point will occur, and estimate the return on investment that will accrue over five years (and ten years, if possible). Discuss in detail how you plan to control the costs and risks associated with development of the CWS initiative and how you will measure the results over time.

Expect members of the top management team to play the "what if" game. Be prepared to answer questions. A rehearsal with the CLT sponsor will help the preparation. By thoroughly reviewing the case—the rationale, the constraints and criteria, all possible alternatives, range of benefits for each alternative, adequate explanation, and top management's needs—you are likely to have an answer ready when needed, even if it is, "We will find out and get back to you tomorrow." Also be prepared to answer these questions: (1) "Who else has done this?" (2) "How are they making it work?" and (3) "How are they benefiting from their CWS initiative?"

The top management team may have concerns over the ability of the CLT to implement the CWS initiative. Be prepared to show that you have built expertise, assembled an appropriate team, and aligned with strong supplemental resources, so it is clear that the know-how is available and being applied to the CWS initiative.

Suggested Agenda for the Presentation

1. *Overview:* brief description of the CWS initiative and its components leading toward a focus on benefits (estimated time: 5 minutes)

2. *Benefits:* identify all the ways the CWS initiative will pay off for the organization, including the intangible ways, such as faster response to customer requests, more innovation, stronger employee ownership, and so forth (estimated time: 10 minutes)

3. *Costs:* focus on the bottom-line costs; be ready for follow-up if someone wants details; avoid arguing about minute details with someone who may want to derail the initiative (estimated time: 5 minutes)

4. *Financial payoffs:* use bullet points to identify expected financial returns from the CWS investment (estimated time: 10 minutes)

5. *Timeline:* identify general milestones and when the break-even point will be reached (leave it loose, so problems in rollout will not invalidate the schedule); include kickoffs for each phase, pilot tests, assessment dates, and so forth (estimated time: 5 minutes)

6. *Strengths of the CLT:* demonstrate the capability of the CLT, including prior experience with similar challenges (estimated time: 5 minutes)

7. *Question and answer period:* invite as many questions and comments from the top management team as time allows; take notes; plan to follow up on any points that indicate change is necessary in the business case or plan

Note: The approximate times shown in this agenda may be extended if more time is available. The minimum desirable presentation time is 40 minutes (as shown, with additional time for question and answer period); 60 minutes is preferable.

Conclusion

Continually build the business case for building collaborative capacity. Articulate how the change work will add value to the organization. Frame the case so that alignment with other initiatives leverages resources. When other initiatives and issues displace CWS in the top management group's minds, support will wane. Communicate with top management regularly to maintain their commitment and enhance their understanding.

Keys to the Chapter

- Top management support is essential to effectively launching and sustaining the CWS initiative.

- Building an effective business case will take thought and time; investing now will pay off later.

- Focus on the business payoffs of investing in the CWS initiative.

- Prepare a well-written business case covering the issues of concern the top management team will consider in deciding to commit resources to the CWS initiative.

- Prepare for the presentation of the business case, and rehearse so it goes smoothly and your team is ready to answer questions that may come up.

- Present a draft of the business plan to the CLT sponsor before presenting to the whole top management team.

Chapter Wrap-Up

- What ideas did this chapter trigger for you and your group? List them in the action planning worksheet at the end of this chapter.

- Review the ideas list. Which of these do you want to implement? List the action item, person or group responsible, and target due dates in the action planning worksheet.

- Were any significant decisions made? Include them at the bottom of the action planning worksheet.

- How can you communicate the pertinent material generated by your work on this chapter to different audiences? Discuss and consider adding action items based on your discussion.

- How can you use the resources list for additional help?

- What chapter should you go through next? Refer back to Guiding Assessment results in Chapter 3 for suggestions of next steps.

- What can you do tomorrow or within the next week based on what you learned in this chapter? Have each person share what he or she will do, and then follow up.

- What is your biggest learning from this chapter? Ask each person to share. This is a nice way to end the session. Include any resulting ideas or action items in the action planning worksheet.

Resources

Adler, P. S., & Kwon, S. (2002). Social capital: Prospects for a new concept. *Academy of Management Review, 27*(1), 17–41.

Beer, M. (2001). How to develop an organization capable of sustained high performance: Embrace the drive for results-capability development paradox. *Organizational Dynamics, 29*(4), 233–248.

Chatzkel, J. (2001). A conversation with Sharon L. Oriel of the Dow Chemical Company. *Journal of Intellectual Capital, 2*(1), 42–52.

Graphite Software. (1994–2002). *101 tips for a winning business plan.* Retrieved May 31, 2003, from www.graphitesoftware.com/101tips1.htm

Haeckel, S. H. (1999). *The adaptive enterprise.* Boston: Harvard Business School Press.

Hinrichs, G., & Ricke, K. (2003). Gaining commitment to high performance work systems: John Deere case study. In M. Beyerlein, C. McGee, G. Klein, J. Nemiro, & L. Broedling (Eds.), *The collaborative work systems fieldbook* (pp. 287–306). San Francisco: Jossey-Bass/Pfeiffer.

Kennedy, F. (2003). Return on teaming initiative (ROTI): Measuring teaming outcomes to optimize their performance. In M. Beyerlein, C. McGee, G. Klein, J. Nemiro, & L. Broedling (Eds.), *The collaborative work systems fieldbook* (pp. 89–101). San Francisco: Jossey-Bass/Pfeiffer.

Leifer, R., O'Connor, G. C., & Rice, M. (2001). Implementing radical innovation in mature firms: The role of hubs. *Academy of Management Executive, 15*(3), 102–114.

Levenson, A. (2003). ROI and strategy for teams and collaborative work systems. In M. Beyerlein, C. McGee, G. Klein, J. Nemiro, & L. Broedling (Eds.), *The collaborative work systems fieldbook* (pp. 103–115). San Francisco: Jossey-Bass/Pfeiffer.

Low, J. (2000). The value creation index. *Journal of Intellectual Capital, 1*(3), 252–262.

Mentzer, J. T., Foggin, J. H., & Golicic, S. L. (2000). Collaboration: The enablers, impediments, and benefits. *Supply Chain Management Review, 4*(4), 52–58.

Nerdrum, L., & Erikson, T. (2001). Intellectual capital: A human capital perspective. *Journal of Intellectual Capital, 2*(2), 127–135.

Project management templates. (n.d.) Retrieved May 31, 2003, from Tasmanian State Government Web site: www.projectmanagement.tas.gov.au/about/site_map_kbase.htm

Rifkin, G. (1996, June/July). Buckman Labs is nothing but net. *Fast Company,* no. 3, p. 118. Also available: www.fastcompany.com/online/03/buckman.html

Saint-Onge, H., & Wallace, D. (2002). *Leveraging communities of practice for strategic advantage.* Burlington, MA: Butterworth-Heinemann.

Sommer, B. (2002, January). A new kind of business case. *Optimize: Strategy and Execution for Business Technology Executives.* Also available: www.bettermanagement.com/Library/Library.aspx?LibraryID=5011

Treasury Board of Canada Secretariat. *Creating and using a business case for information technology projects.* Available: www3.gov.ab.ca/cio/costbenefit/toc.htm

Wenger, E., McDermott, R., & Snyder, W. M. (2000). *Cultivating communities of practice.* Cambridge, MA: Harvard Business School Press.

Wylie, I. (2002, July). There is no alternative to. . . . *Fast Company,* no. 60, p. 106. Also available: www.fastcompany.com/online/60/tina.html

Action Planning and Summary Sheet

Ideas Generated from This Chapter

1	
2	
3	
4	
5	

#	Action Item	Target Date	Person/Group Responsible
1			
2			
3			
4			
5			
6			

Significant Decisions Made

1	
2	
3	
4	

## CHAPTER 9

Identify Needs and Assess Progress

Where Are We in the Strategic Design Process?

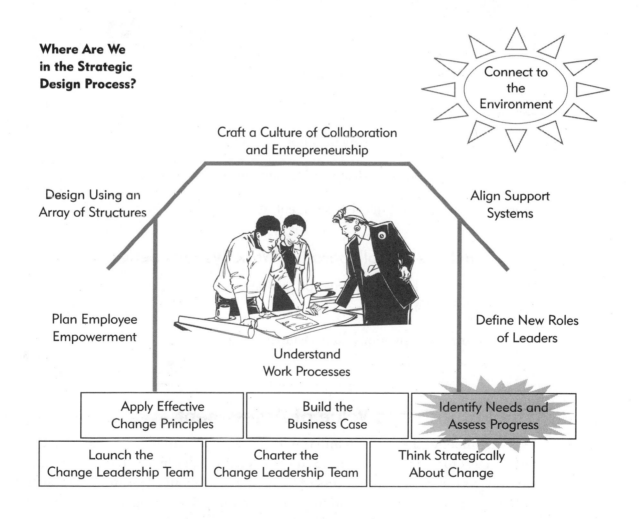

Connect to the Environment

Craft a Culture of Collaboration and Entrepreneurship

Design Using an Array of Structures

Align Support Systems

Plan Employee Empowerment

Understand Work Processes

Define New Roles of Leaders

Apply Effective Change Principles	Build the Business Case	Identify Needs and Assess Progress
Launch the Change Leadership Team	Charter the Change Leadership Team	Think Strategically About Change

? Key Question of This Chapter

How can we track our progress toward the CWS initiative vision?

Quick Look
Overview

An effective change program should be data-driven. Data can be hard or soft, easy or difficult to quantify. Data provides a baseline at the time of program launch and checkpoints along the journey that demonstrate progress and identify areas that require extra attention. A number of assessment tools for gathering data are presented in this chapter. Assessments build energy and credibility by showing the value added by the CWS initiative and the CLT activities. When results are not so positive, they point toward changes that need to be made. Outcomes for this chapter include a quality check on the CLT's measurement methods, an inventory of within and between measures, and a list of measurement instruments to use in the assessment process.

Chapter Plan

Topic				
The Purpose and Value of Assessment	✓	✓		
Quality of Assessment Methods	✓		✓	
Assess Collaboration at the Organizational Level	✓	✓	✓	
Assess Collaboration at the Team and Group Level	✓			✓
Abide by Principles of Ethical Assessment	✓			

Principles of Collaborative Work Systems Series

Create higher standards for discussion, dialogue, and sharing of information

Align authority, information and decision making

The Purpose and Value of Assessment

Every member of the CLT is familiar with assessment. Experiences may range from taking a test for a driver's license to running quality experiments to filling out morale surveys. Assessment is the process of gathering data about a specific situation, individual, or group for purposes of introducing appropriate change. Assessment often involves quantitative data (numbers), but may use qualitative data (words) also. Assessment is used to:

- Establish clear, measurable expected outcomes for the CWS initiative
- Systematically gather, analyze, and interpret evidence to determine how well performance matches those expectations

- Understand and improve the initiative and the decision making that supports it

- Evaluate how the work on critical success factors for the CWS initiative is progressing and determine whether they are contributing to the development of organizational effectiveness

- Provide feedback to the CLT and to the top management team so that they can improve their approach to the CWS initiative

- Guide the use of resources on the CWS initiative, including time and energy

- Identify the strengths and weaknesses of the organization and the initiative

- Aid in prioritizing efforts so that focus on the areas of best payoff is maintained

- Sustain the credibility of the initiative and the support of the top management team

- Communicate results to stakeholders other than the CLT and top management, such as corporate, the union(s), and the employees

The CLT will need assessment skills and tools for monitoring the work done in Part II of this workbook, implementation of the CWS initiative. The assessment process should continue throughout the CWS initiative. It helps put numbers on the vision and the gap between current and desired realities, provides feedback when the CWS initiative is off target, and defines in a data-based way what success will look like. Begin preparation for assessment by discussing the following issues.

Discussion

1. How will we determine where we are now? (The gap analysis in Chapter 3 is a useful source of such information.)

2. How will we determine how well the implementation of the CWS initiative is going?

3. How will we know what needs to change in the initiative?

4. How will we know what needs to change in the organization? (Consider process, output, resources, work flow, information flow, relationships, and so on, and the critical success factors covered by chapters in Part II of the workbook.)

5. What is our work worth to the organization? How can we demonstrate that value? (Part of the business case work in Chapter 8 addressed this issue.)

6. How can we predict the long-term impact of the CWS initiative?

Quality of Assessment Methods

A variety of methods are available for assessment. Table 7.2 provided descriptions of seven ways to collect the data that will help answer the above discussion questions. The quality of the information that comes from an assessment depends on the quality of the assessment tool, the process of data collection, the handling of the data, and the process of converting data into useful information. The old saying "garbage in, garbage out" applies here. Worksheet 9.1 describes some steps that can be taken to raise the quality level. Expert assistance can also help. However, even with everything working well, take assessment results with a grain of salt. None of the data the CLT will collect will be perfect. There are too many sources of error and bias in data and in assessment processes. Use data and its interpretation as a guide for action, not as a sample of "truth."

Assessment: Quality of Assessment Methods

Time Requirement: Approximately 45 minutes

Supplies: Worksheet 9.1, flip chart, masking tape, markers

Overview: Surveys and interviews can produce good information or garbage or a mix of the two. In this activity, you will assess the current quality level of your selected assessment methods.

Instructions

1. Work as a team to answer the questions in Worksheet 9.1.

2. For any items for which the response is "No," discuss the situation to create a new framework and action plan for justifying a "Yes" answer.

3. Reuse this table each time the CLT chooses a new assessment method or process.

When conducting your assessment, you'll need to use both a macro and a micro evaluation. A macro evaluation examines the entire organization for good organizational fit with the CWS initiative. A micro evaluation looks at each particular part of the organization to ensure that it is working properly.

Worksheet 9.1.   Quality Check for Assessment Methods

	No	Yes
Are the questions (for the questionnaire, interview, and so on) appropriate? (Questions need to fit the purpose of the survey or interview and be understandable to the participants—literacy and native language issues are important here as well.)	No	Yes
Are directions to participants clear? (Pilot-test this with target audiences and make changes based on their feedback.)	No	Yes
Is the wording for each question clear? (Pilot-test them and make changes based on feedback.)	No	Yes
Are we capturing what was really said in interviews and focus groups instead of what the CLT member wanted to hear in the session?	No	Yes
Is anonymity of the answers guaranteed? (People who fear their names will be linked with specific answers will either leave blanks or write in politically correct answers; anonymity is the best way to make people feel safe about disclosing their feelings and ideas, and one leak will contaminate the whole process.)	No	Yes
Is the process of administration standardized so that all participants have the same assessment experience? (When people fill out the questionnaires at home rather than at work or have an interview at lunch rather than in an office, answers may change. Work for consistent conditions.)	No	Yes
Are distractions during assessment minimal? (Noise, interruptions, unscheduled breaks, and other distractions disrupt the process and introduce error.)	No	Yes
Did we use the most appropriate media for the assessment? (For example, don't use an English language survey with Spanish-speaking employees or a Web-based survey with people who have no access to or comfort with computers.)	No	Yes
Are we triangulating—that is, looking at the same issue from different angles—using multiple methods (such as questionnaires, focus groups, and observation) and multiple sources of data (such as customers, suppliers, support personnel, managers, and team members), then combining their results to distill a dependable result?	No	Yes

Assess Collaboration at the Organizational Level

Analysis at the organization level must be designed to provide information in a form that best serves the organization. In other words, begin with the end in mind when creating the assessment. How will the information be used by the organization? What format will best serve the organization's needs? Once you can answer these questions, you will have a better idea of how to create an assessment methodology.

The CLT or a cross-functional subteam of its members should conduct an internal audit of the relationship between the collaborative critical success factors and the organization. The audit team must be given autonomy to conduct the assessment and be free from repercussion from top management. Bad news should be welcomed by top management as a red flag that requires immediate attention, not as a reason to "kill the messenger." If the CLT members feel at risk in presenting assessment results, they will tend to minimize the negative and maximize the positive for self-protection. The sponsor can also help with presentations in such cases.

Each chapter in Part II of this workbook provides some assessment tools at the organizational level. These will be a good start in keeping track of the progress of the CWS initiative and assessing the needs of the organization. The tools described in this chapter provide supplemental methods for tailoring the assessment process to your organization.

The internal audit team should answer five questions to determine how the organization is working as a collaborative work system. Record the answers to the questions as part of planning your assessment process.

Discussion

1. *Did top management do its job?* Is top management carrying through on its commitment to the CWS initiative and CLT?

   If the answer is "no," the CLT should check whether management:

   - Understood how the CWS initiative works

   - Determined the impact of the CWS initiative on the organization

   - Invested resources to determine whether or not the organization was ready for the CWS initiative

   - Developed a strategic vision for the organization that provided a framework for the CLT's vision

   - Changed the business strategy significantly enough to reduce the appropriateness of the CWS initiative

   If top management falls short on any of these items, the CLT should present the issue to its sponsor and co-design steps for correcting the situation.

> *Lessons:* Without visible commitment of top management, the rest of the organization will assume it is "business as usual" and no culture change will occur.

2. *Is the CLT a success?* Assessment of the CLT's effectiveness acts as a diagnostic process for improving the work of the group. Several assessment tools are available in Chapters 3, 4, 5, and 6 to help the CLT with self-examination.

Ask: What is our process for using self-assessment tools?

> *Lessons:* The CLT has significant responsibility, including designing the change initiative, modeling good collaborative behavior, implementing the phases of the initiative, and so forth. Each aspect of CLT responsibility should be assessed formally and informally.

3. *Is there both a between and a within focus?* Most approaches to implementing collaborative work systems focus on work teams. The focus is usually *within* the team. It is important to move outward and upward to cover the whole organization. A *between* focus looks at the relationships and spaces between teams, departments, projects, programs, functions, disciplines, levels of the hierarchy, customers and suppliers (internal and external), and organizations. Perhaps 80 percent of the payoff from the CWS initiative will come from the between focus. This is more challenging to assess but also more important. (See Worksheet 9.2 at the end of this section for more help with this issue.)

4. *What is the benchmark for progress?* There are several ways to benchmark the collaborative capability of the organization:

- You can compare the changed organization to the original organization by reviewing the baseline (the initial current assessment) from the gap analysis (Chapter 3)

- You can compare the changed organization to the goal by comparing the desired state to the current state with the gap analysis (Chapter 3)

- You can compare the changed organization to other organizations, benchmarking through visiting their sites, researching public records, and seeing their presentations at conferences. (A number of research organizations provide benchmark data, such as the Center for the Study of Work Teams, *Industry Week,* American Center for Quality and Productivity, and Best Manufacturing Practices, as do most published assessments, where benchmarks are called "norms.")

Ask: What is our plan for comparing our measures of collaborative capability to benchmarks?

Lessons: Numbers have no meaning by themselves. The meaning comes from comparing the numbers to some type of benchmark. Multiple benchmarks may make the numbers from assessment most meaningful and so most useful.

---

5. *Can we show progress?* The CWS initiative is a major program of change, as all parts of the organization are affected. Therefore, it takes time to achieve the goals and vision the CLT articulated. However, small successes may occur constantly in scattered parts of the organization to indicate progress:

- Minor trends in metrics that show improvements in a variety of locations

- Stories about success of the CWS initiative from team members and leaders

- Growing trends in measures of organizational performance, such as quality, efficiency, effectiveness, return on investment (ROI), return on assets (ROA), return on equity (ROE), and others

Ask: How will we collect, archive, integrate, and report both hard and soft data showing the progress of the CWS initiative?

> *Lessons:* Change on a scale that involves organizational, cultural, and employee issues takes time. Rather than rushing or truncating it, allow time for a developmental process. This is a marathon, not a sprint. Don't make time the key variable of success; rather, make the key variable change in business results.

Assessment: Within or Between Focus

Time Requirement: Approximately 45 minutes

Supplies: Worksheet 9.2, flip chart, markers, masking tape

Overview: To determine whether the focus of assessment and the focus of the CWS initiative include both the within-team area and the between-team area, a listing of planned activities can be useful. Areas of assessment can include skills, processes, relationships, perceptions, attitudes, and so forth.

Instructions

1. As a team, brainstorm the names of the departments, programs, customers, and others that the CWS initiative will involve. Most of this information was created by the CLT with completion of Worksheet 5.6 and can be reused here. Enter each name/group in the left-hand column of Worksheet 9.2. Some examples are provided at the top of the worksheet.

2. Work as a team to determine how collaborative capability and potential will be assessed *within* each of those areas of the organization and write the ideas in column 2. Note that there may be multiple answers in some boxes.

3. Work as a team to determine how collaborative capability and potential will be assessed *between* each of those areas and the other areas they work with. Write those ideas in column 3.

4. Look at the patterns in the final answers. Consider questions like the following:

   • Are there any blank spaces that need further thought and planning and possibly some research?

Worksheet 9.2.   Within and Between Efforts

Sample

Area of the Organization	Within Focus	Between Focus
Human Resources	• Assess the department for collaborative practices among its members • Assess collaborative skills of HR members	• Assess collaborative relationships with HR's customers • Assess attitudes of HR employees toward the CWS initiative
Engineering	• Assess each project team for attitudes and skills of members related to working well together	• Assess the way various project teams support each other through sharing knowledge and other resources
Finance	• Assess collaborative practices within the department	• Assess how well financial statements reflect the value of intangibles like collaboration or the value of change initiatives affecting the whole organization

Worksheet

Area of the Organization	Within Focus	Between Focus
Human Resources		
Engineering		
Finance		
Quality		

Worksheet 9.2. (continued)

Area of the Organization	Within Focus	Between Focus
Sales		
Top Management Team		
Operations		
Shipping and Receiving		
Purchasing		
Other:		
Other:		
Other:		

- Are there answers in multiple boxes that relate enough to each other that a single assessment method or process can cover a set of them?
- Is there a balance of within and between efforts? Where there is an imbalance, more attention is needed to build collaborative capability.

Assess Collaboration at the Team and Group Level

After the organizational audit, the next step is to review individual team performance using a micro evaluation. Work is now done by work teams and project teams more often than by individuals. The CWS initiative should increase the effectiveness of these work units. That increase or its absence should be assessed as one of the ways of determining whether or not the initiative is being implemented effectively and whether or not the initiative is generating the desired business results. The same types of benchmarks can be used for the teams as for the organization as a whole—baseline, gap analysis, and comparison with other teams.

Comparing the numbers that result from completion and analysis of team and group questionnaires to benchmarks provides valuable feedback to the CLT and to the individual teams. The feedback provides diagnostic information that shows what is working well and what needs attention. Table 9.1 provides an overview of a number of assessment tools that can be applied to individuals, teams, and organizations, beginning with the one in Chapter 3. Part II of this workbook includes others at the organizational level. Advice of experts can make choices more efficient and more effective. A combination of methods that covers both micro and macro levels is the best.

Planning: Selection of Assessment Instruments

Time Requirement: Approximately 45 minutes

Supplies: Worksheet 9.3, flip chart, masking tape, markers

Overview: In this activity, the team will begin selecting the instruments that will be used to assess progress of the initiative.

Instructions

1. In column 2 of Worksheet 9.3, as a group describe the various purposes that instruments might serve. This column is filled out first so the choices of instruments are purpose-driven.

2. In the first column, list assessment instruments that will meet each purpose. Making this determination will require some research. Research on the Web, conversations with researchers, and calls to test publishers will provide other options. Look at samples of tests in print or online and compare the design and content to the goals of the CWS initiative. Make careful choices. Add to the table gradually. Several examples are already provided. Retain those you plan to use and strike out any others.

3. Specify the dates when the instrument will be used, so ordering, pilot-testing, and administration details can be arranged in time to avoid the errors of last-minute preparation.

Table 9.1. Published Assessment Tools at Individual, Team, and Organization Levels

Name	Focus	Special Features
1. The Guiding Assessment from Chapter 3	Gap analysis of the critical success factors for collaborative work systems	The centerpiece of this workbook and the launch point for the CWS initiative; also online with benchmark comparisons available in reports
2. Team Feedback System (TFS)	Team competencies using a 360-degree view where team members rate themselves and one another	Online survey with reports at individual and team levels; benchmarking across teams and organizations available in reports; can be tailored to organization's choice of key competencies
3. Team Return on Investment (TROI)	Diagnosis of the team system, including team skills, alignment of support systems, and the financial value of process innovations created by the teams	Online survey; benchmark across time, teams, and organizations; capture best practices; quantify the value of team innovations in dollars; tool for building an innovation culture
4. Technical Professional Survey (TPS)	Perceptions of individual job, team, and organization on sixty-six short scales	Benchmark sample includes engineering, finance, HR, and others
5. Support Systems Survey (3S)	Survey assessing alignment of support systems with teams	Basis of work in Chapter 16; nine support systems covered; three versions: brief form—three items per system, regular form—fifteen items per system, long form for in-depth diagnosis—forty-five items per system
6. Campbell-Hallam Team Development Survey (TDS)	Strengths and weaknesses of a team	Facilitators and team members complete it
7. Group Styles Inventory (GSI)	Patterns of behavior emerging during team's work on a particular problem	Both constructive and defensive elements of process are assessed
8. Job Descriptive Index (JDI)	Individual's feelings about his/her job on five dimensions adding up to job satisfaction	Extensive research base
9. Organizational Culture Inventory (OCI)	Corporate culture—adaptive and unadaptive	Can focus on either current or ideal culture
10. Organizational Effectiveness Inventory (OEI)	Organizational processes and outcomes rather than behaviors	Links results to levers for change

(continued)

Table 9.1. Published Assessment Tools at Individual, Team, and Organization Levels (continued)

Name	Focus	Special Features
11. Team Climate Inventory (TCI)	Team vision, participative safety, task orientation, support for innovation, and interaction frequency	Available in several languages
12. Survey of Organizational Excellence (SOE)	Group and organizational strengths and weaknesses	Includes demands on the individual, such as stress; benchmarks include government organizations
13. Team Effectiveness Profile (TEP)	Issues of effective teamwork including mission, planning, goal setting, processes, and relationships	Surfaces obstacles to effectiveness
14. Job Diagnostic Survey (JDS)	Job characteristics assessed include autonomy, feedback, significance of the work, wholeness of the task, and variety	Five job factors fit knowledge work well; fairly extensive research base
15. Team Development Survey (TDS)	Characteristics of an effective team, including clarity of purpose, civilized disagreement, and listening	Has been used with a wide variety of teams

Sources:
1. Chapter 3 and Center for the Study of Work Teams at http://www.workteams.unt.edu/assessment.htm
2., 3. Center for the Study of Work Teams at http://www.workteams.unt.edu/assessment.htm
4., 5. Center for the Study of Work Teams, 940-565-3096
6. NCS Testing at www.ncs.com
7. Human Synergistics at http://www.humansyn.co.uk/products/gsi.html
8. Bowling Green State University at http://www.bgsu.edu/departments/psych/JDI
9., 10. Human Synergistics at www.humansyn.co.uk/products/oei.html
11. Hanover House in the UK or Professor Michael West at m.a.west@aston.ac.uk
12. Survey of Organizational Excellence, University of Texas, Austin, at http://www.utexas.edu/research/cswr/survey
13. HRDQ at http://www.hrdq.com/products/load-tep.htm
14. CapitalWorks at http://www.capworks.com/jds/
15. Consulting Psychologists Press at 1-800-624-1765 or Glenn Parker at http://www.glennparker.com

Combining Micro-Level and Macro-Level Assessment

The top management team works at a high level and often uses macro-level data, but a good sense of what is happening at the micro level is equally important. Micro-level assessment of teams and collaborative practices needs to roll up to the top of the organization. The example in Figure 9.1 illustrates how team assessment information was used in six organizations. Each of the teams was assessed through a focus group interview to determine what innovations had been made in the last quarter. The value of the innovations was calculated and recorded. The totals were rolled upward to the strategic decision makers. They compared results to goals and made changes in plans to build core competencies so that performance would improve. The teams also completed questionnaires that indicated how well the support systems were providing necessary inputs (see Chapter 16 for more on support systems). When using this method, if the value of innovations is insufficient, the support systems results are examined to

Worksheet 9.3.   Selected Assessment Instruments

Instrument	Purpose	Target Dates
The Guiding Assessment from Chapter 3	Baseline needs assessment	Done at the beginning of the CWS initiative, repeated annually
Team Return on Investment (TROI)	Generate diagnostic information for the team system and generate financial feedback for top management	Before launching CLT work on Part II of this workbook
Team Feedback System (TFS)	Provide developmental feedback to teams as part of the performance management support system	When the CLT reaches Chapter 16 in this workbook

Figure 9.1. Combining Micro and Macro Assessments

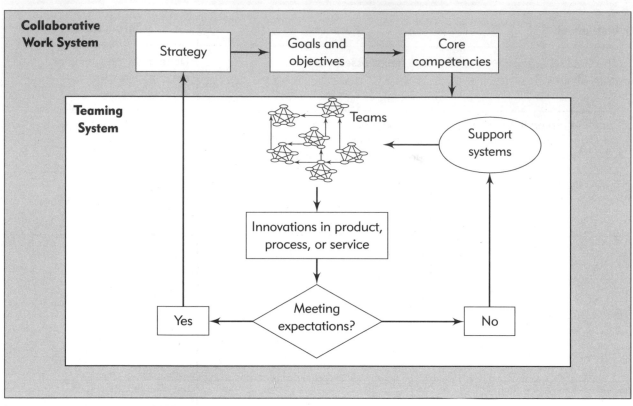

Source: Adapted from Kennedy, 2003.

determine whether the problem is due to training or reward systems or communications and so on. Thus, a within-team focus is combined with a between-team focus to get a picture of the whole organization's collaborative functioning for decision-making purposes.

Abide by Principles of Ethical Assessment

Assessment is not a casual activity, except for informal observation. It requires preparation, including training of assessors. There are too many ways to contaminate the results when assessors do not follow proper procedures.

Think of your own willingness to answer questions in interviews, focus groups, or surveys. When do you feel safe enough to be frank? Jot down notes about the assessment situations where you did or did not feel safe (school tests, certification exams, driver's license test, civil service exams, employment applications, loan applications assessing credit risk, and so on).

Share the answers as a group and capture the factors that increased or reduced the sense of safety (for example: "The test administrator kept looking over my shoulder during the exam," "They wanted too much personal information on the form," or "There were people in the room watching us take the exam whom we did not know"). Discuss the patterns the list suggests.

Participant Rights to Informed Consent, Voluntary Participation, and Anonymity

Participants have an absolute right to full disclosure about the purpose of the assessment, how data will be used, and who will receive the summary report. *Before* starting the focus group or questionnaire administration, assessors should clearly communicate the following to participants:

- Attendance at the session is entirely voluntary.

- Participants can leave the group or end the session at any time.

- If the CLT members take notes or make an audiotape of the session, participants have the right to review the material for accuracy and request revisions; taking notes on flip charts simplifies this, as the record is made public during the session.

- Assessors will record the names of participants, but only for internal use in case follow-up questions are needed, and names are *never* linked to individual responses.

- The CLT should provide a summary report that all focus group and survey participants should have access to, perhaps one copy at the front desk to be checked out or one in the company library, at minimum.

- The assessment will not start until the group's questions have been satisfactorily answered.

At the end of the session, assessors should be available to answer any follow-up questions. Participants should be able to contact a CLT liaison to discuss any unresolved concerns. These steps may seem excessive, but they are designed to do three things: (1) protect the individual from any retribution for sharing negative opinions; (2) create a safe environment so that people will be frank and the data will be of high quality; and (3) protect the assessment process so that people will participate and see the results as a valid picture of the organization.

Focus groups work best when the participants are at the same level in the organization, so supervisors cannot intimidate direct reports in the session. However, assessors should expect, and proactively address, concerns that excluding managers may create mistrust later on. We recommend frank discussion about the goals of assessment and the possible dampening effects of management participation. If managers and supervisors participate in a session with unit members, assessors should communicate the possible effects of that decision.

Sharing Results

The most effective way to share the results of an assessment is by presenting them to the small groups or teams who completed the questionnaire. Many organizations also hold town hall meetings to provide everyone with an overview of the results at one time. The feedback session can be used to answer questions, clarify the meaning of responses, and benchmark the team against the overall organization. Most importantly, the session is an opportunity to develop action plans based on ideas brought out in the discussion and gain commitment on the plans. One company of 1,500 people generated 1,000 ideas from these survey-feedback meetings and acted on 500 of them over the next year.

Conclusion

A healthy CWS initiative is data-driven. The quality of the decisions depends on the quality of the data. The collection of qualitative and quantitative data provides information for assessing the impact of the actions the CLT takes to implement the initiative, the degree to which the initiative is on or off target, and the location of problem areas. Using dependable measurement instruments and combining their results with observation and interview data enables the CLT to construct a picture of the whole situation for both decision making and reporting purposes. Protecting the individual participants in the data-collection process protects the credibility of the data, the initiative, and the CLT. There is a lot to measure, so be sure each measurement has a purpose that fits with the CWS initiative.

Keys to the Chapter

- Be clear about what the CLT wants to assess to improve the viability and outcomes of the CWS initiative.

- Use multiple methods of assessment and combine the results to get a better picture of the situation.

- Try to adopt a strategic approach to assessment, making long-term plans that build over time.

- Assess both the within and the between levels of collaborative capability.

- Protect the credibility of the assessment by protecting participants through ethical procedures.

- Protect the quality of the assessment results by following standardized procedures for data collection, analysis, and reporting.

Chapter Wrap-Up

- What ideas did this chapter trigger for you and your group? List them in the action planning worksheet at the end of this chapter.

- Review the ideas list. Which of these do you want to implement? List the action item, person or group responsible, and target due dates in the action planning worksheet.

- Were any significant decisions made? Include them at the bottom of the action planning worksheet.

- How can you communicate the pertinent material generated by your work on this chapter to different audiences? Discuss and consider adding action items based on your discussion.

- How can you use the resources list for additional help?

- What chapter should you go through next? Refer back to Guiding Assessment results in Chapter 3 for suggestions of next steps.

- What can you do tomorrow or within the next week based on what you learned in this chapter? Have each person share what he or she will do, and follow up.

- What is your biggest learning from this chapter? Ask each person to share. This is a nice way to end the session. Include any resulting ideas or action items in the action planning Worksheet.

Resources

Campion, M. A., Medsker, G. J., & Higgs, A. C. (1993). Relations between work group characteristics and effectiveness: Implications for designing effective work groups. *Personnel Psychology, 46*, 823–850.

Church, A. (2001). Is there a method to our madness? The impact of data collection methodology on organizational survey results. *Personnel Psychology, 54*, 937–970.

Church, A. H., Waclawski, J., & Kraut, A. I. (2001). *Designing and using organizational surveys: A seven-step process.* San Francisco: Jossey-Bass.

Cohen, S. G. (1994). Designing effective self-managing work teams. In M. Beyerlein & D. Johnson (Eds.), *Advances in interdisciplinary studies of work teams: Vol. 1. Theories of self-managing work teams.* (pp. 67–102). Greenwich, CT: JAI Press.

Dammen, K. (2001, March 19) *Research update* [Review of Tools @ work: Nine ways to evaluate the effectiveness of your team-based organization. *Journal for Quality and Participation, 23*(2).] Retrieved May 31, 2003, from University of Wisconsin–Stout, College of Technology, Engineering and Management, People Process Culture Web site: www.ppc.uwstout.edu/ru/3_19_01.htm

Filipczak, B. (1995). Critical mass: Putting whole-systems thinking into practice. *Training, 32*(9), 33–41.

Galbraith, J. R. (1994). *Competing with flexible lateral organizations* (2nd ed.). Reading, MA: Addison-Wesley.

Henderson, D., & Green, F. (1997). Measuring self-managed work teams. *Journal for Quality & Participation, 20*, 52–58.

Keen, T. R., & Keen, C. N. (1998). Conducting a team audit. *Training & Development, 52*(2), 13–16.

Kennedy, F. (2003). Return on teaming initiative (ROTI): Measuring teaming outcomes to optimize their performance. In M. Beyerlein, C. McGee, G. Klein, J. Nemiro, & L. Broedling (Eds.), *The collaborative work systems fieldbook* (pp. 89–101). San Francisco: Jossey-Bass/Pfeiffer.

Miles, R. E., Coleman, H. J., Jr., & Creed, W. E. (1995). Keys to success in corporate redesign. *California Management Review, 37*, 128–145.

Rupp, K. (2003). UATTRA performance assessment for fast formed teams. In M. Beyerlein, C. McGee, G. Klein, J. Nemiro, & L. Broedling (Eds.), *The collaborative work systems fieldbook* (pp. 513–542). San Francisco: Jossey-Bass/Pfeiffer.

Wohlfarth, T., & Stevens, M. (2003). Creating and measuring ways to win together. In M. Beyerlein, C. McGee, G. Klein, J. Nemiro, & L. Broedling (Eds.), *The collaborative work systems fieldbook* (pp. 465–477). San Francisco: Jossey-Bass/Pfeiffer.

Action Planning and Summary Sheet

Ideas Generated from This Chapter

1

2

3

4

5

#	Action Item	Target Date	Person/Group Responsible
1			
2			
3			
4			
5			
6			

Significant Decisions Made

1

2

3

4

## PART II

Align the Organization for Collaboration

IN PART II, we build on the foundation laid in Part I to redesign your organization for collaboration. The design process requires connections to elements that are not easily changed—the environment outside and work inside the organization (Chapters 10 and 12). The pieces that should align with the environment and the work include culture and structures (Chapters 11 and 13), employee behavior and leadership roles (Chapters 14 and 15), and support systems (Chapter 16). The Conclusion (Chapter 17) pulls together all the material generated in the workbook.

Key Questions in Each Chapter

Chapter	Key Questions
10 Connect to the Environment	How can we connect and adapt to our environment?
11 Craft a Culture of Collaboration and Entrepreneurship	What kind of culture supports collaboration, and how can we move toward a collaborative culture?
12 Understand Work Processes	What are the key work processes, and how can we better understand them?
13 Design Using an Array of Structures	What collaborative structures can be incorporated into our target organization design?
14 Plan Employee Empowerment	What is empowerment, and how can empowerment plans be used to define it?
15 Define New Roles of Leaders	How should roles of leaders change in a collaborative work system?
16 Align Support Systems	How can the organizational context support collaboration?
17 Conclusion: Working Toward the Future	What have we accomplished, what resources have we created, and what is our next goal?

## CHAPTER 10

Connect to the Environment

Where Are We in the Strategic Design Process?

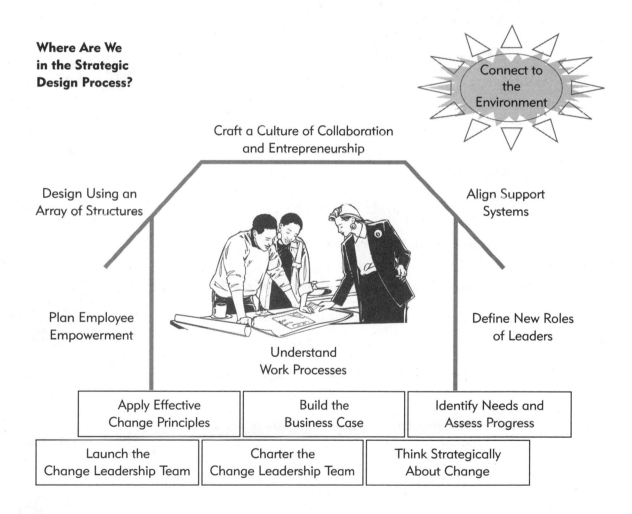

Connect to the Environment

Craft a Culture of Collaboration and Entrepreneurship

Design Using an Array of Structures

Align Support Systems

Plan Employee Empowerment

Understand Work Processes

Define New Roles of Leaders

| Apply Effective Change Principles | Build the Business Case | Identify Needs and Assess Progress |
| Launch the Change Leadership Team | Charter the Change Leadership Team | Think Strategically About Change |

Key Question of This Chapter

How can we connect and adapt to our environment?

Quick Look

Overview

The environment of the organization includes the surrounding conditions, influences, or forces that shape organizational growth and development. Examples range from customers and suppliers to the industry and economy. By attending to the environment and responding reactively or proactively, the organization becomes adaptive and is better suited to survive in today's fast-changing world. Building in mechanisms for scanning the environment and acting on that information helps to make adaptability a habit. The outcomes of this chapter include an assessment of how well the organization connects to elements of the environment, identification of mechanisms to improve those connections, processes for acting on information collected, and understanding of the types of information that different people in the organization can provide and ideas for capturing and using that information.

Chapter Plan

Topic				
What Is the Environment?	✓			
Build Mechanisms to Create Awareness of the Environment	✓		✓	✓
Act on Awareness of the Environment	✓			✓
Create Ways for All Members to Contribute	✓			✓

Principles of Collaborative Work Systems Series

Focus collaboration on achieving business results

Manage complex trade-off decisions

Create higher standards for discussion, dialogue, and sharing of information

Foster personal accountability

What Is the Environment?

The environment is the surrounding conditions, influences, or forces that shape organizational growth and development. The environment exists both within the organization and outside the organization. What is considered the environment depends

Table 10.1.   Elements of the Environment from a Site Perspective

Element	Description
Customers	The users of the site's products or services
Suppliers	People who provide inputs (materials ranging from equipment to physical materials to information) for the site to create products or services
Government regulators	Federal, state, and local regulatory agencies that affect aspects of the work
Unions	Any unions that oversee labor-management relations
Corporate office	Individuals or groups within the corporation to whom your site reports
Other sites in the corporation	Other sites in your organization that may have to work with your site and may learn from your example
Community	Families of employees and community citizenship
Shareholders	The shareholders or owners of your corporation or site
Political climate	The overall viewpoint of the people in political power that may affect aspects of the business through laws, financial regulations, ability to obtain government contracts, and so forth
Economy	The system or range of economic activity in the world, country, or community (The economy affects things such as the job market, the business a site is able to bring in, and resulting growth or decline of the organization.)
Competitors	Other corporations that are in competition for the work in the industry
Partner organizations	Organizations with whom your site or corporation has strategic alliances, shared contracts, or any other form of partnership
The industry	Advances in expertise affecting the organization's field or industry, including new techniques, processes, and technology

on perspective. To a team, other teams and individuals, the manager, the department, site, and corporate office are parts of the environment in addition to the environment outside the organization. This workbook focuses on the site level of the organization, and this chapter focuses on the elements of the environment from the perspective of the site. See Table 10.1 for a list of environmental elements at the site level. When designing at levels within the site such as teams and departments, also consider the relevant elements of the environment within the site.

Current Environmental Trends

Some of the general environmental trends creating a need for increased collaboration in organizations include globalization; fast pace of change; technology; increased complexity; and permeable organizational boundaries.

Why Connect to the Environment?

Connecting to the environment provides information about the environment. Having the information is just the first step. Acting on that information allows the organization to become adaptable. Adaptability represents the ability to make organizational changes in response to changes in the environment. The organization must be aware of its environment and able to respond both proactively and reactively in order to survive and thrive in today's fast-changing world. Adaptability means the organization is more agile and flexible. Any major change initiative (especially the CWS initiative) within an organization must have adaptability as one of its primary goals.

Adapting effectively depends on collaboration in several ways: obtaining information from the environment, sharing information so all are informed, working together to create solutions to new demands from the environment, and working together informally to maximize the speed and flexibility necessary for fast response to the environment. Collaborative capability ought to make adaptation more effective.

Each group in the organization, including departments, teams, groups, and business units, would benefit from gaining some understanding of its current environment. While it is impossible to predict the future, some things are foreseeable, and some educated guesses can be made. By anticipating the future environment, you can take upcoming changes into consideration when implementing your plans.

Build Mechanisms to Create Awareness of the Environment

To create awareness of the environment, a significant intelligence function is required—scanning and making sense of the environment and understanding the competition and the customer. An important part of this is promoting open lines of communication among employees, customers, and suppliers.

In general, a healthy system has numerous and effective connections to suppliers and to customers (both internal and external). The more active and positive connections the system has to others in the environment, the more viable it is. Organizations that invest in building a healthy web of relationships will be more informed, prepared, and agile.

The exercises in this section will help you identify the most important parts of the environment to link to, identify the specific information needed, and develop ways to gather that information.

Assessment: Elements of Environmental Awareness

Time Requirement: Approximately 1 hour

Supplies: Assessment 10.1, flip chart, markers

Overview: In this activity, you'll assess your current and ideal level of environmental awareness and then identify the gaps and create ideas for closing them.

Instructions

1. Choose the appropriate method for completing the assessment. Refer back to Table 3.2 for methods and pros and cons for each.

2. Brainstorm environmental elements that are important to your organization, but are not included in Assessment 10.1. List them in the empty spaces at the end of the tool.

3. For each item on the tool, assess the extent to which the organization links to that environmental element. Use a circle to indicate where your organization is now.

4. Review the items again. This time, use a square to indicate where your organization would like to be at the highest level of CWS.

5. Discuss the answers, using the following questions:

   • What are the biggest gaps between where you are now and where you want to be?

   • In what order do you need to address the gaps? Create a prioritized list for addressing the gaps, based on your discussion.

   • What can you do short term and long term to close those gaps? Brainstorm ideas.

6. List ideas generated in this discussion in your action planning worksheet at the end of the chapter.

Planning: Create Environmental Scanning Mechanisms

Time Requirement: Approximately 1 hour

Supplies: Completed Assessment 10.1, Worksheet 10.1, flip chart, and markers for each small group

Overview: After assessing current connections to the environment using Assessment 10.1, use this planning activity to begin identifying mechanisms that will improve those links.

Instructions

1. Using the results of Assessment 10.1 and resulting conversation, identify the top five most important environmental elements to which your organization needs to attend. List them in Worksheet 10.1.

2. Form small groups of three to five people. Assign one or more elements to each small group.

3. Each small group should discuss and record the information requested for each element assigned using Worksheet 10.1. A scribe from each group can also record the discussion results on a flip chart.

4. Each small group should take a turn reviewing its results with the entire group. The facilitator may want to reproduce the activity sheet on a flip chart to capture the discussion. Encourage the entire group to take their own notes during the discussion. Encourage clarifying questions.

5. Capture resulting ideas in the action planning worksheet at the end of this chapter.

Assessment 10.1.   Gap Analysis: Elements of Environmental Awareness

Environmental Elements	Rating				
How well does your site link to each environmental element?	**Low**				**High**
Customers	1	2	3	4	5
Suppliers	1	2	3	4	5
Government regulators	1	2	3	4	5
Unions	1	2	3	4	5
Corporate office	1	2	3	4	5
Other sites in the corporation	1	2	3	4	5
Community	1	2	3	4	5
Shareholders	1	2	3	4	5
Political climate	1	2	3	4	5
Economy	1	2	3	4	5
Competitors	1	2	3	4	5
Partner organizations	1	2	3	4	5
The industry	1	2	3	4	5
Other: _____	1	2	3	4	5
Other: _____	1	2	3	4	5
Other: _____	1	2	3	4	5

Worksheet 10.1. Creating Environmental Scanning Mechanisms

Environmental Element	Specific Information Needed	Ways to Gather That Information

Act on Awareness of the Environment

Collecting information about your environment is worthless unless it is distributed to the right people and acted on. The more distribution and implementation processes can be built into the system, the more likely it is that the habit of linking to the environment will be formed.

Deciding Who Needs the Information

It is often difficult to decide who needs the information, but a good rule of thumb is that it is better to share information with too many people than with too few. One option may be to consciously bring up the topic of who needs what information periodically to make sure everyone is getting what he or she needs (see Chapter 7 on how this ties to resistance).

Distributing the Information

The method for distributing the information depends on the information itself, the audience, and the communication methods that you have available. Some methods for distributing the information, examples of using each method, and guidelines for appropriate use of each method are included in Table 10.2.

Building Implementation Processes

Once information is distributed, how can you ensure that something is done about it? Whenever possible, create processes to make sure the information is reviewed and necessary actions taken. This may take the form of periodic environmental scanning meetings with action items assigned, individuals or groups assigned to take on the role of environmental scanner, or whatever other options are appropriate for your group.

Planning: Act on Environmental Information

Time Requirement: Approximately 1 hour

Supplies: Completed Worksheet 10.1, Worksheet 10.2, flip charts, markers

Overview: After identifying mechanisms to improve your organization's links to the environment in the previous planning activity (captured in Worksheet 10.1), use this planning activity to begin creating processes to ensure that the information is acted on.

Instructions

1. Using the results of the previous activity (captured in Worksheet 10.1) and resulting conversation, identify the most important information elements that your organization needs to attend to. List them on Worksheet 10.2.

2. Form small groups of three or four people each. Assign one or more elements to each small group.

3. Have the small groups complete the remaining columns in Worksheet 10.2 for their assigned element(s). A scribe from each small group can also record the results on a flip chart.

Table 10.2.   Methods of Distributing Information

Method	Examples	Guidelines for Use
Meetings	• Face-to-face or virtual • Different levels (department, group/team, site, business unit, corporate-wide) • In-house or off-site	• Follow an agenda • Assign meeting roles • Make sure the appropriate people are participating • Have clear time expectations • Write and distribute notes and action items
Electronic technology	• E-mail • Shared drives • Web sites, Internet • Chat	• A supplement to, not a substitute for, personal interaction • Keep all information and distribution lists current • Don't force people to read messages/information that don't pertain to them • Standardize software versions
Integration mechanisms (see Chapter 13)	• Members of multiple groups • Integration teams	• Use when integration between groups is needed • Be clear about what information can be shared and what cannot • Be clear about decision-making power; can the representative from a group make decisions for that group in an integration meeting? • Share relevant information that applies to those integrating; do not withhold, but do not cloud the issue by sharing irrelevant information
Phone technology	• Phone calls • Voicemail • Conference calls • Videoconferencing	• Pay attention to the conversation even when it is not directly pertinent to you • Avoid talking over others • Minimize interruptions • Be sensitive to voice volume • Use printed material to increase clarity • Respect time zones
Publications	• Newsletters • Memos	• Distribute on a regular basis • Focus on one subject at a time • Obtain contributions from all levels of the organization
Signs	• Bulletin board material • Charts and graphs • Big signs throughout site	• Use signs as reminders of things shared in more detailed ways (for example, "Safety first!") • Make sure signs are clear, relatively simple, and self-explanatory • If using bulletin boards, create norms to ensure that they are checked regularly

Worksheet 10.2.   Acting on Environmental Information

Information	Who Needs It?	How Can They Get It?	How Can They Act on It?

4. Each small group should take a turn reviewing its results with the entire group. You may want to reproduce Worksheet 10.2 on a flip chart to capture the discussion. Encourage the entire group to take their own notes during the discussion. Encourage clarifying questions.

5. Capture resulting ideas in the action planning worksheet at the end of this chapter.

Create Ways for All Members to Contribute

Connecting to the environment is traditionally the responsibility of top management, with little involvement from lower levels. In a CWS, all levels should contribute to connecting to the environment. Not only must the environment be attended to, but there must be a way for all employees to contribute information about the environment in a way that makes tracking, using, and archiving by the organization reasonably easy.

One person has a limited experience of the environment. Gaining the viewpoints of multiple people broadens the "picture" of the environment. Since successful strategic planning requires an accurate understanding of the environment, it makes sense to involve as many people as possible in the planning process. For example, there is a hierarchy of customers. CEOs may have frequent contact with executives in customer organizations, but they may never have contact with the bottom-level customer. Frontline teams will have this contact, so their viewpoint is critical. Upward flow of the information gained from that contact is essential for informing strategic decisions.

Involving everyone in the process of understanding and adapting to the environment requires people working together to develop creative and adaptive solutions. As more people "pool" their knowledge of the environment, chances for developing new opportunities for the organization should occur.

Planning: Develop Ways for All Members to Contribute

Time Requirement: Approximately 1 hour

Supplies: Flip chart and markers for each small group, Worksheet 10.3, completed Worksheets 10.1 and 10.2

Overview: Use this activity to start developing ways for all members to contribute environmental information.

Instructions

1. As a group, determine the levels of membership you will use for this planning activity. List the levels in Worksheet 10.3. Use levels that make sense for your organization. Examples include top managers, middle managers, coaches, direct supervisors, and employees. (You could also further categorize employees into different functions, teams, or departments.)

2. Break into small groups of three or four people and assign a level to each group. Attempt to put individuals into groups that match their expertise (for example, if you have an engineer category, put an engineer in that group).

Worksheet 10.3.   Develop Ways for All Members to Contribute

Membership Level	Unique Access to What Information?	How to Capture That Information

3. Have small groups complete Worksheet 10.3. Use completed worksheets from earlier in the chapter to jump-start the discussion and fill in details as needed. In the middle column, determine the unique information that the level can access due to contact with different groups in daily work, access to professional groups, and so on. In the right column, brainstorm mechanisms to capture that information. Ask someone from each group to write the results on a flip chart.

4. Each small group should take a turn reviewing its results with the entire group. You may want to reproduce Worksheet 10.3 on a flip chart to capture the discussion. Encourage the entire group to take notes during the discussion. Encourage clarifying questions.

5. Capture resulting ideas in the action planning worksheet at the end of this chapter.

Conclusion

The key question for this chapter is, "How can we connect and adapt to our environment?" The environment is the surrounding conditions, influences, or forces that shape organizational growth and development. Intentionally creating environmental scanning mechanisms and processes for acting on that information will improve adaptability and contribute to long-term success of the organization.

Keys to the Chapter

- The environment exists both within the organization and outside the organization. What is considered the environment depends on perspective.

- Connecting to the environment provides information about the environment. Construct mechanisms to create awareness of the environment.

- Having the information is just the first step; acting on that information allows the organization to become adaptable.

- Adaptability represents the ability to make organizational changes in response to changes in the environment. Without adaptability, no organization can survive in a changing environment.

- Collaborative capability ought to make adaptation more effective.

- Everyone has a different perspective and access to different information that can add to the big picture. Develop ways for all members of the organization to contribute knowledge of the environment.

Chapter Wrap-Up

- What ideas did this chapter trigger for you and your group? List them in the action planning worksheet at the end of this chapter.

- Review the ideas list. Which of these do you want to implement? List the action item, person or group responsible, and target due dates in the action planning worksheet.

- Were any significant decisions made? Include them at the bottom of the action planning worksheet.

- How can you communicate the pertinent material generated by your work on this chapter to different audiences? Discuss and consider adding action items based on your discussion.

- How can you use the resources list for additional help?

- What chapter should you go through next? Refer back to Guiding Assessment results in Chapter 3 for suggestions of next steps.

- What can you do tomorrow or within the next week based on what you learned in this chapter? Have each person share what he or she will do, and follow up.

- What is your biggest learning from this chapter? Ask each person to share. This is a nice way to end the session. Include any resulting ideas or action items in the action planning worksheet.

Resources

Astley, W. G. (1984). Toward an appreciation of collective strategy. *Academy of Management Review, 9*(3), 526–536.

Brogniez, J., & Hall, S. (2001). *Attracting perfect customers: The power of strategic synchronicity.* San Francisco: Berrett-Koehler.

Connolly, M., Rianoshek, R., & Merten, G. (2002). *The communication catalyst: The fast (but not stupid) track to value for customers, investors, and employees.* Chicago: Dearborn Trade Publishing.

Fuld, L. M. (1994). *The new competitor intelligence: The complete resource for finding, analyzing, and using information about your competitors* (2nd ed.). Hoboken, NJ: Wiley.

Galinsky, E. (1994). Families and work: The importance of the quality of the work environment. In S. L. Kagan & B. Weissbourd (Eds.), *Putting families first: America's family support movement and the challenge of change* (pp. 112–136). San Francisco: Jossey-Bass.

Laseter, T. M. (1998). *Balanced sourcing: Cooperation and competition in supplier relationships.* San Francisco: Jossey-Bass.

Marr, J. W., & Walker, S. F. (2001). *Stakeholder power: A winning plan for building stakeholder commitment and driving corporate growth.* Cambridge, MA: Perseus.

McCarthy, M. P., Stein, J., & McCarthy, M. (2002). *Agile business for fragile times: Strategies for enhancing competitive resiliency and stakeholder trust.* New York: McGraw-Hill.

Miles, R., & Snow, C. (1994). *Fit, failure, and the hall of fame: How companies succeed or fail.* Hoboken, NJ: Wiley.

Miller, D. (1992). Environmental fit versus internal fit. *Organizational Science: A Journal of the Institute of Management Sciences, 3*(2), 159–179.

Moore, R. A. (2001). *The science of high-performance supplier management: A systematic approach to improving procurement costs, quality, and relationships.* New York: AMACOM.

Porter, M. E. (1998). *Competitive strategy: Techniques for analyzing industries and competitors.* New York: Free Press.

Zaltman, G. (2003). *How customers think: Essential insights into the mind of the market.* Cambridge, MA: Harvard Business School Press.

Action Planning and Summary Sheet

Ideas Generated from This Chapter

#	
1	
2	
3	
4	
5	

#	Action Item	Target Date	Person/Group Responsible
1			
2			
3			
4			
5			
6			

Significant Decisions Made

#	
1	
2	
3	
4	

Craft a Culture of Collaboration and Entrepreneurship

Where Are We in the Strategic Design Process?

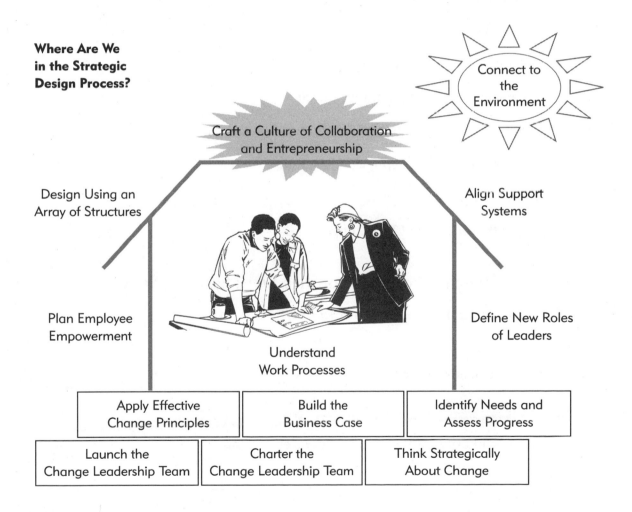

Connect to the Environment

Craft a Culture of Collaboration and Entrepreneurship

Design Using an Array of Structures

Align Support Systems

Plan Employee Empowerment

Understand Work Processes

Define New Roles of Leaders

Apply Effective Change Principles	Build the Business Case	Identify Needs and Assess Progress
Launch the Change Leadership Team	Charter the Change Leadership Team	Think Strategically About Change

Key Question of This Chapter

What kind of culture supports collaboration, and how can we move toward a collaborative culture?

Quick Look

Overview

Culture is a fuzzy term we use to refer to the way work really gets done. By identifying your current culture and envisioning your ideal culture, you can begin to get an understanding of required changes in the organization. The outcomes of this chapter include a vision statement for your culture and key values and design principles to guide your CWS initiative.

Chapter Plan

Topic	ABC	👥	🔍	🧍
What Is Culture?	✓	✓		
Why Change Culture?	✓	✓		
Identify Current Culture			✓	
Characteristics of Collaborative Culture	✓		✓	
Align Organizational Subcultures	✓	✓		
Characteristics of Entrepreneurial Culture	✓		✓	
Envision Ideal Culture	✓	✓		✓
Begin the Journey to Ideal Culture	✓	✓		

Principles of Collaborative Work Systems Series

Articulate and enforce "a few strict rules"

A few strict rules

Foster personal accountability

RESPONSIBILITIES

Align authority, information, and decision making

What Is Culture?

Culture is a pattern of shared organizational values, basic underlying assumptions, and informal norms that guide the way work is accomplished in an organization. It is the unwritten way work really gets done and does not necessarily align with formal policies and procedures.

We take a practical view of culture in this chapter. We suggest using culture as a way to understand current values of the organization, envision the ideal values, and use the ideal values as "signposts" for changes in the organization. Every change decision should be checked with these "signposts"—are we going in the right direction?

Following are some definitions for terms that frequently come up in discussions about culture:

Values—beliefs of a person or group in which they have an investment. A principle, standard, or quality considered worthwhile or desirable. For example, "Trust in workers to get the job done" is an organizational value.

Assumptions—statements that are assumed to be true and from which a conclusion can be drawn; an idea that is taken for granted. For example, "People are inherently good" is an assumption.

Norm—a standard, model, or pattern regarded as typical. For example, "Meetings never start on time" can be a group norm. A positive example would be, "We help when someone has a problem."

Practice—a habitual or customary action or way of doing something. For example, "Turn off the machine before going home" is a practice. Practices do not always align with policies and procedures. No matter how standardized policies and procedures seem to be, effective practice requires individuals to make adjustments according to the situation.

Discussion

1. What does the word "culture" mean to you?

2. What does "culture" mean in your organization? Give some examples.

3. How does the work really get done, beyond the rules and regulations?

4. Think of a group you belong to. What are some of the group's norms?

5. Consider the same group. What practices does the group have in use?

6. What are the values and assumptions behind the practices?

Why Change Culture?

Culture is one of the most important organizational components to be changed for successful collaborative work systems. Unfortunately, it is also perhaps the most difficult component to change, requiring years of effort for real change to occur. However, there are strong reasons for changing culture in a CWS initiative:

- *Successful collaboration.* Traditional organizational culture emphasizes individuals and competition, not collaboration and cooperation. Unless culture is changed (indirectly through systems, leaders, and structures) to support collaboration, the success of any CWS change effort will be limited. When culture is truly collaborative, collaboration emerges spontaneously and does not always require formal team structure and charter.

- *Direction setting.* When you create a culture that is aligned with the business strategy, everyone's values, norms, and assumptions support it rather than conflict. That includes alignment with collaboration. Everyone knows the strategy, so they have similar criteria when making decisions.

Discussion

Why are you trying to change the culture in your organization?

Planning: Identify Current Culture

Time Requirement: Approximately 1½ hours

Supplies: Flip chart and markers for each small group, Worksheet 11.1

Overview: Before making efforts to change culture, it is important to have an understanding of your current situation. This activity will help you identify aspects of your culture.

Instructions

1. As a group, answer the question, "What are the characteristics of our culture today?" (the unwritten rules, assumptions, beliefs, and values; the way work really gets done). Use the results of your discussion in the What Is Culture? section of the workbook to trigger your answers. Some examples include:

   - We can't do the job without overtime.

   - People have great ideas but there is minimal follow-through.

   - Management trusts employees.

2. Record the main points in the discussion on a flip chart.

3. Look at your list and connect similar ideas with numbers or lines. This should help you create themes. For example, "computers available to share information," "learn from each other," and "share plant successes" could all go under the theme of "share information."

4. Form small groups of three or four members. Assign one or more themes to each small group to further define each theme using Worksheet 11.1. Each group should select a scribe to record the discussion results on a flip chart.

5. Each small group should take a turn reviewing its results with the entire group. You may want to reproduce Worksheet 11.1 on a flip chart to capture the discussion. Encourage the entire group to take notes during the discussion.

6. Encourage discussion using the following questions:

   - Does your organization have gaps between policies and procedures (the "rules") and practices (the "actions")? What are the gaps?

   - Why do you have these gaps?

7. List ideas generated in this discussion in your action planning worksheet at the end of the chapter.

Characteristics of Collaborative Culture

In a collaborative culture, people want to work together. To highlight aspects of collaborative culture, an extreme contrast is shown in Table 11.1. In a "blame" culture, people work against each other. These extremes are shown to make a point, but most organizations fall somewhere on a continuum between these two points.

For collaborative work systems to be most effective, the organization's values, assumptions, and norms must support collaboration and cooperation. Some characteristics of a collaborative culture are listed in Assessment 11.1.

Assessment: Collaborative Culture

Time Requirement: Approximately 1 hour

Supplies: Assessment 11.1, flip chart, markers

Worksheet 11.1.   Identify Your Current Culture

Theme	What Does It Look Like in Practice?	How Is It Reflected in Policies and Procedures?

Table 11.1. Blame vs. Collaborative Cultures

Blame	Collaborative
Time and energy spent looking for scapegoats	Time and energy spent looking for partners
Little time spent solving problems	Spontaneous problem solving
Collaboration is forced, not natural	Collaboration is efficient and habitual
When a problem arises, impulse is to shift blame, avoid the problem, or point fingers	When a problem arises, impulse is to solve it in a group of appropriate individuals
Committed to working against each other	Committed to cooperation and collaboration
No clue of how to pull a group together to work on something, and no desire to do so	Understand how to pull a group together to work on something

Overview: Assess your current and ideal level of collaborative culture. Identify the gaps and create ideas for closing them.

Instructions

1. Choose the appropriate method for completing the assessment. Refer back to Table 3.2 for methods and pros and cons for each.

2. For each item in Assessment 11.1, assess the extent to which that item is part of your organization's culture. Use a circle to indicate where your organization is now.

3. Review the items again. This time, use a square to indicate where your organization would like to be at the highest level of CWS.

4. Discuss the answers, using the following questions:

   - What are the biggest gaps between where you are now and where you want to be?

   - In what order do you need to address the gaps? Create a prioritized list for addressing the gaps, based on your discussion.

   - What can you do short term and long term to close those gaps? Brainstorm ideas.

5. List ideas generated in this discussion on the action planning worksheet at the end of the chapter.

Align Organizational Subcultures

We refer to *organization culture* as the overall feeling about the way things are done in an organization. However, there are lots of different subcultures within an organization. A *subculture* is a group within the organization that has distinctive patterns of behavior and beliefs. Some types of subcultures include: management, labor, engineering, production, marketing, quality assurance, union employees, nonunion employees, and different races, nationalities, and religions.

Assessment 11.1.   Collaborative Culture Gap Analysis

Collaborative Culture Characteristic	Rating Low				High
A "cooperation" mindset, where collaboration is efficient and habitual	1	2	3	4	5
Respect for expertise instead of position	1	2	3	4	5
Continuous improvement	1	2	3	4	5
Shared responsibility	1	2	3	4	5
Decision making, responsibility, and authority are placed where the work is actually done	1	2	3	4	5
Employees fully engaged mentally, physically, and emotionally in their work	1	2	3	4	5
Commitment of all employees to the success of the organization	1	2	3	4	5
Not a "me" but a "we" mindset	1	2	3	4	5
Open atmosphere of trust and respect	1	2	3	4	5
Partnership instead of dictatorship	1	2	3	4	5
Decisions made collaboratively, when appropriate	1	2	3	4	5
Employees are involved in decision making	1	2	3	4	5
A natural tendency to select collaborative methods for reaching solutions	1	2	3	4	5
A focus on relationship building	1	2	3	4	5
Formal and informal collaboration promoted	1	2	3	4	5
Support for natural, informal processes of learning and communication	1	2	3	4	5
Different functions and departments work together without disruptive conflict	1	2	3	4	5
People of different races, genders, and religions work together in harmony	1	2	3	4	5

Figure 11.1.   Culture and Subcultures

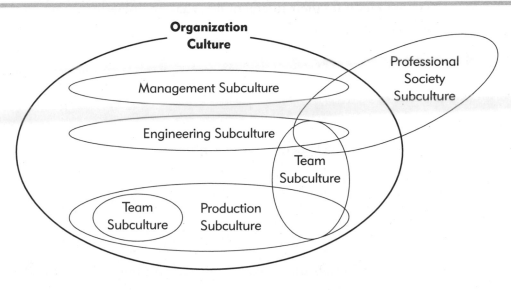

Schein (1997) suggests that the differences in culture between management, engineering, and production are so large that it is as if they are living in different countries. Alignment across these boundaries can be achieved through participation in the CWS initiative. Creating a change leadership team with a vertical slice of the organization as a membership criterion provides the opportunity for input from all the subgroups, so shared understanding can unite them across their current boundaries.

The relationship between the organization's culture and its various subcultures is shown in Figure 11.1.

Each subculture will respond to the CWS initiative differently. There will be different components of conflict and differing compatibility between the subculture and the CWS initiative's value set. The CLT must take into account these differences and act accordingly.

Discussion

1. Create a list of the subcultures within your organization.

2. How do people interact within their subculture? What values and practices do you see for each one?

3. How do the different subcultures interact with each other? What organizational factors facilitate their interaction? What organizational factors inhibit their interaction?

4. What can you do to help align subcultures?

5. How will each subculture respond to the CWS initiative differently?

6. How can the CLT deal with those differences?

Characteristics of Entrepreneurial Culture

What Is an Entrepreneur?

An entrepreneur is "a person who organizes, operates, and assumes the risk for a business venture." Successful entrepreneurs are highly self-motivated, personally involved, assertive, opportunistic, optimistic, responsive, and responsible.

Why Entrepreneurship?

In a CWS, where the organization structure is flatter and empowerment of all employees is greater, a spirit of entrepreneurship is important. The goal is to create a culture in which all work groups perform as if they owned the business. The focus should be quality, cost, and results—and on whatever it takes to meet customer needs.

Supporting Entrepreneurship

For a spirit of entrepreneurship to occur, the organization must provide space for it to develop. Resources (for example, time, money, information) should be provided for entrepreneurial activities. Employees should be encouraged to take calculated, intelligent risks, without fear of being disciplined if they fail. The idea is for employees to become partners in the business, so they need developmental opportunities for increased business sense, knowledge, and skill.

Assessment: Entrepreneurial Culture

Time Requirement: Approximately 1½ hours

Supplies: Assessment 11.2, completed Assessment 11.1, flip chart, markers

Overview: Assess your current and ideal level of entrepreneurial culture. Identify the gaps and create ideas for closing them.

Instructions

1. Choose the appropriate method for completing the assessment. Refer back to Table 3.2 for methods and pros and cons for each.

2. For each item in Assessment 11.2, assess the extent to which that item is part of your organization's culture. Use a circle to indicate where your organization is now.

3. Review the items again. This time, use a square to indicate where your organization would like to be at the highest level of CWS.

4. Discuss the answers, using the following questions:

   - What are the biggest gaps between where you are now and where you want to be?

   - In what order do you need to address the gaps? Create a prioritized list for addressing the gaps, based on your discussion.

   - What can you do in the short term and long term to close those gaps? Brainstorm ideas.

5. Compare collaborative (Assessment 11.1) and entrepreneurial (Assessment 11.2) assessment results. Discuss the following questions:

   - How are the results the same? How do they differ?

   - How do the results fit together?

   - What additional ideas develop from reviewing the results together?

6. List ideas generated in this discussion in your action planning worksheet at the end of the chapter.

Envision Ideal Culture

Many culture "types" have been used as the guiding forces in organizational change. Some examples are listed in Table 11.2.

Whatever culture "type" (or combination of types) you select, whether it is on this list or not, it is important to pick one (or a compatible set), stick with it, and do everything it takes to support outstanding organizational performance. Creating a consistent language to describe your CWS initiative also helps create understanding in the organization as to the purpose of the change.

Assessment 11.2.   Entrepreneurial Culture Gap Analysis

Entrepreneurial Culture Characteristic	Rating				
	Low				High
Employees are highly self-motivated and personally involved in their work.	1	2	3	4	5
Employees are responsive to problems.	1	2	3	4	5
Employees take responsibility for their actions.	1	2	3	4	5
Work groups perform as if they owned the business.	1	2	3	4	5
Work groups focus on meeting customer needs.	1	2	3	4	5
Work groups focus on quality.	1	2	3	4	5
Work groups focus on cost and results.	1	2	3	4	5
Resources (for example, time, money, and information) are provided for entrepreneurial activities.	1	2	3	4	5
Employees are encouraged to take calculated, intelligent risks, without fear of being disciplined if they fail.	1	2	3	4	5
Employees feel as though they are partners in the business.	1	2	3	4	5
Employees have opportunities (for example, training sessions, access to information) to develop their understanding of the business.	1	2	3	4	5
Each employee knows who his or her customers are and what customers need	1	2	3	4	5
Employees have goals and measure their progress toward them frequently.	1	2	3	4	5
Employees have opportunities to make decisions about their work.	1	2	3	4	5
Leaders support employees rather than direct them in reaching their goals.	1	2	3	4	5
There is an assumption that "if you want to find out how best to improve a job, ask the person doing it."	1	2	3	4	5
Employees focus on both internal and external customer satisfaction.	1	2	3	4	5

Table 11.2. Culture Types

Culture Type	Explanation
Collaborative	A culture where collaboration is efficient and habitual. Time and energy are spent looking for partners. When a problem arises, impulse is to solve it in a group of appropriate individuals.
Entrepreneurial	A culture where all work groups perform as if they own the business. The focus is quality, cost, and results—and on anything to meet customer needs.
Innovation	A culture focused on creating new ideas and ways of solving old problems.
Empowerment	A culture focused on giving authority and responsibility to all employees, holding them accountable, and rewarding them for fulfilling these responsibilities.
Employee as most valuable asset	A culture focused on the value of the employee. Programs and policies focus on supporting the employee—for example, extra learning and development opportunities, in-house day-care and fitness facilities.
Command and control	A culture where leaders are focused on commanding and controlling employees and processes. Usually very rigid rules and processes are used.
Laissez-faire	A culture where "anything goes," usually involving very hands-off management and very few rules to guide the work process.
Involvement	A culture focused on involving employees in decision making.
Learning	A culture focused on understanding the environment, reacting (or acting proactively) accordingly, learning from these situations, and building the learning into the organization.
Quality	A culture focused on the quality of the product or service, including doing it right the first time and eliminating rework.

Discussion

1. What culture "type" (or types) is most like what you want to create?

2. Why do you believe that is the one (or ones) to select?

Planning: Envision Ideal Culture, Part 1

Time Requirement: 1 hour for Steps 1 through 6; 1 hour for Steps 7 and 8; Step 9 depends on the method of creating the vision statement; 30 minutes for Steps 10 and 11

Supplies: Worksheet 5.7 (previously completed); your organization's mission, vision, and strategy statements; Worksheets 11.2 and 11.3; two flip charts; markers; masking tape

Overview: Before making efforts to change culture, it is important to have a vision of your ideal culture. This section will help you visualize your ideal culture.

Instructions

1. In Worksheet 11.2, have each person write his or her vision of what the ideal culture will look like in three to five years. What will the organization look like? What will be some of the unwritten rules?

2. Ask each individual to share his or her ideal vision. Record the main points on a flip chart.

3. Number each point on the flip chart.

4. On another flip chart, brainstorm vision themes. What themes came out of the individual visions?

5. Go through numbered points one-by-one and put them into vision themes. Cross the point off when you have it listed with a theme. Add themes as appropriate.

6. Refer to any relevant work you may have done in Chapter 5. Your ideal culture should align with your organization's strategy, mission, and vision, and to whatever mission and vision statements you have already created for the CWS initiative. Pull together copies of your organization's mission, vision, and strategy statements and the mission and vision statements developed for the CWS initiative. Based on these documents, and on your previous cultural assessments in this chapter, determine what elements of your organization's culture need to be expanded or downplayed and what missing elements need to be added. Add themes as needed.

7. Form small groups and assign one or more themes to each group. Ask each group to complete Worksheet 11.3, keeping in mind that they are focusing on ideal conditions. Select a scribe from each group to record the discussion results.

8. Each small group should take a turn reviewing its results with the entire group. You may want to reproduce Worksheet 11.3 on a flip chart to capture the discussion. Encourage the entire group to take notes during the discussion. Encourage clarifying questions.

9. Develop a vision statement based on the material you have created. You might do this in one of two ways:

    • Work on the vision statement as a group, writing it together and gaining consensus on every point, or

Worksheet 11.2.　Individual Vision for Organization

My vision of the ideal culture in our organization in three to five years:

_____

_____

_____

_____

_____

_____

_____

Worksheet 11.3.　Envision Your Ideal Culture

Theme	What Does It Look Like in Practice?	How Is It Reflected in Policies and Procedures?

- Assign a few small groups to each write a vision statement. Bring the small groups back together to discuss their results. Lead the whole group in choosing the points they like best, and craft the vision statement based on those points.

10. Determine whether this statement needs to be communicated differently to different audiences. For example, some people need more detail than others, but some may respond better to a visual representation that could be placed around the site as a reminder. What ideas do you have for this?

11. List ideas developed from this activity in the action planning worksheet at the end of this chapter.

Planning: Envision Ideal Culture, Part 2

Time Requirement: Approximately 2 hours

Supplies: Worksheet 5.4 (previously completed), completed vision statement from previous activity, flip chart, markers, Worksheet 11.4

Overview: Now that you have a vision of your ideal culture, it is important to create a values list and set of design goals to guide your CWS initiative. You can use these lists as criteria for weighing each decision regarding the CWS initiative.

Instructions

1. Refer to any relevant work the group may have done in Chapter 5.

2. Look at the vision statement created in the last section. Brainstorm (and list on flip chart) a list of key values that come out of this statement.

3. Determine the three to five key values that will guide your CWS initiative. If this has become clear from the vision statement discussion, then confirm consensus and move on. If not, discuss with the group until a consensus is reached.

4. Write the three to five key values in the left column of Worksheet 11.4.

5. Translate your values list into design goals. For example, if your value is "employee involvement," a design goal might be "When possible, we will involve employees in decision making." Design goals should be specific enough to be understood, yet general enough to provide discretionary space within the bounds of the principles. Don't make the "rules" too rigid or they will inhibit the effort rather than help it. Each value can have as many design goals as desired, but try to keep the number small, as it will be difficult to focus on too many design goals. Refer to these goals when you get to more "concrete" parts of the CWS initiative (see Chapters 12 through 16).
   Other examples include:

   - Move as much self-management as possible into teams.
   - Share leadership responsibilities among employees.

6. Discuss the design goals until you develop the key few (no more than ten). Be sure to develop consensus around these.

Worksheet 11.4.   Ideal Culture Values and Design Goals

Values	Design Goals

7. Write the design goals in the right column of Worksheet 11.4.

8. List ideas developed from this activity in the action planning worksheet at the end of this chapter.

Begin the Journey to Ideal Culture

The journey to your ideal culture will be long and difficult, but worth the effort. Before beginning the journey, take some time to anticipate the difficulties.

Realize the Difficulties in True Culture Change

True culture change is a slow, difficult, resource-intensive, and time-intensive process. Some of the potential issues include the following:

- *Resources:* Employee time and financial investment in education and training are just two of the resources required. The CWS initiative requires long-term investment through reward, modeling, and selection.

- *Setbacks:* Sudden unexpected changes can derail a CWS initiative. A dramatic event that caused a setback for many companies was the attacks of September 11. Most setbacks are much less dramatic, but provide problems nonetheless.

- *Time:* Many believe that it takes at least five years for true culture change to occur!

- *Persistence:* Because it takes such a long time for true change to occur, many give up before results are realized.

- *Resistance to change:* People in the organization may resist change, especially if they have seen multiple change efforts come and go through the years, showing no results.

Discussion

1. What potential difficulties do you foresee for the CWS initiative?

2. What can you do ahead of time to prevent these difficulties?

Table 11.3. Links to Other Chapters

Topic	Chapter
Connect to the Environment	10
Understand Work Processes	12
Design Using an Array of Structures	13
Create a Plan for Employee Empowerment	14
Define New Roles of Leaders	15
Align Support Systems for Collaboration	16

Changing Culture

As mentioned earlier in this chapter, culture is very intangible and abstract and is *difficult or impossible to change directly.* Instead, you can *change the more concrete parts* of the organization, which leads to culture change. The "concrete" pieces of the organization that lead to culture change are discussed elsewhere in the workbook. These topics and corresponding chapters are listed in Table 11.3.

The vision and desired values list created in the previous section serve as signposts guiding the CWS initiative as you change the "concrete" pieces of the organization.

Discussion

1. What can you do to close the gap between the current and ideal future?

2. What are some immediate steps you can take?

3. What are some long-term steps?

4. What resources do you need to start the change?

Conclusion

The key question for this chapter is, "What kind of culture supports collaboration, and how can we move toward a collaborative culture?" In a collaborative culture, people want to work together, and work groups perform as if they own the business. Use culture as a way to understand current values of the organization, envision the ideal values, and use the ideal values as signposts for changes in the organization.

Keys to the Chapter

- Culture is a pattern of shared organizational values, basic underlying assumptions, and informal norms that guide the way work is accomplished in an organization. It is the way work really gets done.

- By identifying your current culture and envisioning your ideal culture, you can begin to get an understanding of required changes in the organization.

- Culture is one of the most important organizational components to be changed for successful collaborative work systems. Unfortunately, it is also perhaps the most difficult component to change, requiring years of effort for real change to occur. Realize the difficulties of true culture change and plan accordingly.

- Culture change happens indirectly; when an organization changes structures, employee and leader roles, and systems, culture eventually shifts.

- Obtain input from all affected subcultures (different functions, managers, and employees) in your design process.

- Identify the gaps between your current and ideal culture. Periodically reassess culture to measure change, using the gap analysis tools in this chapter, or create your own gap analysis tool, using your key values and design principles.

Chapter Wrap-Up

- What ideas did this chapter trigger for you and your group? List them in the action planning worksheet at the end of this chapter.

- Review the ideas list. Which of these do you want to implement? List the action item, person or group responsible, and target due dates on the action planning worksheet.

- Were any significant decisions made? Include them at the bottom of the action planning worksheet.

- How can you communicate the pertinent material generated by your work on this chapter to different audiences? Discuss and consider adding action items based on your discussion.

- How can you use the resources list for additional help?

- What chapter should you go through next? Refer back to Guiding Assessment results in Chapter 3 for suggestions of next steps.

- What can you do tomorrow or within the next week based on what you learned in this chapter? Have each person share what he or she will do, and follow up.

- What is your biggest learning from this chapter? Ask each person to share. This is a nice way to end the session. Include any resulting ideas or action items on the action planning worksheet.

Resources

Cameron, K. S., & Quinn, R. E. (1999). *Diagnosing and changing organizational culture: Based on the competing values framework.* Reading, MA: Addison-Wesley.

Carter, L., Giber, D., & Goldsmith, M. (Eds.) (2001). *Best practices in organization development and change: Culture, leadership, retention, performance, coaching.* San Francisco: Jossey-Bass/Pfeiffer.

Childress, J. R., & Senn, L. E. (1999). *The secret of a winning culture: Building high-performance teams.* Los Angeles: Leadership Press.

Randolph, W. A. (2000). Re-thinking empowerment: Why is it so hard to achieve? *Organizational Dynamics, 29*(2), 94–107.

Schein, E. H. (1997). *Organizational culture and leadership* (2nd ed.). San Francisco: Jossey-Bass.

Sherriton, J., & Stern, J. L. (1997). *Corporate culture team culture: Removing the hidden barriers to team success.* New York: AMACOM.

Shonk, J. H. (1997). *Team-based organizations: Developing a successful team environment.* Homewood, IL: Irwin.

Action Planning and Summary Sheet

Ideas Generated from This Chapter

1
2
3
4
5

#	Action Item	Target Date	Person/Group Responsible
1			
2			
3			
4			
5			
6			

Significant Decisions Made

1
2
3
4

Understand Work Processes

Where Are We in the Strategic Design Process?

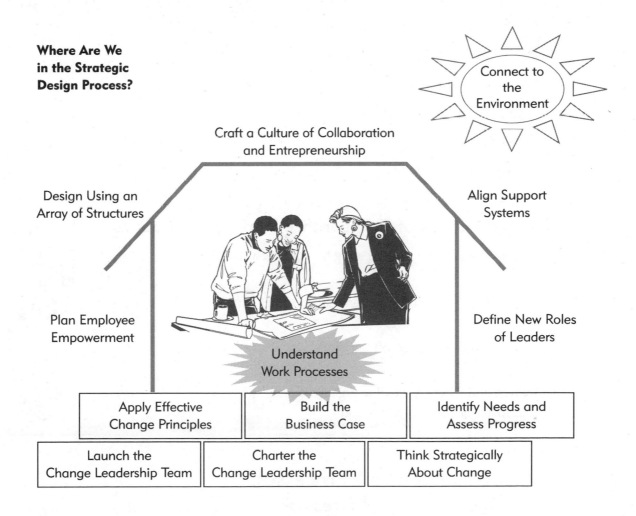

Connect to the Environment

Craft a Culture of Collaboration and Entrepreneurship

Design Using an Array of Structures

Align Support Systems

Plan Employee Empowerment

Define New Roles of Leaders

Understand Work Processes

Apply Effective Change Principles	Build the Business Case	Identify Needs and Assess Progress
Launch the Change Leadership Team	Charter the Change Leadership Team	Think Strategically About Change

Key Question of This Chapter

What are the key work processes, and how can we better understand them?

Quick Look

Overview

Work encompasses the tasks to be completed for the business to thrive. Work processes break down those tasks into sequential steps. An effective CWS initiative enhances the completion of work and anchors all the components of the initiative, especially the design of organization structure (see Chapter 13) with an understanding of the work. The outcomes of this chapter include identification of key work processes, mapping of those processes, analysis of the maps, and understanding of customer, supplier, and regulator expectations for the key work processes.

Chapter Plan

Topic				
Why Focus on Work Processes?	✓			✓
Map Work Processes	✓			✓
Analyze Work Processes	✓			✓
Understand Customer, Supplier, and Regulator Requirements	✓			✓

Principles of Collaborative Work Systems Series

Focus collaboration on achieving business results

Exploit the rhythm of divergence and convergence

Manage complex trade-off decisions

Design and promote flexible organizations
that foster needed collaboration

Why Focus on Work Processes?

What Are Work Processes?

The work encompasses the tasks to be completed in order for the business to thrive. Work processes break down those tasks into sequential steps. For example, in an airline organization, the work consists of flying passengers from one city to another. Some processes may include selling tickets to customers, preparing the airplane for the journey, the trip itself, and finishing the journey at the destination. And, of course, there are many subprocesses to these processes.

Why Is It Important to Understand Work Processes?

Placing work in the center of our organizing model (see Figure 1.1) emphasizes the point that the purpose of organizations is to complete their business, whatever that may be. An effective CWS initiative enhances the completion of work and anchors all components of the initiative with an understanding of the work.

Understanding the work is especially important in determining the appropriate structure to carry out that work. It is critical to match the type of work to the appropriate mechanism for carrying out the work, whether it is a team, individual, or some other structure. This chapter focuses on understanding the work and looking for opportunities for collaboration; Chapter 13 concentrates on designing organization structures to carry out the work.

Planning: Identify Key Work Processes

Time Requirement: Approximately 15 minutes

Supplies: Flip chart and markers

Overview: Identify the key work processes in your organization so you can map and analyze them later in this chapter. Understanding the work provides the grounding for the CWS initiative.

Instructions

1. As a group, brainstorm a list of the important processes or products in your organization.

2. Review the list. How similar are the processes or products? Can any of them be reviewed together?

3. Choose two key processes or products to analyze in this chapter. Pick ones that you think have the best opportunities to further the CWS initiative. You may decide to analyze more processes or products later, but two will be enough to start. List the two key processes or products below.

Key Processes or Products to Analyze in This Chapter

1. _____

   _____

   _____

2. _____

   _____

   _____

Map Work Processes

One method of carefully examining the work is work process mapping.

A work process map is a technique for visually representing work processes at a high level. It is not the very detailed engineering-driven version of work process mapping that many use as part of a quality improvement process, although those detailed versions may be helpful in subsequent rounds. Figure 12.1 shows a simplified example of a work process map. The hypothetical widget production begins in marketing when the customer order is received. Over time, the process is handed off to various functions in the organization. Finally, the widgets are sent to the customer at the end of the process.

Guidelines for Work Process Mapping

1. *Develop a map that works for you.* Work process mapping is more of an art than a science. There are no "right" answers. The map itself is not important; instead, it is the discussion and understanding of the work that develop out of the mapping process.

2. *Illustrate the appropriate level of detail.* Start at a conceptually high level of the work process and avoid getting into every little detail. Focus on the big steps in the

Figure 12.1. Sample Work Process Map

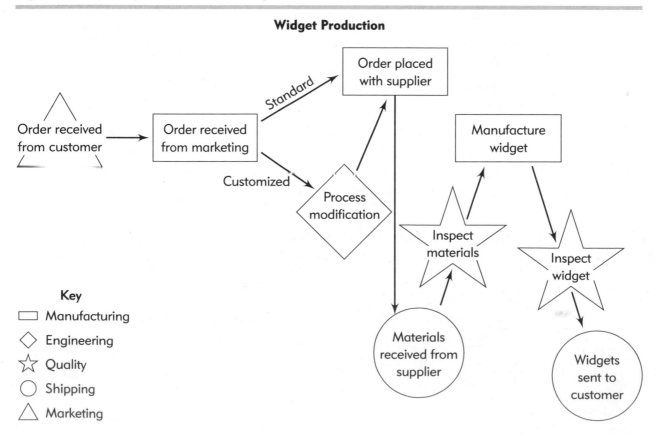

process, not the little ones. "Manufacturing accomplishes extrusion; then quality checks the parts for defects" is at an appropriately high level of detail, whereas "Joe hands the part to Martha to turn a screw; then she hands it to Juan to seal the screw" is too much detail for initial work process maps. As you get further into the CWS initiative, you may want to have each potential team or group create a work process map at a higher level of detail.

3. *Focus on handoffs between functions.* Handoffs between functions indicate interdependencies that will be important in the analysis of the work process map later in this chapter. Also, focusing on the handoffs between functions will help keep the group at a higher level of detail.

4. *Identify how support groups interact with key work processes.* Groups such as purchasing and human resources may not interact as direct parts of the work process, but it is important nonetheless to understand how these support groups interact with the key work processes.

5. *Determine appropriate boundaries for the work process.* In most cases, you will want to map the work process within your organization only and show handoffs from suppliers and customers at the beginning and the end of the work process map. However, if your organization is highly interdependent with customers, suppliers, or other organizations, you may need to include some of their work process within your work process map. Again, this is an art, not a science, so do what works best for your organization.

6. *Use a facilitator with expertise leading groups through complex tasks.* Work process mapping is a difficult process, as it is easy to become too focused on the details. Someone with experience keeping the group focused at a conceptual level who can move the process along is invaluable. Experience in work process mapping is a plus, but since this is a different form of work process mapping than the detailed engineering-driven version, work process mapping experience is not a requirement.

7. *Involve appropriate work process expertise.* Members of the CLT should be involved in the work mapping process as well as appropriate members of the organization with expertise in the work process being mapped. Bringing in people with knowledge of the work process will not only enhance the work process map, but also develop their ownership of the CWS initiative.

8. *Focus on key work processes identified in the previous planning activity.* Start with maps of the two important work processes identified earlier in this chapter. After the first round of work process mapping, you can decide what other processes, if any, should be mapped.

Planning: Create a Work Process Map

Time Requirement: Approximately 90 minutes for each map

Supplies: Figure 12.2, flip chart, markers, masking tape; colored sticky notes (optional)

Overview: In this activity, you'll map the key work processes identified earlier in the chapter. These maps will be analyzed later in the chapter. The goal of work process mapping is to gain further understanding of the work processes. This understanding will be crucial for all parts of the CWS initiative, but especially in designing organizational structure (see Chapter 13).

Instructions

1. Invite people to the work process mapping session. Involve appropriate CLT members and other employees with expertise in the work process to be mapped.

2. Prepare for the work process mapping session.

    - Identify and prepare facilitators of the process. Find one or more individuals with expertise in work process mapping and group facilitation to lead the process. If possible, have one person lead the mapping process and have a second person observe the group with the goal of making suggestions to help move the group along. Give these facilitators whatever materials they need to help them understand the CWS initiative and the group to participate in the activity.

    - Prepare materials. Tape together flip chart paper as shown in Figure 12.2. Prepare the paper as shown. Write the work process to be discussed at the top of the page. Have a flip chart nearby with the key (as shown).

3. Create the key for the functions—for example, engineering and manufacturing. Use different colors of sticky notes to distinguish different functions, or create a shape code as in the example (Figure 12.1).

4. Create the work process map. Refer back to the example in Figure 12.1 for guidance.

Figure 12.2.   Blank Work Process Map

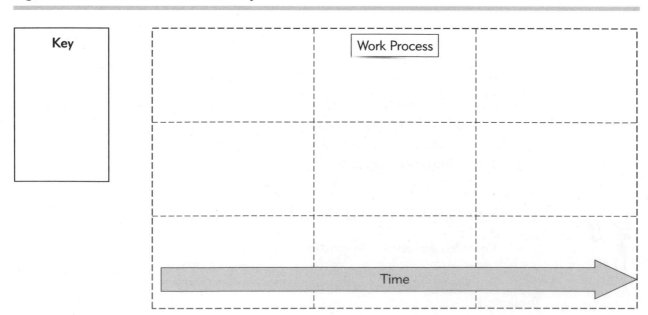

- At a very high level, discuss the workflow over time in terms of these functions. Start from the time the product (or process) comes "in the door" at the organization, to the time it goes "out the door."

- Use arrows to indicate handoffs between steps. Focus on transitions and exchanges between steps.

- As the mapping process develops, it might become necessary to add meaning to the map through different mechanisms such as extra color or shape coding or special lines. Some of the items you may want to differentiate include direct handoffs, people required to support part of the process, special case handoffs, and what happens in the case of a problem.

- When necessary, ask participants to further explain the work process by helping the facilitator draw it.

5. Use some of the following questions to guide the activity, if needed:

   - What is the process for making your output (whether it is a physical product, information, customer transaction, or whatever)?

   - How many people per function?

   - How does each function relate to the process or product?

   - How does each function relate to other functions?

   - How are the functions interdependent?

   - How does shift work play into the process?

   - What is the length of the process or product cycle? Is it continuous?

   - Is a work unit currently organized around the entire product or process, or are small parts of a much larger process or product completed by multiple work units?

   - In the next year, do you expect any major changes in the work process?

6. Once each map is completed, the facilitator or a team member should create a clean copy of the map and distribute a copy to each team member so it can be used in subsequent activities in this chapter and in Chapter 13.

7. Add any action ideas that come out of this activity to the action planning worksheet at the end of this chapter.

Analyze Work Processes

Now that you have completed your first round of work process mapping, it is time to look for opportunities for collaboration. Some characteristics of collaborative work are identified below. A planning activity follows that will lead you through analyzing your work processes.

Characteristics of Collaborative Work

Requires interdependent work. For the CWS initiative to be successful, the organization must have work that is appropriate for collaboration—that is, interdependent tasks that require more than one person to complete them. This interdependence requires the integration of the knowledge and work of different individuals. In other words, simple, single-function tasks, such as turning a screw to complete a roller skate, would be less appropriate for a team than assembly and inspection of an entire roller skate. In teams, members depend on each other to achieve work goals.

Requires whole pieces of work. In a CWS, workers are organized around whole pieces of work, as opposed to segmented work with many transitions between different groups or departments during production of the product or process. When the overall task is too complex for a single team (for example, building an airplane), then the work of the team represents a complete piece of the larger project, for example, the paint team handling the entire exterior of the plane rather than breaking it into tail section, wings, or fuselage for separate work groups, resulting in the work having less segmentation. Collaborative structures often are organized around processes, products, or customers in order to maximize the use of cross-functional teams that bring diverse experience and expertise together. For example, a team could be responsible for an entire assembly line, rather than the traditional approach where each individual does his or her part and throws it to the next person, without regard for the final product.

Requires different types of expertise to perform the work. Collaboration is needed when the work process requires input from multiple types of expertise. As a prerequisite for designing structure, work should be analyzed to determine the types of expertise required to perform the work. Look at the types of expertise in two categories. Types of expertise needed to routinely perform the work are required in the work process almost daily. Key supporters either only affect the work in special situations or only occasionally are involved with the work.

Identify Opportunities to Redesign Work

Some situations may warrant redesign of the work to become more suitable for a team. While the characteristics of the work in most situations are fairly set, the task can be reframed through work process redesign. If work is not amenable to teams, then perhaps it should be. Not all work is teamwork, but some work that looks like individual work can be redesigned to be teamwork and can be better as a result. Collaboration could also occur through offline teams or informally working together.

When Is Work Redesign Appropriate?

If you can answer "yes" to the following questions, work redesign may be appropriate:

- Are there opportunities for improving the work processes or outcomes through increased collaboration? How can this occur?

- Would a team accomplish the work better than would individuals? What kind of team would be needed? (See Chapter 13 for the array of team options.)

- Are there "hidden" interdependencies that suggest the use of a team? These "hidden" interdependencies might become apparent when a work process map is drawn.

- Would value be added by accomplishing the task with a team?

Work process mapping is one effective tool for identifying these opportunities graphically.

Planning: Analyze the Work Process Map

Time Requirement: Approximately 90 minutes for each work process map

Supplies: Completed work process maps, markers, flip charts, masking tape, Worksheet 12.1, Worksheet 12.2

Overview: This planning activity helps you analyze the work process maps to find opportunities for collaboration, as a prerequisite for developing collaborative structure in Chapter 13.

Instructions

1. Invite people to the work process mapping session. Involve appropriate CLT members and other employees with expertise in the work process.

2. Identify work processes to be analyzed. Work on one at a time, and then repeat this planning activity for each work process.

3. Identify interdependent work. Look at the work process map and identify areas with lots of arrows between functions. These arrows show areas of interdependency, where different functions need to work together closely to ensure an effective work process. Circle the areas with the most interdependence.

4. Look at the work process map and identify whole processes or subprocesses. Mark these with squares. These may be the same as the interdependent work identified in Step 3. As you will see in Chapter 13, when possible, employees should be organized around whole processes or subprocesses. List each whole process or subprocess in Worksheet 12.1. Use additional pieces of paper as needed.

5. Identify types of expertise required to routinely perform work. For each whole process or subprocess identified in Step 4, identify the functions routinely required to perform the work. These are the functions that are the most interdependent in the process and are needed almost daily. List results in Worksheet 12.1.

6. Identify key supporters. These are the functions that are required only periodically or sporadically in the work process. List results in Worksheet 12.1.

7. Identify opportunities to redesign work. Review the questions under the "when is work redesign appropriate" section above. Do you see opportunities for work redesign? If so, follow up appropriately.

8. Develop design considerations. Given what you have learned in this planning activity and in this chapter so far, what are the key work issues or goals to consider when designing work structures, for example, customer drives the process, better integration of support group to shift teams needed, or identification of areas of potential team design? List the design considerations in Worksheet 12.2. These design issues and goals will be carried over into Chapter 13.

Worksheet 12.1.   Whole Processes and Expertise Required

Process or subprocess

_____

Functions required

_____

Key supporters

Process or subprocess

_____

Functions required

_____

Key supporters

Process or subprocess

_____

Functions required

_____

Key supporters

Worksheet 12.2.   Design Considerations

Understand Customer, Supplier, and Regulator Requirements

An important aspect of understanding the work is to be familiar with customer, supplier, and regulator requirements and how they relate to work processes.

Customers are people internal or external who receive outputs (products or services) of the work process.

Suppliers are people internal or external who provide inputs (raw materials) to the work process.

Regulators are federal, state, and local regulatory agencies that affect aspects of the work process. Unions could be considered regulators as well.

The best way to identify customer, supplier, and regulator requirements is to ask them. After you complete the next planning exercise, you may decide to follow up by talking to your customers, suppliers, and regulators. Some methods for asking for their requirements include surveys, focus groups, site visits, meetings, and phone conversations. Details about some of these methods are available in Chapter 9.

Planning: Understand Customer, Supplier, and Regulator Requirements

Time Requirement: Approximately 1 hour for each work process

Supplies: Completed work process maps, completed Worksheet 12.1, and copies of Worksheet 12.3; markers and flip charts (optional)

Overview: Understanding customer, supplier, and regulator requirements and how they relate to key work processes is vital to the effectiveness of the CWS initiative. In this planning activity, you will identify the requirements of customers, suppliers, and regulators through small-group discussion. If needed, you should plan to follow up directly with customers, suppliers, and regulators.

Instructions

1. Invite people to the session. Involve appropriate CLT members and other employees with expertise in the work process to be discussed. See Chapter 5 for more ideas on accomplishing this.

2. Identify work processes to be analyzed (see completed Worksheet 12.1 for ideas). Work on one at a time, then repeat this planning activity for each work process.

3. Form three small groups. Assign each group a category—customers, suppliers, or regulators. Ensure that participants with appropriate expertise are assigned to the groups.

4. Ask each small group to complete the appropriate category of Worksheet 12.3. Select a scribe from each group to capture the discussion results directly on the worksheet or on a flip chart.

Worksheet 12.3.   Customer, Supplier, and Regulator Requirements

Work Process: _____

	Name	**Requirements of Work Process**
Customers		
Suppliers		
Regulators		

5. Each small group should take a turn reviewing its results with the entire group. You may want to reproduce the activity sheet on a flip chart to capture the discussion. Encourage the entire group to take notes during the discussion. Encourage clarifying questions.

6. Repeat the planning activity for each work process (Steps 3 through 5).

7. Determine next steps, if any. Some possibilities include the following:

   • Follow up with customers, suppliers, or regulators. Did any questions come up that need further clarification? Do you feel that this activity was sufficient to identify requirements, or is further investigation necessary?

   • Communicate requirements to others. Should others in the organization see some form of the material you generated in this planning activity? Who should see it? How can this material be leveraged for further effectiveness. (For example, can you develop new effectiveness measures? If so, who should get the material to make sure this happens?)

   • Revise work process maps. Did any of the information obtained warrant changes on the work process maps?

8. Develop design considerations. Given what you have learned in this planning activity and in this chapter so far, what are the key work issues or goals to consider when designing work structures? Add any new design considerations to Worksheet 12.2. These design issues and goals will be carried over into Chapter 13.

9. Add any new action ideas to the action planning worksheet at the end of the chapter.

Conclusion

The key question for this chapter is, "What are the key work processes, and how can we better understand them?" Work encompasses the tasks to be completed for the business to thrive. An effective CWS initiative enhances the completion of work and anchors all the components of the initiative, especially the design of organization structure, with an understanding of the work. Take the material created in this chapter to design structures in Chapter 13, and use the information as needed throughout the CWS initiative.

Keys to the Chapter

• The purpose of an organization is to complete its business, whatever that may be. An effective CWS initiative enhances the completion of work and anchors all components of the initiative with an understanding of the work.

• The work encompasses the tasks to be completed for the business to thrive. Work processes break down those tasks into sequential steps. A work process map is a technique for visually representing work processes at a high level.

- Understanding the work is especially important in determining the appropriate structure (including both formal and informal collaborative structures) to carry out that work.

- A crucial part of understanding the work is to be familiar with customer, supplier, and regulator requirements and how they relate to work processes.

- Link the work to all parts of the CWS initiative by analyzing the work and developing design considerations to guide the CWS initiative.

Chapter Wrap-Up

- What ideas did this chapter trigger for you and your group? List them in the action planning worksheet at the end of this chapter.

- Review the ideas list. Which of these do you want to implement? List the action item, person or group responsible, and target due dates in the action planning worksheet.

- Were any significant decisions made? Include them at the bottom of the action planning worksheet.

- How can you communicate the pertinent material generated by your work on this chapter to different audiences? Discuss and consider adding action items based on your discussion.

- How can you use the resources list for additional help?

- What chapter should you go through next? Refer back to Guiding Assessment results in Chapter 3 for suggestions of next steps.

- What can you do tomorrow or within the next week based on what you learned in this chapter? Have each person share what he or she will do, and follow up.

- What is your biggest learning from this chapter? Ask each person to share. This is a nice way to end the session. Include any resulting ideas or action items in the action planning worksheet.

Resources

Beyerlein, M., Johnson, D., & Beyerlein, S. (Eds.). (1995). *Advances in interdisciplinary studies of work teams: Vol. 2. Knowledge work in teams.* Greenwich, CT: JAI Press.

Beyerlein, M., Johnson, D., & Beyerlein, S. (Eds.). (1999). *Advances in interdisciplinary studies of work teams: Vol. 5. Product development teams.* Greenwich, CT: JAI Press.

Beyerlein, M., Johnson, D., & Beyerlein, S. (Eds.). (2001). *Advances in interdisciplinary studies of work teams: Vol. 8. Virtual teams.* London: Elsevier Science.

Beyerlein, M., McGee, C., Klein, G., Nemiro, J., & Broedling, L. (Eds.) (2003). *The collaborative work systems fieldbook: Strategies, tools, and techniques.* San Francisco: Jossey-Bass/Pfeiffer.

Cross, R. (2000). Looking before you leap: Assessing the jump to teams in knowledge-based work. *Business Horizons, 43*(5), 29–36

Lytle, W. O. (1998). *Designing a high-performance organization: A guide to the whole-systems approach.* Clark, NJ: Block Petrella Weisbord.

Mock, T., Mock, B., & Britt, H. (1998). Integrate work processes to cut plant life-cycle costs. *Chemical Engineering, 105*(11), 130–137.

Mohrman, S. A., & Mohrman, A. M., Jr. (1997). *Designing and leading team-based organizations: A workbook for organizational self-design.* San Francisco: Jossey-Bass.

Pasmore, W. A. (1988). *Designing effective organizations: The sociotechnical systems perspective.* Hoboken, NJ: Wiley.

Purser, R. E., & Cabana, S. (1998). *The self managing organization: How leading companies are transforming the work of teams for real impact.* New York: Free Press.

Valle, R., Martin, F., Romero, P. M., & Dolan, S. L. (2000). Business strategy, work processes and human resources training: Are they congruent? *Journal of Organizational Behavior, 21*(3) 283–297.

Action Planning and Summary Sheet

Ideas Generated from This Chapter

1	
2	
3	
4	
5	

#	Action Item	Target Date	Person/Group Responsible
1			
2			
3			
4			
5			
6			

Significant Decisions Made

1	
2	
3	
4	

Design Using an Array of Structures

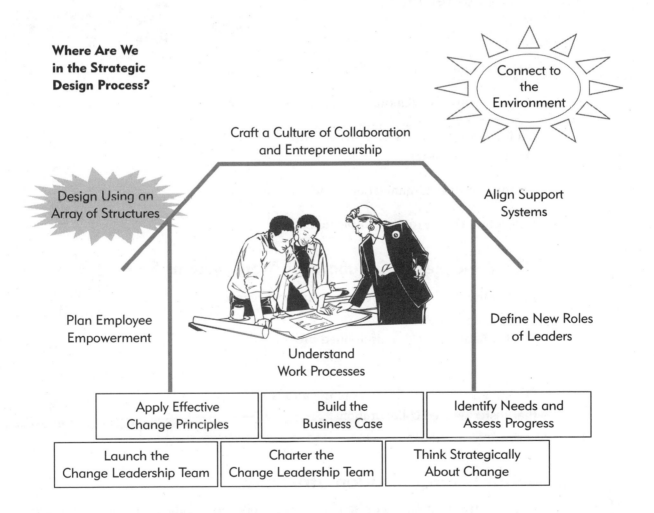

Connect to the Environment

Craft a Culture of Collaboration and Entrepreneurship

Design Using an Array of Structures

Align Support Systems

Plan Employee Empowerment

Understand Work Processes

Define New Roles of Leaders

Apply Effective Change Principles	Build the Business Case	Identify Needs and Assess Progress
Launch the Change Leadership Team	Charter the Change Leadership Team	Think Strategically About Change

Key Question of This Chapter

What collaborative structures can be incorporated into our target organization design?

Quick Look
Overview

Organizational structure represents the way people are organized to carry out the work. In a CWS, structure should support collaboration when collaboration is appropriate. The choice of collaborative structures within the organization should be linked to the selection of target CWS organization type (see Chapter 2) and should support the work (see Chapter 12). The outcomes of this chapter include an analysis of current organization structure, an assessment of how well different forms of collaborative structure are currently being used, a list of realities that affect future design, a visualization of future organization structure, and a determination of where to start implementing the future organization structure.

Chapter Plan

Topic				
What Is Organization Structure?	✓			✓
Use an Array of Collaborative Structures	✓		✓	
Understand Realities That Affect Future Organization Design				✓
Visualize Future Organization Structure				✓
Determine Where to Start Implementation				✓

Principles of Collaborative Work Systems Series

Exploit the rhythm of divergence and convergence

Treat collaboration as a disciplined process

Design and promote flexible organizations
that foster needed collaboration

What Is Organization Structure?

Organization structure represents the way people are organized to carry out the work. An organization chart is how this is traditionally depicted, although the organization chart does not always adequately reflect how things are really done. In a CWS, structure is designed to support collaboration through groups, individuals, and integrating mechanisms. Both formal (for example, a team) and informal (for example, a learning network) structures are used to meet the needs of the situation.

The choice of collaborative structures within the organization should be linked to the selection of target CWS organization type (see Chapter 2). Each option in the typology, whether it is a traditional bureaucracy, an organization using teams, a spontaneous cooperation organization, a team-based organization, a collaborative organization, or something in between, affects the design of collaborative structures.

Why Is Organizational Structure Important?

The formal reporting relationships of the organization often determine to whom people communicate. Structure creates barriers between one reporting group and another. For the sake of everyday functioning, these barriers are necessary. If they are designed incorrectly, people may have to go up and down chains of command to make decisions and may not have direct access to people who are crucial links in their work.

Organization structure must evolve with changes in the work, business strategy, and environment. Creating a fluid, flexible structure ensures adaptability.

Base Organization Structure on a Thorough Assessment of Work

Organizational structure design should be based on a thorough assessment of work processes and an understanding of the types of skills and abilities needed to perform those work processes (see Chapter 12 for more on understanding the work). Structure must facilitate, not hinder, the work. Often organizational structure is created for the convenience of management, with less regard for the work itself. For example, we often hear, "He reports to me because there was no one else to do it." It is important to organize around the work instead of against it. Remove any hurdles in the way, and create formal and informal processes to facilitate it.

Notes About Designing Structure

Organization design is not an exact science. The chapter gives a broad, general framework and process for designing collaborative structures, but these should not be used in lockstep fashion. Instead, use material to facilitate discussion and allow the organization design to emerge. Relate the material to your organization and make it work for you.

We strongly recommend the use of someone with expertise in organization design when completing this chapter. This person should be able to move the group along in its discussions, be flexible in allowing the design to emerge through discussion, and add insights to improve the design.

Planning: Understand Current Organization Structure

Time Requirement: Approximately 90 minutes

Supplies: Information about your organization's structure (see Step 1), Worksheets 11.4 and 12.2 (previously completed), Worksheets 13.1 and 13.2, flip chart, markers, masking tape; gumdrops and toothpicks (optional), Tinkertoys® (optional)

Overview: Understanding your current organization structure, its strengths and weaknesses, and what can and cannot be changed provides the preparation for what your new organization design can be.

Instructions

1. Prepare for the planning activity. Secure the assistance of someone with organization design expertise to lead the activity. Gather the most current information about your organization structure (for example, organization charts). Bring forward any relevant material from Chapters 2, 3, and 12. Compile material as needed and make copies for all participants of the activity.

2. When the team meets, using the materials gathered on current organization structure as resources, draw a picture of the current organization design on a flip chart. Some alternatives to drawing a picture include having the group demonstrate the structure using gumdrops and toothpicks or Tinkertoys. Whatever method you choose, the goals of this step are

   - To understand the real structure of the organization, not just what is written on official documents

   - To gain an understanding of the reporting structure of the organization (who reports to whom and why)

3. Use these questions to guide the discussion, if needed:

   - What departments or functions are in your organization?

   - What formal levels of reporting are in your organization?

   - How many people report directly to each member of management?

   - What informal (unwritten) reporting relationships are important?

   - In the next year, do you expect that there will be major changes in your organization's structure? If so, what?

4. Compare the analysis of work from Chapter 12 to your drawing of the current structure. Answer the following questions and any others that arise through your discussion. Write your answers on Worksheet 13.1

   - What are the strengths of the current structure in relation to your work?

   - What are the weaknesses of the current structure in relation to your work? How can these be improved? (Consider adding design goals based on the discussion.)

   - What are the parts of the structure that the CLT can change?

   - What are the parts of the structure that are beyond the CLT's power to change? Can the CLT influence others to make changes, or are there certain "givens" that simply cannot be changed?

5. Given what you have learned in this planning activity, what are the goals or issues to consider when designing work structures? Use the design considerations developed in Worksheets 11.4 and 12.2. This will help you link to the work through the analyses your team did in Chapter 12. List the design considerations on Worksheet 13.2.

Worksheet 13.1.   Analysis of Current Organization Structure

Strengths of current structure

Weaknesses of current structure

Parts of current structure that the CLT can change

Parts of current structure that the CLT cannot change

Worksheet 13.2.   Design Considerations

6. Conduct a planning activity with other groups. You may want to gather the perceptions of others in the organization. We suggest involving a cross-section of the organization (employees from different functions and different levels of the organization) to gain a more holistic perception of the strengths and weaknesses of your current organization structure.

Use an Array of Collaborative Structures

Because flexibility and adaptability are so important to meeting the demands of the ever-changing business environment, organizational structure of a CWS must be able to flex and change as well. Because of the different needs, many different types of collaborative structures exist. A mix of structures is used to meet the needs of each situation.

Figure 13.1 demonstrates how different collaborative structures can be used together within an organization. The figure demonstrates both formal (such as teams) and informal (such as learning networks) structures, at both the individual and group levels. Integration mechanisms (such as integration teams or liaisons) serve to connect groups.

Figure 13.1. Visual Representation of Collaborative Structures

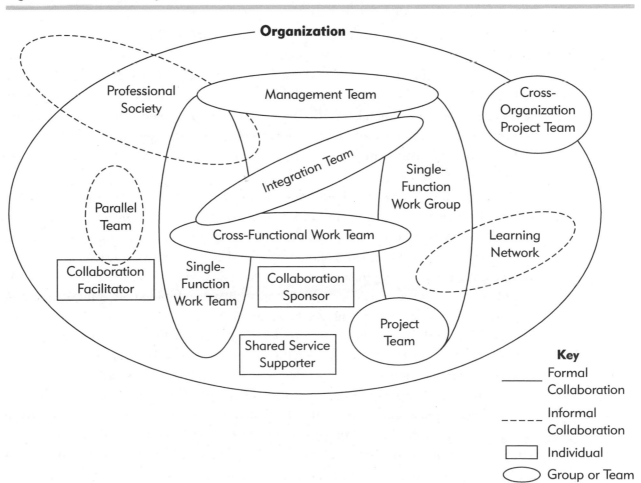

Ideally, an organization promotes both formal and informal forms of collaborative structure, but the choice must be made by each organization. Some of the structures overlap, as individuals can be members of multiple structures. As organization boundaries become more permeable and more organizations develop partnerships to conduct work together, collaborative structures may extend beyond the boundaries of the organization. Types of collaborative structures are defined in Table 13.1.

Determine When to Collaborate

Organizations using CWSs often fall into the trap of thinking that every decision must be made collaboratively. This is unrealistic and often counterproductive. Instead, the organization must create an understanding for when to collaborate and when to work individually. This understanding must occur both at the design level (When is a team appropriate and when is an individual appropriate?) and within teams or groups (When does the team make a decision and when is it acceptable for a team member to make a decision?).

Collaboration comes at a cost of time, effort, and other resources needed to integrate and communicate effectively. Teams represent a complex solution that is too costly when individuals can do the job, but a wise investment when outcomes depend on collaboration.

For more on when to collaborate, see Chapter 5.

Categories of Collaborative Structures

We categorize collaborative structures into groups, individuals, and integration mechanisms. Each category is explained briefly below. Table 13.1 describes the structures within each category. Please note that the descriptions in the group category have more detail than those in the individual and integration mechanisms levels. In practice, group level terminology is much better defined and commonly used across organizations, whereas individual level and integration mechanisms are general concepts that are defined and used differently across organizations. The different level of detail in the categories reflects this.

Groups include formal collaborative structures, such as teams and work groups, and informal structures, such as communities of practices. Groups can be temporary or permanent, single function or multifunction (cross-functional), and co-located or distributed (virtual). As the boundaries of organizations become more permeable, groups may have members from more than one organization (such as different organizations working together to complete a government contract like developing new military aircraft). For more on management teams, see Chapter 15.

Individuals include shared service providers and other individuals who play collaborative roles by supporting or working with different groups, but either have jobs that are not very interdependent with others or have specialized skills that warrant working with many different groups. For more on the individual role of leaders, see Chapter 15.

Integration mechanisms connect interdependent groups (for example, groups providing different services to the same customers or different parts of the same service) to enhance communication and cooperation and limit competition. Integration mechanisms can also connect groups and individuals to the outside environment and connect the CWS site to other sites and the corporate entity. For more on integration, see Chapter 16.

Table 13.1. An Array of Collaborative Structures

	Group
Work team	*Characteristics:* formal, permanent, long-term, both single- and multifunctional, plan their work, develop their own processes to enhance the work
	A group of employees who have shared goals and are jointly accountable to each other and to organization for a piece of work or service. Members work together to improve operations, handle daily problems, and plan their work.
Work group	*Characteristics:* formal, permanent, long-term, both single and multifunctional, does not plan own work or develop their own processes
	A group of employees responsible for a piece of work or service but who do not have shared goals and joint accountability. Members may share ideas informally but do not formally come together to plan their work and improve their work processes.
Project team	*Characteristics:* formal, temporary, short-term, multifunctional
	A cross-functional group that is brought together to complete clearly defined tasks, lasting from several months to years, and quickly disbands once the project is complete (for example, product development teams). Task is usually assigned by management. The team members may not be involved in the whole project and may be called in as needed.
Management team (can also be considered an integration mechanism)	*Characteristics:* formal, permanent, multifunctional
	Comprises management members from multiple functions, each usually concerned with particular issues. Responsible for coordinating, integrating, and providing direction to other teams.
Parallel team	*Characteristics:* informal, temporary, multifunctional, limited authority
	Comprises individuals from different areas of the organization, parallel teams are short-term teams with limited authority (usually with recommendation power only) that exist in parallel to existing organizational structure.
Community of practice	*Characteristics:* informal, long-term, voluntary membership, no authority
	Groups of people who share similar goals and interests and, in pursuit of these goals and interests, apply common practices, use the same tools, and express themselves in a common language (for example, Xerox copier repair technicians). Storytelling is a common method of learning.
Learning network	*Characteristics:* informal, long-term, voluntary membership, no authority
	Groups of people with similar interests and needs who get together either virtually or face-to-face to share learnings (for example, oil rig technicians). Often develop their own knowledge management systems (for example, Web sites, shared databases) to capture and share knowledge.

(continued)

Table 13.1. An Array of Collaborative Structures (continued)

Professional society	*Characteristics:* informal, long-term, voluntary membership, no authority
	Groups of people with similar professional interests (for example, engineering) who join together to develop professional standards, share their work, and advance their profession.

Individual

Shared service supporter	An individual in a specialized role or with rare knowledge who becomes a contract worker to teams and groups rather than an official member of lots of teams and groups.
Individual contributor	An individual contributor who works on tasks with little to no interdependence and so has no reason to be formally connected to any group.
Collaboration sponsor	An individual with no formal authority over groups or teams he or she assists and who acts as a mentor to teams or groups by checking on their progress toward developing their own processes, working with them to determine needs, championing them to other parts of the organization, and helping them get resources to develop them as groups or teams.
Collaboration facilitator	Facilitates team processes in order to help teams to be more effective. This may include facilitation of meetings, conflict resolution, authority transfer, goal development, leadership emergence, and interpersonal cooperation.
Collaboration consultant	An individual with expertise in collaboration who acts as resource to the CLT to help develop the CWS. Resource areas may include organization design, development of support systems, design of assessment of coaching behaviors, continued skill development, debriefing sessions, behavioral observations, and process suggestions.

Integration

Starpoints	Team members who take lead responsibility for dealing with their team's issues relating to a particular aspect (for example, quality, safety and health, administrative, training, customer service) for the team. Each team has a person fulfilling a starpoint role for each of the designated areas. Starpoints across teams for the same aspect (for example, safety and health) meet to address needs in their area of responsibility.
Boundary workers	Individuals who are members of more than one team or group who are responsible for communicating relevant issues from each team or group to the other team or group.
Integration teams	Representatives from multiple teams or groups who work together to integrate the work of the represented teams or groups. They may be responsible for elements such as prioritizing tasks, identifying problems, or determining how a change in one team or group affects another.
Liaisons	Members of one group or team who are responsible for acting as an "ambassador" by bringing issues to another group or team.

Assessment: Collaborative Structure Utilization

Time Requirement: Approximately 2 hours

Supplies: Copies of latest draft of Worksheet 13.2, Assessment 13.1, relevant material from Chapter 12, flip chart and markers

Overview: Are you making appropriate use of all types of collaborative structures available in your toolbox? Use this gap analysis tool to evaluate your current and ideal use of collaborative structures.

Instructions

1. As a group, go through each collaborative structure listed in Assessment 13.1. Identify examples of that type of structure in your current design and list those in the appropriate column. If your organization does not use that structure, mark "N/A" for not applicable.

2. Individually or as a group, complete Assessment 13.1.

   - For each collaborative structure, assess the extent to which that structure is used now in your organization. Use a circle to indicate where your organization is now.

   - Review the structures again. This time, use a square to indicate where your organization would like to be at the highest level of CWS. Refer back to appropriate information generated in Chapter 12 to help you with this analysis.

3. Discuss the answers, using the following questions:

   - What types of collaborative structure do you use the most? Why?

   - What types of collaborative structure do you use the least? Why?

   - Looking back at the analysis of the work created in Chapter 12, what types of collaborative structures can be used to support that work and where?

4. Translate into organization design goals. Given what you have learned in this planning activity and in this chapter so far, what are the key goals to consider when designing work structures? Add design goals to Worksheet 13.2.

Planning: Understand Realities That Affect Future Organization Design

Time Requirement: Approximately 1 hour for each round of Steps 1 through 4, 1 hour for Step 5

Supplies: Completed assessments and planning worksheets from all chapters, Worksheet 13.3, flip chart, markers

Overview: Before developing the future organization design, reflect on what has been learned in the workbook so far and develop a list of realities that affect future design. This list will affect the organization design created in the next planning activity.

Assessment 13.1.   Utilization of Collaborative Structures

Collaborative Structure	Example from Your Organization	Rating Low				High
Work team		1	2	3	4	5
Work group		1	2	3	4	5
Project team		1	2	3	4	5
Management team		1	2	3	4	5
Parallel team		1	2	3	4	5
Community of practice		1	2	3	4	5
Learning network		1	2	3	4	5
Professional society		1	2	3	4	5
Shared service supporter		1	2	3	4	5
Individual contributor		1	2	3	4	5
Collaboration sponsor		1	2	3	4	5
Collaboration facilitator		1	2	3	4	5
Collaboration consultant		1	2	3	4	5
Starpoints		1	2	3	4	5
Boundary workers		1	2	3	4	5
Integration teams		1	2	3	4	5
Liaison roles		1	2	3	4	5

Instructions

1. Create small groups of three or four people each. Assign each group a completed workbook chapter. Consider having multiple groups review Chapter 12, since understanding the work is so crucial to designing effective organization structure.

2. Small groups review their assigned chapters, especially products completed by the group, to identify any realities that affect future design. (For example, from Chapter 12, a reality might be something that comes from analysis of regulators of the work process. For example, in the airline industry, FAA regulations might affect the way a plane is built, and this in turn might affect organization design.) Anything that might affect design should be listed.

3. Back in the large group, small groups should take turns sharing results. Have someone compile results from all groups on a flip chart.

4. Repeat this process until all chapters have been reviewed.

5. Review the compiled results to remove redundancies and confirm agreement. Write the refined list on Worksheet 13.3.

6. Use the refined list to guide the future organization design planning activity.

Planning: Visualize Future Organization Structure

Time Requirement: Approximately 3 hours for Steps 1 through 5; a few weeks to compile, define, and confirm design with appropriate people

Supplies: Copies of material generated in Chapter 12 (especially Worksheet 12.1) and previously in this chapter (Worksheets 13.1, 13.2, and 13.3, and Assessment 13.1), Worksheet 13.4, flip charts, markers, and masking tape for each small group

Overview: In this planning activity, you will take everything you have learned about organization design and apply it to your work processes reviewed in Chapter 12 to create your future organization design. Use the list of realities in Worksheet 13.3 and design goals in Worksheet 13.2 to guide the organization design.

Instructions

1. Prepare for the planning activity. Find someone with expertise in organization design to lead the activity. From Chapter 12, bring copies of work process maps, design considerations, and any other relevant material generated. From this chapter, bring copies of the current structure analysis, design goals, current collaborative structure assessment, list of realities, and any other relevant material.

2. Create small groups of three to six people from members of the CLT and other people (for example, key decision makers, a cross-section of the organization) as determined by the CLT. Ensure a mix of expertise in each group (in other words, do not put all the engineers in the same group) to provide a more holistic picture.

3. Brainstorm future organization structure in small groups.

   - Given what you learned in Chapter 12 about your key work processes and the material created previously in this chapter, draw pictures of what your future organization design could look like.

Worksheet 13.3. Realities That Affect Future Design

- Keep a list of any issues that come up that need to be addressed by the organization design.

- Get creative and "dream" a little bit. This is the "brainstorm" part of the process. The actual design will be narrowed down later.

4. Use these points to guide the discussion as needed:

    - On the work process map, look at the arrows between skill sets to identify interdependencies.

    - Draw circles around the parts suggesting different collaborative structures. Consider using a color-coding system to coordinate with different types of collaborative structures. You may even want to lay work process maps on the floor and use pieces of string to create circles. The advantage of string is that you can move it easily.

    - The less interdependent parts of the process are still important to the different collaborative structures, but perhaps do not need to be full-time members of that collaborative structure.

    - How will you integrate your teams and employees?

5. Review small-group designs.

    - Have each small group present its designs to the large group. Each should also share its list of issues.

    - After each group has presented its designs, develop lists of strengths and weaknesses of each design.

6. Using the strengths and weaknesses identified in Step 5, develop an improved "compiled" design. You may want to commission a small group to develop the design and bring it to a later meeting.

7. Further define the design. Assign structures to small groups. Small groups look at the "compiled" design and further define each structure using Worksheet 13.4. This is an extension of Worksheet 12.1 created in the analysis of the work, so some of the work in this step may already be complete. Use the material developed in Worksheet 12.1 and modify it given your "compiled" design. Have each small group report to the whole group and make changes as needed.

8. Review and confirm desired design.

    - Confirm the design within the CLT. Does the design meet the design goals created in Worksheet 13.2? Does the design address the realities in Worksheet 13.3?

    - Share the organization design with key decision makers and work with them until consensus is met.

    - Share the organization design with a cross-section of the organization to test how well it will be received and find any "holes."

Worksheet 13.4. Defining Each Structure

Type of structure

Process or subprocess

Functions required

Key supporters

Type of structure

Process or subprocess

Functions required

Key supporters

Type of structure

Process or subprocess

Functions required

Key supporters

Planning: Determine Where to Start Implementation

Time Requirement: Approximately 4 hours, but depends on the size of the organization being changed

Supplies: Confirmed desired design (see last planning activity), completed Worksheet 13.4, Worksheet 13.5, flip chart, markers

Overview: After determining and confirming the future organization design, begin to create plans for implementing that design.

Instructions

1. Prepare for the planning activity. Find someone with expertise in organization design to lead the activity.

2. Given what you have decided about the design of your work structures, where will you start implementation? Create a list of areas to evaluate; any area where change will eventually occur should be listed. Depending on the size of your CWS initiative, you may have from two to twenty or more areas where change is expected to occur. If you completed Worksheet 13.4, list each area here. The top of Worksheet 13.5 contains some examples. Write the areas to be evaluated in the left-hand column of Worksheet 13.5.

3. Develop criteria for selecting areas to work on first. When developing criteria, consider any factors that may promote or inhibit successful change. Some example criteria are listed at the top of Worksheet 13.5. Write these on a flip chart. Brainstorm a list, review the list for redundancies and eliminate those, then, finally, narrow the criteria down to the top ten most important. List these across the top of Worksheet 13.5.

4. Using Worksheet 13.5, review each area against the criteria developed in Step 3. You may want to reproduce Worksheet 13.5 on a flip chart. Indicate results with a + for positive, − for negative, +/− for neutral, ? for unsure, and N/A for not applicable. If possible, follow up on the unsure responses. In the example shown on Worksheet 13.5, the cross-functional work team received positive ratings for being highly visible and having quick success potential, but only had a neutral response to current and near future (some uncertainty looms ahead). The area received negative ratings for the manager's openness to change (the manager has a very traditional, controlling style).

5. Review the results of Worksheet 13.5. Look at the patterns of symbols that emerge and discuss their meaning. Continuing the cross-functional work team example from Step 4, the positive ratings of criteria 1 and 2 suggest that the cross-functional team is a good place to start implementation. However, the negative rating of the manager's openness to change (criterion 3) may be a "showstopper" that prohibits change in this area until the manager issue can be resolved. Issues such as these should come out in your discussion and help you determine where to start implementing change. If further analysis is needed, consider developing a list of strengths and weaknesses for each area. Determine

Worksheet 13.5. Comparing Structures to Criteria

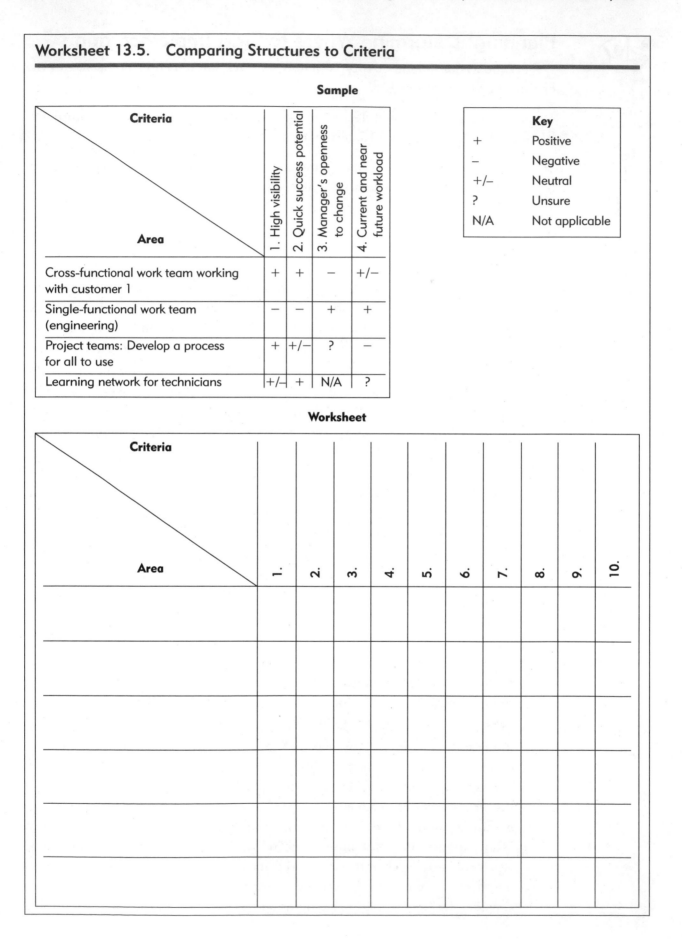

Sample

Criteria / Area	1. High visibility	2. Quick success potential	3. Manager's openness to change	4. Current and near future workload
Cross-functional work team working with customer 1	+	+	−	+/−
Single-functional work team (engineering)	−	−	+	+
Project teams: Develop a process for all to use	+	+/−	?	−
Learning network for technicians	+/−	+	N/A	?

Key

+	Positive
−	Negative
+/−	Neutral
?	Unsure
N/A	Not applicable

Worksheet

Criteria / Area	1.	2.	3.	4.	5.	6.	7.	8.	9.	10.

Worksheet 13.5. (continued)

Worksheet

	1.	2.	3.	4.	5.	6.	7.	8.	9.	10.
Criteria / Area										

the areas where you want to begin implementation of collaborative work structures. If possible, create a list of the order in which you recommend that implementation take place.

6. Determine next steps. Consider the following:

   • What steps are needed to refine and confirm the plan? How can you involve others (such as those who might be affected) in developing the plan?

   • What needs to be done to gain commitment from key decision makers for this plan?

   • What needs to be done to gain commitment from affected groups and individuals for this plan?

   • What are the next steps in turning the plan into reality?

   • What is your timeline for implementation?

   • How will you communicate this plan to the organization as a whole, the affected groups, key decision makers, and any other relevant groups?

   • When will you return to this activity to evaluate the subsequent areas where you wish to implement change?

7. Write any relevant ideas and action ideas in the action planning worksheet at the end of this chapter.

Conclusion

The key question for this chapter is, "What collaborative structures can be incorporated into our target organization design?" Organizational structure represents the way people are organized to carry out the work. In a CWS, structure is designed to support collaboration through groups, individuals, and integrating mechanisms. The outcomes of this chapter include an analysis of current organization structure, an assessment of how well different forms of collaborative structure are currently being used, a list of realities that affect future design, a visualization of future organization structure, and a determination of where to start implementing the future organization structure.

Keys to the Chapter

   • The choice of collaborative structures within the organization should be linked to the target CWS organization type.

   • Organization structure must evolve with changes in the work, business strategy, and environment. Creating a fluid, flexible structure ensures adaptability.

   • Design of organizational structure should be based on a thorough assessment of work processes and an understanding of the types of skills and abilities needed to perform those work processes.

   • Because of the different needs presented by the work, many different types of collaborative structures exist. A mix of structures both formal (for example, a team) and informal (for example, a learning network) is used to meet the needs of the situation.

- Groups include formal collaborative structures (such as teams and work groups) and informal structures (such as communities of practices).

- Individuals include shared service providers and other individuals who play collaborative roles by supporting or working with different groups but who either have jobs that are not very interdependent with others or have specialized skills that warrant working with many different groups.

- Integration mechanisms connect interdependent groups (for example, groups providing different services to the same customers or different parts of the same service), to enhance communication and cooperation and limit competition.

Chapter Wrap-Up

- What ideas did this chapter trigger for you and your group? List them in the action planning worksheet at the end of this chapter.

- Review the ideas list. Which of these do you want to implement? List the action item, person or group responsible, and target due dates on the action planning worksheet.

- Were any significant decisions made? Include them at the bottom of the action planning worksheet.

- How can you communicate the pertinent material generated by your work on this chapter to different audiences? Discuss and consider adding action items based on your discussion.

- How can you use the resources list for additional help?

- What chapter should you go through next? Refer back to Guiding Assessment results in Chapter 3 for suggestions of next steps.

- What can you do tomorrow or within the next week based on what you learned in this chapter? Have each person share what he or she will do, and follow up.

- What is your biggest learning from this chapter? Ask each person to share. This is a nice way to end the session. Include any resulting ideas or action items on the action planning worksheet.

Resources

Beyerlein, M., Johnson, D., & Beyerlein, S. (Eds.). (1995). *Advances in interdisciplinary studies of work teams: Vol. 2. Knowledge work in teams.* Greenwich, CT: JAI Press.

Beyerlein, M., Johnson, D., & Beyerlein, S. (Eds.). (1999). *Advances in interdisciplinary studies of work teams: Vol. 5. Product development teams.* Greenwich, CT: JAI Press.

Beyerlein, M., Johnson, D., & Beyerlein, S. (Eds.). (2001). *Advances in interdisciplinary studies of work teams: Vol. 8. Virtual teams.* London: Elsevier Science.

Campion, M. A., Medsker, G. J., & Higgs, A. C. (1993). Relations between work group characteristics and effectiveness: Implications for designing effective work groups. *Personnel Psychology, 49,* 429–452.

Cross, R. L., Yan, A., & Louis, M. R. (2000). Boundary activities in "boundaryless" organizations: A case study of a transformation to a team-based structure. *Human Relations, 53*(6), 841.

Hackman, J. R. (1987). The design of work teams. In J. W. Lorsch (Ed.), *Handbook of organizational behavior* (pp. 315–342). Englewood Cliffs, NJ: Prentice Hall.

Mohrman, S. A., Cohen, S. G., & Mohrman, A. M., Jr. (1995). *Designing team-based organizations: New forms for knowledge work.* San Francisco: Jossey-Bass.

Mohrman, S. A., Cohen, S. G., & Mohrman, A. M., Jr. (1997). *Designing and leading team-based organizations: A workbook for organizational self-design.* San Francisco: Jossey-Bass.

Mohrman, S. A., & Quam, K. F. (2000). Consulting to team-based organizations: An organizational design and learning approach. *Consulting Psychology Journal: Practice and Research, (2)*1, 20–35.

Purser, R. E., & Cabana, S. (1998). *The self managing organization: How leading companies are transforming the work of teams for real impact.* New York: Free Press.

Wageman, R. (2001). How leaders foster self-managing team effectiveness: Design choices versus hands-on coaching. *Organization Science, 12*(5), 559–577.

Action Planning and Summary Sheet

Ideas Generated from This Chapter

#	
1	
2	
3	
4	
5	

#	Action Item	Target Date	Person/Group Responsible
1			
2			
3			
4			
5			
6			

Significant Decisions Made

#	
1	
2	
3	
4	

Plan Employee Empowerment

Where Are We in the Strategic Design Process?

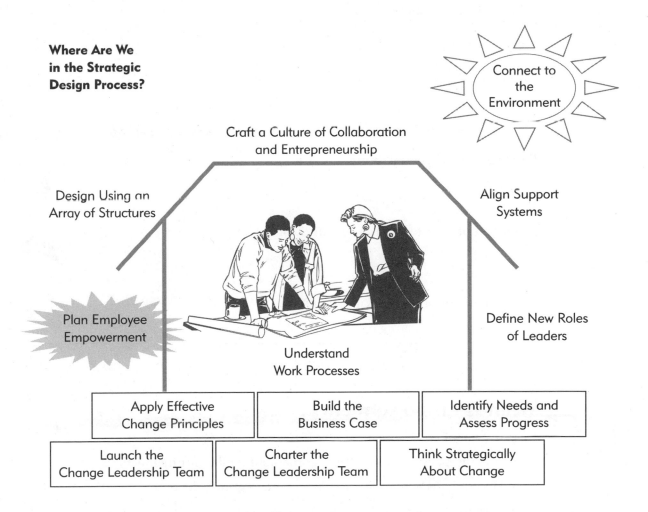

Connect to the Environment

Craft a Culture of Collaboration and Entrepreneurship

Design Using an Array of Structures

Align Support Systems

Plan Employee Empowerment

Define New Roles of Leaders

Understand Work Processes

Apply Effective Change Principles	Build the Business Case	Identify Needs and Assess Progress

Launch the Change Leadership Team	Charter the Change Leadership Team	Think Strategically About Change

Key Question of This Chapter

What is empowerment, and how can empowerment plans be used to define it?

Quick Look

Overview

Empowerment means increasing authority, ability, and accountability of employees to accomplish their work. Empowerment planning is a method of laying out expectations for how employee behavior should change as a result of empowerment. The outcomes of this chapter include assessment of current and ideal empowerment in your organization, identification of limits of empowerment, and the first draft of the empowerment plan.

Chapter Plan

Topic				
What Is Empowerment?	✓	✓	✓	
Identify Limits of Empowerment	✓			✓
Design the Empowerment Plan	✓	✓		✓

Principles of Collaborative Work Systems Series

Foster personal accountability

Align authority, information, and decision making

Treat collaboration as a disciplined process

What Is Empowerment?

Empowerment is

- Giving people responsibility and accountability for their actions
- Driving decision making down to the employee level
- Providing increased authority to employees
- Creating employee accountability and responsibility for results
- Providing opportunities for employees to develop new skills and abilities

It is *not* the freedom to act in whatever way you wish, without understanding the sharing or risks and responsibilities involved.

Components of Empowerment

The three main components of empowerment are authority, accountability, and ability. All three components must be in place for true empowerment to occur.

Authority means giving employees the power and freedom to manage and accomplish tasks and make relevant decisions.

Accountability means holding individuals and groups answerable for accomplishing assigned tasks.

Ability means having the necessary information, skills, and knowledge for effective decision making and task completion.

What Does Empowerment Accomplish?

- Unleashes the hearts and minds of the individual employees and the synergies that emerge from effective collaboration

- Improves personal and organizational performance

- Creates shared leadership

- Provides the backbone of successful teams

- Increases involvement and commitment while keeping individual and team decisions in alignment with organizational goals

- Enhances personal development as employees gain new skills

The Empowerment Implementation Triangle

This chapter focuses on the development of employee empowerment. The empowerment implementation triangle (Figure 14.1) shows that employee empowerment is only one part of the equation. Leaders must support employee empowerment and become more empowered themselves for employee empowerment to be effective. For more on the leader transition, see Chapter 15. Support systems such as training, performance management, and compensation must support employee empowerment or employees will get mixed messages about what is truly desired and revert to old habits. For more on support systems development, see Chapter 16. The three parts of the triangle must be aligned for empowerment to occur.

Empowerment and Managers

Empowerment is often perceived as sharing power, but it is more about creating power. Empowerment means shifting responsibility for some of the managers' daily tasks to employees. As employees become more empowered, managers have more time for strategic activities (such as improving processes and seeking out new customers) to improve the business. In essence, empowerment of managers should increase along with that of employees. Figure 14.2 shows the relationship between employee and management empowerment. Managers often fear empowerment because they think it takes away their jobs. We argue that empowerment should create new organization-enhancing strategic roles for managers. As the team (or employee) becomes more empowered and takes on more responsibility, the manager is able to shift his or her

Figure 14.1.   The Empowerment Implementation Triangle

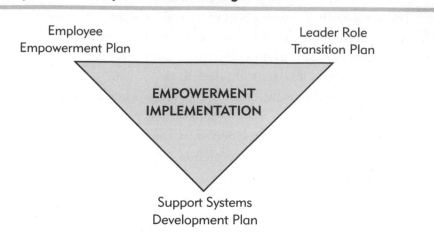

Figure 14.2.   Relationship Between Employee and Management Empowerment

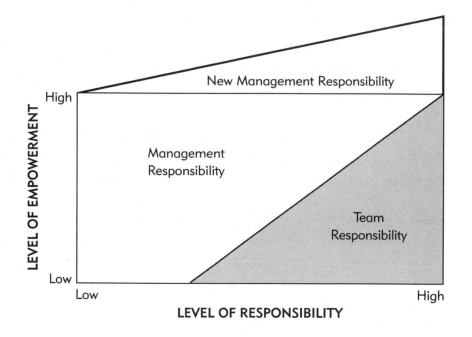

daily responsibilities to the team. This leaves the manager free to take on new, more strategic responsibilities (as indicated by the top triangle). Before empowerment, it takes the manager and the team to achieve responsibilities in the box. As can be seen, empowerment allows the manager and team to both achieve more.

Implementing Empowerment

There are a number of steps an organization can take to encourage empowerment, some of which are detailed in this section.

Create a foundation of trust. True empowerment requires a foundation of trust. Trust requires respect, consistency, clarity, openness, and honesty. Managers may fail to trust employees to be accountable when empowered. Employees may suspect hidden motives and agendas. Trust can be supported by creating environments in which people are involved in decision making, communication goes in all directions, and employees are truly heard and their suggestions implemented.

Create freedom to risk with safety net. Empowerment sometimes means letting groups take risks so they can learn from their mistakes. Having check systems in place for decisions (such as criteria for a good decision, approval from management) provides a safety net.

Clarify decision-making responsibility. Clarify who makes what decisions where (for example, use a decision-making responsibility chart), and under what conditions those decisions may be overturned. Create guidelines for when decisions should be escalated and how those escalated decisions should be handled.

Set a tone for empowerment through leaders. Leaders create conditions under which empowerment can occur by sharing power, information, and decision making. Leaders must back up their talk about empowerment with their actions. Traditional leaders often cave in to pressure from others in organization to "make that person do his (or her) job"; empowered leaders must resist the pressure to micro-manage.

Empower informally as well as formally, rather than waiting for the empowerment plan. We focus on the formal part of empowerment in this chapter, but do not forget about the informal part. It can be as easy as a manager asking an employee to take a customer call that the manager would normally take, or an employee taking responsibility to analyze and solve a chronic problem that no one else has ever taken the time to address. Look for empowerment opportunities in your daily life. Do not wait until the formal plan is in place to start your own empowering behavior. Figure out ways you can change your behavior now.

Discussion

1. What does empowerment mean to you? Create your own definition that you can share with others.

2. How can you share this definition with others?

Assessment: Empowerment

Time Requirement: Approximately 1 hour

Supplies: Assessment 14.1, flip chart, markers

Overview: Assess your current and ideal level of empowerment. Identify the gaps and create ideas for closing them.

Instructions

1. Choose the appropriate method for completing Assessment 14.1. Refer back to Table 3.2 for methods and pros and cons for each.

2. For each item in Assessment 14.1, assess the extent to which that item is true for your organization. Use a circle to indicate where your organization is now.

3. Review the items again. This time, use a square to indicate where your organization would like to be at the highest level of CWS.

4. Discuss the answers, using the following questions:

   • What are the biggest gaps between where you are now and where you want to be?

   • In what order do you need to address the gaps? Create a prioritized list for addressing the gaps, based on your discussion.

   • What can you do in the short term and long term to close those gaps? Brainstorm ideas.

   • List ideas generated in this discussion on your action planning worksheet at the end of the chapter.

Identify Limits of Empowerment

How empowered an organization must be to be successful varies by organization, and this empowerment level should be consciously chosen by the leadership (Guillory & Galindo, 1995). An extension of this principle is that the empowerment level of each structure (teams, groups, and individuals) in the organization must be consciously chosen.

Considerations When Choosing Empowerment Level

• *Direct control desired by management.* Is management comfortable with empowering its workforce with decision-making authority and responsibility? Choose levels of empowerment that management can handle.

• *Team or group maturity.* Does the team or group have experience working together? Do members have a history of working well together?

• *Trust.* To what degree do employees have trust in each other, in the management, and in the organization?

• *Ability.* To what extent does the team, group, or individual have the abilities (for example, technical skills, interpersonal skills, business knowledge) to take on the responsibilities empowerment brings?

Assessment 14.1. Empowerment Gap Analysis

Empowerment Elements	Rating				
	Low				High
Employees have the skills and abilities required to accomplish assigned tasks.	1	2	3	4	5
Leaders share power, information, and decision-making responsibilities with their employees.	1	2	3	4	5
Employees are given the freedom to take risks without fear of being punished for failure.	1	2	3	4	5
Decision-making responsibility (who makes what decisions and when decisions should be escalated to the next level) is clear.	1	2	3	4	5
Employees are given responsibility for tasks and the authority to get those tasks done.	1	2	3	4	5
Employees are held accountable for their responsibilities.	1	2	3	4	5
Members of the organization trust each other.	1	2	3	4	5
The meaning of the word empowerment is clear and shared.	1	2	3	4	5
Representatives from appropriate parts of the organization are involved in planning empowerment.	1	2	3	4	5
Members of the organization understand the limits to empowerment.	1	2	3	4	5
Employee empowerment is supported by a shift in leader role.	1	2	3	4	5

- *Unions and outside regulators.* Do union contracts and other regulators (for example, the health care industry is regulated by the FDA, insurance companies, and many others) prohibit certain tasks from being done by employees?

- *Experience.* Does the team, group, or individual have the necessary experience to accomplish the task?

- *Authority.* Can the organization provide the team, group, or individual with the power to accomplish the task? Will others in the organization accept that power?

- *Accountability.* Can the organization hold the team, group, or individual accountable for the tasks?

Planning: Identify Limits of Empowerment

Time Requirement: Approximately 1 hour

Supplies: Paper and pen for each participant, flip chart and markers, Worksheets 14.1 and 14.2

Overview: Before creating the empowerment plan, identify the limits of empowerment. Empowerment does not mean "We get to do whatever we want"; instead, the organization should set limits on empowerment and make sure they are communicated.

Instructions

1. Individually, write a list of tasks or behaviors that employees will absolutely not be able to do even at the highest level of empowerment. However, you may decide that employees can suggest, recommend, and have input on these ideas.

2. Share as a group. Each person shares one idea until all ideas have been shared. Have someone list the ideas on a flip chart. Ask questions for clarification only.

3. Confirm limits. Review each idea. Ask whether anyone has objections to the idea. If there is an objection, discuss as a group and make changes until consensus is met. List your limits in Worksheet 14.1.

4. Identify limits for each structure. Now that you have overall limits for all employees, you may want to identify limits for each structure. Discuss whether further defining limits for each structure is useful for your organization. If so, use Worksheet 14.2 to summarize your results.

Design the Empowerment Plan

A major hurdle to effective empowerment is lack of a plan. Empowerment should proceed in steps that correspond to the developing capabilities of the team. A study of empowerment steps across 117 teams in nine companies by the Center for the Study of Work Teams showed that the first steps in empowerment were usually team responsibility for problem solving and safety decisions. The last steps were those dealing with disciplining, hiring, and firing of employees. Many other responsibilities were arranged in between these extremes of safety and risk.

Worksheet 14.1.   Limits to Empowerment for All Employees

Sample

Limits to Empowerment for All Employees

Employees cannot change work processes (but can make recommendations).

Employees cannot change safety regulations.

Employees cannot fire other employees.

Employees cannot create a new job opening (but can make recommendations).

Worksheet

Limits to Empowerment for All Employees

Worksheet 14.2.   Limits for Each Structure

Sample

Structure	Limits
Project teams	• Cannot recruit new members without approval • Cannot start a new project without approval • Cannot utilize resources not specified in their charter without approval
Quality improvement teams	• Cannot implement process solutions without approval of relevant parties • Cannot determine what problem they will work on; it's given to them by management

Worksheet

Structure	Limits

Worksheet 14.2.   Limits for Each Structure

An empowerment plan is a tool that

- Describes how you want employee behavior to change as a result of empowerment

- Helps you develop a common mindset about what empowerment will look like in your organization

- Can be used to communicate to others

- Helps employees understand what it is they have to do to continue their development

Operationalizing empowerment is a difficult challenge, but must be done for employees to understand what needs to be done to get to the next level. A sample empowerment plan can be found in Figure 14.3.

Figure 14.3.   Sample Empowerment Plan

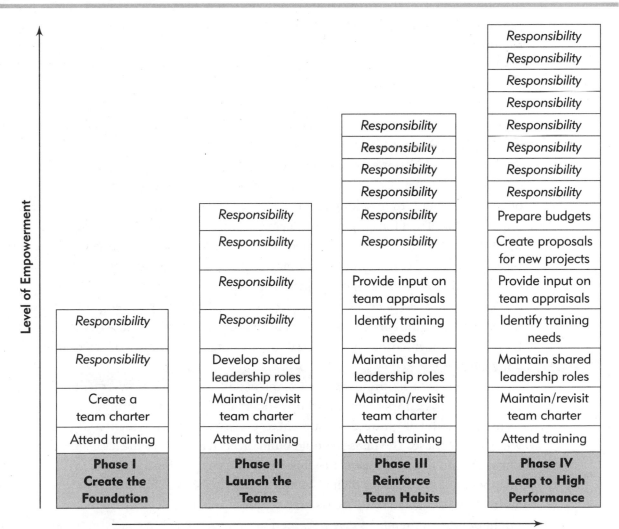

Source: Harris & Bodner, 2003, p. 315. Used with permission.

Considerations When Creating an Empowerment Plan

In the next activity, you'll begin drafting an empowerment plan. Before you begin, however, be aware of the following considerations that will affect the plan.

The foundation of the CWS initiative. The empowerment plan is an important step in defining how you want employee behavior to change. It represents a more detailed vision of your CWS initiative and starts to put actions to the vision. After the empowerment plan is complete, the leader role transition (see Chapter 15) and support systems development (see Chapter 16) can be planned to support the empowerment plan.

Involvement. Involve a cross-section of the organization when developing the empowerment plan.

Time required for development of empowerment plan. A lot of time should be spent on the empowerment plan, as it becomes the foundation of your CWS initiative. In addition to the entire CLT working on the empowerment plan, some time in small groups outside of regular meetings will be necessary. Development could take from two to six weeks or even more, depending on the circumstances (such as how much time CLT members devote to that work). Everyone in the planning process should be able to support the empowerment plan when it is complete so that they can show their support to others outside the process. The more up-front understanding of what you want empowerment to look like in your organization, the more likely you will be able to implement that vision.

A living document. No matter how much time you spend developing your empowerment plan, some changes will be needed periodically. Create mechanisms for updating the empowerment plan as needed.

Certification. You may decide to create a "certification" program to enforce your empowerment plan. This may take the form of developing requirements for each level of empowerment, then asking teams and employees to show proof of meeting those requirements. Then the employee or team becomes certified in that phase of empowerment. If you take this approach, remember to make the requirements general enough to meet the needs of your audience. You may wish to tailor requirements for different types of teams and individuals or allow them some input into tailoring requirements.

Appropriate level of detail. Avoid getting too detailed in your empowerment plan. Instead, create guidelines that can be tailored by each team, group, or employee to fit their work. On the other hand, detail must be enough for employees to understand your meaning.

Phasing approach. Empowerment plans usually depict empowerment as occurring in phases. For example, you could use Tuckman's "forming, norming, storming, performing" model of group development as phases of empowerment and include tasks within each phase. The phases should build on each other, and the tasks going into each phase should follow a logical progression. For example, the end goal may be for team members to be able to do their own hiring, but they have skills to develop and lots to learn about the selection process before participating in selection processes. Phase 1 might be "Team members give new member requirements to coach but coach does all the hiring," phase 2 might be "Team members interview candidates with coach and give recommendations but coach makes the final decision," phase 3 might be "Team members interview candidates with coach and they make hiring decisions together," and phase 4 might be "Team members hire new members using coach as a resource." This example may be more detailed than you want in your empowerment plan, but it gives you a sense of the step-by-step progression of the phases. Naming the phases helps develop shared meaning around empowerment. Figure 14.3 provides an example of phase names. Most empowerment plans have from three to seven phases. The goal is to find the balance between having enough phases to develop a step approach, where one phase builds on the next and adequately represents empowerment, and having too many phases so that they become overwhelming to implement and scary to those trying to achieve them. There is no "right" answer. Use the number of phases that works for your organization.

Discussion

Look at the sample empowerment plan in Figure 14.3.

1. What do you like about the plan?

2. What do you not like about the plan?

3. What ideas do you want to borrow for your own plan?

Planning: Build an Employee Empowerment Plan

Time Requirement: Approximately 2 hours

Supplies: Flip charts, medium-sized sticky notes (1 pad per person with a few extra just in case), masking tape and cellophane tape, markers, pens

Overview: Now that you have some understanding of empowerment plans, it is time to create a first draft of your own empowerment plan. This first draft just needs to be a high-level overview of how you want empowerment to develop over time. Later, you can further define and refine your empowerment plan.

Instructions

1. Prepare for the activity. Tape together six sheets of flip chart paper on a wall, according to the following example (dotted lines indicate each piece of flip chart paper).

2. Create parameters, for example:

   - *Number of phases.* Given your discussion in the previous exercise, determine the number of phases you want for your empowerment plan. Most empowerment plans range from three to seven phases. This number is just a start for this activity; you may decide to change it later. You may also decide to name the phases to better create shared meaning. For more on phases of the empowerment plan, see the "Considerations When Creating an Empowerment Plan" listing previously in this chapter. Write the phase numbers across the top of the chart, leaving an equal amount of space for each phase, as indicated in a four-phase example. Draw lines between the phase labels to create a space for each phase.

Phase 1	Phase 2	Phase 3	Phase 4

- *Time span.* How long is your empowerment plan vision?
- *Boundaries.* Keep the limits created in the previous planning activity in mind when completing this planning activity.

3. On sticky notes, have each individual write employee behaviors and tasks that you would want to see at the highest level of empowerment. Think especially of tasks that managers do now that you want employees to take on as they become empowered. Come up with at least twenty each, and write one idea per sticky note. An example might be "Employees freely communicate with other departments as needed."

4. Consolidate ideas in the following manner.
   - Go around the room asking each person to share his or her best idea.
   - Repeat the idea, and ask the others if they need clarification. Make sure that what is written is understandable and it is clear to whom it applies.
   - For now, place each note in the highest phase of empowerment.
   - Have everyone else throw away any sticky notes with similar ideas.
   - Continue around the room until all ideas are given.

5. Confirm agreement with ideas. Read through each idea. Ask group members to signal if it is something they think should not be there. Discuss if needed, and remove or keep it there as the group decides.

6. Ask for more ideas. Is there something missing? Come up with at least two new things to add to the list.

7. Move notes to the appropriate empowerment phase. The group should gather around the flip chart wall and work together to move each note into the appropriate phase of empowerment where that behavior or task begins. Remember that phases should build on each other, so consider sequencing the behaviors or tasks accordingly. Put any sticky notes that are difficult into a separate "parking lot" flip chart to be discussed later. (*Note:* If you decide to move your flip chart wall, first tape down the sticky notes with cellophane tape so they will not fall off.)

8. Congratulations! You have finished the first draft of your empowerment plan! Now it is time to figure out the next steps. Some possibilities are listed below; determine the best steps for your organization. List any action items on the sheet at the end of this chapter.

9. Type the list into a computer file. This will make the information easier to maneuver and communicate to others.

10. Confirm consensus on the empowerment plan. This is a foundational document, so it is important that everyone be able to support it.

11. Divide into areas of responsibility, if desired. In addition to having phases as the columns, the rows can be categorized into levels such as areas of responsibility (for example, administrative, quality, and productivity). Especially if your empowerment plan is quite detailed, this categorization will help as a naming convention when referring to different parts. Dividing the rows into areas may

help create specializations or roles that different team members can take on a rotating basis. Taking these areas of responsibility a step further, you may want to create a starpoint system (see Chapter 13) where shared leadership is created by giving members of groups or teams responsibility for each of these areas.

12. Now that you have a foundation for what you want empowerment to look like, you can decide how to create the conditions for empowerment to occur. What will you do to get the empowerment plan approved by key decision makers? How can you gain input from the employees themselves? How can you communicate the empowerment plan so that it is understood? What are the first steps for rolling out the empowerment plan in your organization?

13. Develop a system to add, modify, or delete items from the empowerment plan. No matter how much effort and thought you put into your empowerment plan, changes will be needed. Treat the empowerment plan like a living document and create mechanisms such as periodic reviews to adjust as needed.

14. Communicate to different audiences. Sharing the empowerment plan in ways that your different audiences understand is crucial to your success. Consider the level of detail and language necessary for your different audiences (employees, executives, and others) and adjust as appropriate. Go beyond written communication; consider using alternate formats, meetings, graphics, signs, and logos. Consider creating a communication plan for how you will share this information periodically.

15. Consider additional parameters.

    • Do you want the same empowerment plan for all employees, or do you need different plans for different structures (such as different types of teams and individuals, see Chapter 13)?

    • How much detail do you want in your plan? Remember to leave room for changes at the local level if needed. Too many details and strict rules will constrain rather than enhance empowerment.

    • Do you want to create estimates on how long it will take to achieve the phases of empowerment? While we recommend that you allow employees and teams to achieve phases of empowerment at their own pace, a timeline will be useful in aiding planning activities, such as creating certification tasks and creating the support systems development plan (see Chapter 16).

 ## Conclusion

The key question for this chapter is, "What is empowerment, and how can empowerment plans be used to define it?" Empowerment means increasing authority, ability, and accountability of employees to accomplish their work. Empowerment planning is a method of laying out expectations for how employee behavior should change as a result of empowerment. The empowerment plan defining employee behavior expectations is only one piece of the empowerment implementation triangle. The other pieces include a leader role transition plan (see Chapter 15) and a support systems development plan (see Chapter 16).

Keys to the Chapter

- Empowerment means increasing authority, ability, and accountability of employees to accomplish their work.

- Empowerment means shifting responsibility for some of the managers' daily tasks to employees, freeing managers to do more strategic work. Empowerment of managers should increase with empowerment of employees.

- Empowerment does NOT mean doing whatever you want. Creating limits on empowerment and communicating them helps identify the things employees and managers will not be able to do, even at the highest level of empowerment.

- Empowerment planning is a method of laying out expectations for how employee behavior should change as a result of empowerment.

- Empowerment must be supported by leader behavior and support systems in order for employee behavior to change.

Chapter Wrap-Up

- What ideas did this chapter trigger for you and your group? List them on the action planning worksheet at the end of this chapter.

- Review the ideas list. Which of these do you want to implement? List the action item, person or group responsible, and target due dates on the action planning worksheet.

- Were any significant decisions made? Include them at the bottom of the action planning worksheet.

- How can you communicate the pertinent material generated by your work on this chapter to different audiences? Discuss and consider adding action items based on your discussion.

- How can you use the resources list for additional help?

- What chapter should you go through next? Refer back to Guiding Assessment results in Chapter 3 for suggestions of next steps.

- What can you do tomorrow or within the next week based on what you learned in this chapter? Have each person share what he or she will do, and follow up.

- What is your biggest learning from this chapter? Ask each person to share. This is a nice way to end the session. Include any resulting ideas or action items on the action planning worksheet.

Resources

Blanchard, K., Carlos, J. P., & Randolph, A. (2001). *Empowerment takes more than a minute.* San Francisco: Berrett-Koehler.

Gerwin, D. (1999). Team empowerment in new product development. *Business Horizons, 42*(4), 29–41.

Guillory, B., & Galindo, L. (1995). *Empowerment for high-performing organizations.* Salt Lake City, UT: Innovation International.

Harris, C., & Bodner, S. (2003). Developing team-based support systems: Conceptual overview and strategic planning workshop. In M. Beyerlein, C. McGee, G. Klein, J. Nemiro, & L. Broedling (Eds.), *The collaborative work systems fieldbook: Strategies, tools, and techniques* (pp. 307–325). San Francisco: Jossey-Bass/Pfeiffer.

Ketchum, L. D., & Trist, E. (1992). *All teams are not created equal: How employee empowerment really works*. Thousand Oaks, CA: Sage.

Kirkman, B. L., & Rosen, B. (1997). A model of work team empowerment. In R. W. Woodman & W. A. Pasmore (Eds.), *Research in organizational change and development* (Vol. 10, pp. 131–167). Greenwich, CT: JAI Press.

Kirkman, B. L., & Rosen, B. (1999). Beyond self-management: Antecedents and consequences of team empowerment. *Academy of Management Journal, 42*(1), 58–74.

Quinn, R. E., & Spreitzer, G. M. (1997, Autumn). The road to empowerment: Seven questions every leader should consider. *Organizational Dynamics*, pp. 37–49.

Randolph, W. A. (2000). Re-thinking empowerment: Why is it so hard to achieve? *Organizational Dynamics, 29*(2), 94–107.

Sewell, G. (2001). What goes around, comes around: Inventing a mythology of teamwork and empowerment. *Journal of Applied Behavioral Science, 37*(1), 70–89.

Wellins, R. S., Byham, W. C., & Wilson, J. M. (1991). *Empowered teams: Creating self-directed work groups that improve quality, productivity, and participation*. San Francisco: Jossey-Bass.

Action Planning and Summary Sheet

Ideas Generated from This Chapter

1
2
3
4
5

#	Action Item	Target Date	Person/Group Responsible
1			
2			
3			
4			
5			
6			

Significant Decisions Made

1
2
3
4

## CHAPTER 15

Define New Roles of Leaders

**Where Are We
in the Strategic
Design Process?**

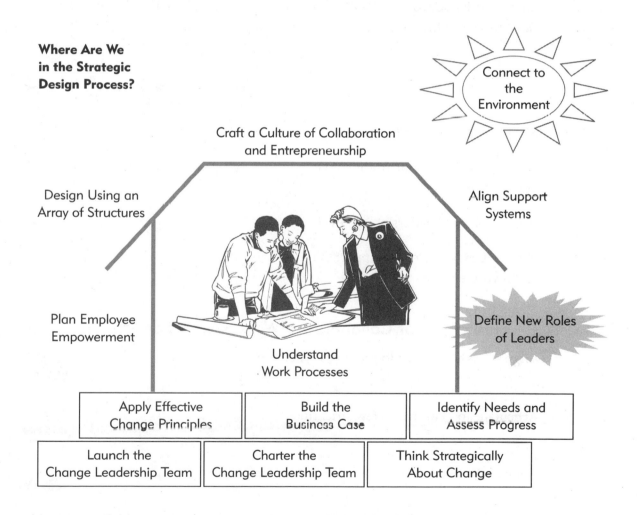

Connect to
the
Environment

Craft a Culture of Collaboration
and Entrepreneurship

Design Using an
Array of Structures

Align Support
Systems

Plan Employee
Empowerment

Define New Roles
of Leaders

Understand
Work Processes

Apply Effective Change Principles	Build the Business Case	Identify Needs and Assess Progress
Launch the Change Leadership Team	Charter the Change Leadership Team	Think Strategically About Change

? ## Key Question of This Chapter

How should roles of leaders change in a collaborative work system?

Quick Look

Overview

Leadership in a CWS is broader than in traditional definitions of leadership. Leadership in a CWS encompasses the people in formal positions of power (such as managers and supervisors), but also includes the worker level. While leaders must be able to apply different styles to different situations, there are some common skills and abilities that leaders must learn in order to support the transition to a CWS. These characteristics look different in leaders at different levels of the organization. The levels of collaborative leadership to be examined here include employees, coaches and special roles, and executive managers. The outcomes of this chapter include an assessment of current and ideal levels of collaborative leadership, identification of the most important characteristics of collaborative leadership for each level of leadership in your organization, a list of leader roles and definitions, and a leader role transition plan to support the empowerment plan developed in Chapter 14.

Chapter Plan

Topic				
What Is Collaborative Leadership?	✓		✓	
Leader Transition from Traditional to Collaborative	✓			
Define Roles of Leaders at All Levels	✓	✓		✓
Identify Leader Roles to Support the Empowerment Plan	✓			✓

Principles of Collaborative Work Systems Series

Align support systems to promote ownership

Articulate and enforce "a few strict rules"

Align authority, information, and decision making

What Is Collaborative Leadership?

A leader is traditionally seen as a person in a formal position of power in the organization. To become a more collaborative organization, formal leaders must empower others, distributing leadership throughout the organization. Since leadership is distributed throughout the organization, it should be viewed as a system. Leadership in a CWS encompasses the people in formal positions of power (such as managers and supervisors), but also includes the worker level.

Collaborative leadership does not mean including everyone in the decision-making process for every decision. Instead, it means involvement when involvement is appropriate. Leaders in a CWS should pick the appropriate style of leadership for each situation. Appropriate leadership style depends on such factors as the maturity or experience of the individual or group, the level in the organization, and the type of decision to be made (simple or complex, routine or non-routine, and so forth).

While leaders must be able to apply different styles to different situations, there are some common skills and abilities that leaders must learn to support the transition to a CWS. Some of the characteristics of collaborative leaders are listed in Table 15.1. These characteristics look different in leaders at different levels of the organization. The goal of this chapter is to show how the roles of leaders change at all levels of the organization.

Why Is Collaborative Leadership Important?

Leaders are responsible for designing and influencing change in the systems, structures, and processes to support collaboration. Without their support, the CWS initiative is doomed to failure. Managers can be huge hurdles in the CWS initiative. Show them their new roles so they are willing to let go of old ones.

The Leader Transition

To support the transition to the collaborative work systems, the role of the leader changes from a traditional command-and-control director to a collaborative supporter of the group. See Figure 15.1 for a visual demonstration. This transition should occur at all levels of the organization. How far to go in the transition depends on the needs of the organization, the needs of the leader's group, and the style or preferences of the leader.

Empowerment Implementation Triangle

This chapter focuses on creating a plan for new roles of leaders. The empowerment implementation triangle (Figure 15.2) shows that the leader transition plan is only one part of the equation. Leaders must support employee empowerment and become more empowered themselves for employee empowerment to be effective. Expectations for how employee behavior and tasks should change as a result of empowerment should be identified and communicated through an empowerment plan. For more on creating an employee empowerment plan, go to Chapter 14. Support systems such as training, performance management, and compensation must support employee empowerment or employees will receive mixed messages about what is truly desired and revert to old habits. For more on support systems development, see Chapter 16. The three parts of the triangle (see the figure) must be aligned for empowerment to occur.

Table 15.1. Characteristics of Collaborative Leadership

Characteristic	Description
Develop organizational context	Build systems, structures, and relationships to support collaboration in the organization and facilitate the accomplishment of work.
Build teams or groups	Create processes within teams or groups to support better collaboration and the accomplishment of work.
Support individual development	Work with individuals to determine opportunities for improvement and develop methods (such as training or experiences) for them to help them improve.
Set direction	Through strategic planning and working with others in the organization, set the direction for the group, team, or organization and communicate it so that all understand.
Actively support the CWS initiative	Participate in groups leading the CWS initiative, give time and other resources to relevant activities, and formally and informally support the effort through words and actions as much as possible.
Model collaboration	Participate in groups or teams when relevant, involve others in decision making, actively discuss the importance of collaboration, and act in accordance with your words.
Provide resources	Seek to understand the resource needs of others and work to get those resources.
Integrate the organization	Act as an integrator and develop interfaces among all parts of the organization.
Interface with the environment	Work to develop open lines of communication with customers, suppliers, regulators, corporate headquarters, and other parts of the environment for all in the organization.
Counsel and coach others	Listen to the concerns of others and provide feedback, encourage signs of progress, and suggest opportunities and means for improvement.
Communicate and provide information	Facilitate communication in all directions, share relevant information, and act as a resource.
Lead performance management	Understand, communicate, and develop progress toward organizational, group or team, and individual goals.

Assessment: Collaborative Leadership

Time Requirement: Approximately 1 hour

Supplies: Copies of Assessment 15.1 for each participant, flip chart, markers

Overview: Assess your current and ideal level of collaborative leadership. Identify the gaps and create ideas for closing them.

Figure 15.1.   The Leader's Transition

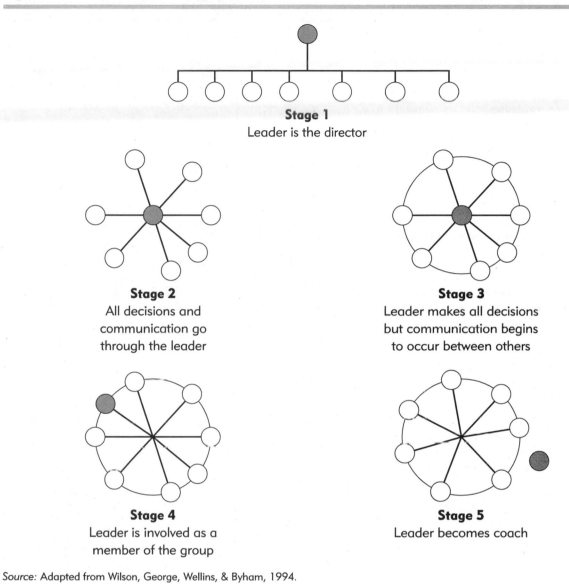

Stage 1
Leader is the director

Stage 2
All decisions and
communication go
through the leader

Stage 3
Leader makes all decisions
but communication begins
to occur between others

Stage 4
Leader is involved as a
member of the group

Stage 5
Leader becomes coach

Source: Adapted from Wilson, George, Wellins, & Byham, 1994.

Figure 15.2.   The Empowerment Implementation Triangle

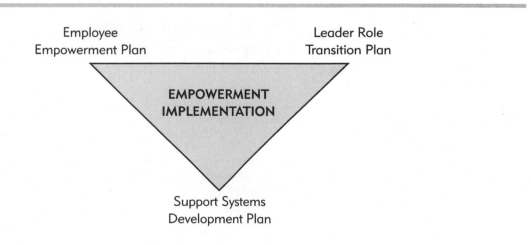

Employee
Empowerment Plan

Leader Role
Transition Plan

EMPOWERMENT
IMPLEMENTATION

Support Systems
Development Plan

Assessment 15.1.   Collaborative Leadership Gap Analysis Tool

Characteristics of Collaborative Leadership	Rating				
Leaders in our organization . . .	Low				High
Build systems, structures, and relationships to support collaboration in the organization and facilitate the accomplishment of work.	1	2	3	4	5
Create processes within teams or groups to support better collaboration and the accomplishment of work.	1	2	3	4	5
Work with individuals to determine opportunities for improvement, and develop methods (training, experiences, and so on) to help them to improve.	1	2	3	4	5
Through strategic planning and working with others in the organization, set the direction for the group, team, or organization and communicate it so that all understand.	1	2	3	4	5
Participate in groups leading the CWS initiative, give time and other resources to relevant activities, and formally and informally support the effort through words and actions as much as possible.	1	2	3	4	5
Participate in groups or teams when relevant, involve others in decision making, actively discuss the importance of collaboration, and act in accordance with their words.	1	2	3	4	5
Seek to understand the resource needs of others and work to obtain those resources.	1	2	3	4	5
Act as an integrator and develop interfaces between all parts of the organization.	1	2	3	4	5
Work to develop open lines of communication with customers, suppliers, regulators, the corporate headquarters, and other parts of the environment for all in the organization.	1	2	3	4	5
Listen to the concerns of others and provide feedback, encourage signs of progress, and suggest opportunities and means for improvement.	1	2	3	4	5
Facilitate communication in all directions, share relevant information, and act as a resource.	1	2	3	4	5
Understand, communicate, and develop progress toward organizational, group or team, and individual goals.	1	2	3	4	5

Instructions

1. Choose the appropriate method for completing the assessment. Refer back to Table 3.2 for methods and pros and cons for each.

2. For each item in Assessment 15.1, assess the extent to which that item is true for the majority of leaders in your organization. Use a circle to indicate where your organization is now.

3. Review the items again. This time, use a square to indicate where you would like the majority of leaders in your organization to be at the highest level of CWS.

4. Discuss the answers, using the following questions:

   • What are the biggest gaps between where you are now and where you want to be?

   • In what order do you need to address the gaps? Create a prioritized list for addressing the gaps, based on your discussion.

   • What can you do in the short term and long term to close those gaps? Brainstorm ideas.

   • List ideas generated in this discussion in your action planning worksheet at the end of the chapter.

Leader Transition from Traditional to Collaborative

Figure 15.3 demonstrates the transition of leaders from a traditional organization to an organization supporting collaboration. Dotted lines connect the level of manager in the traditional organization to the new roles in the organization supporting collaboration. The arrows indicate one-way and two-way communication between leaders.

In the traditional organization, three main levels of leadership exist: Executive managers "live" at the top of the organization, creating a strategic view; middle managers coordinate groups at the bottom and "translate" between the top and the bottom; and direct supervisors oversee daily operations of the workforce. Employees are not considered leaders in the traditional organization. Communication between levels of leaders is primarily top-down and one-way.

In a CWS, three main levels of leadership exist, but they are different from those in the traditional organization. Executive managers remain at the top, but may work in management teams. The organization supporting collaboration is flatter than the traditional organization, so the middle management level no longer exists. Previous middle managers are transitioned to being coaches or into special roles. The second level of leadership includes coaches and special roles, which are the new roles of traditional direct supervisors and middle managers. This second level supports collaboration at the employee level and integrates between the employee level and executive manager level. The third level of leadership is the employee level. In the collaborative system, employees are considered leaders and fill roles such as starpoints (to be discussed later) and take the lead in areas of their expertise. Communication in the system supporting collaboration occurs between all levels and is two-way, promoting extra forms of collaboration between the levels.

Figure 15.3.   Formal Leader Transition from Traditional to Collaborative

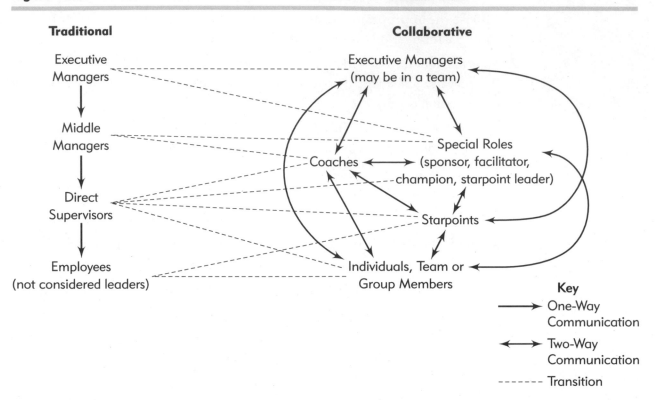

Please note, just because the middle management level of the organization no longer exists in a collaborative system does not mean that those managers should be eliminated in the transition! Middle managers have a wealth of experience and knowledge—valuable intellectual capital—that will be lost if they are removed. Move former middle managers to new roles such as sponsors, champions of the change effort, consultants, integrators (vertical and horizontal), and customer/supplier liaisons. These roles are extremely important to the CWS initiative. They will be described later in Table 15.4.

Define Roles of Leaders at All Levels

Collaborative leadership looks different at different levels of the organization. For each level of leadership—employees, coaches and special roles, and executive managers—the next sections define responsibilities in a CWS organized around the characteristics of collaborative leadership shared in Table 15.1.

Each of these levels will be described collectively. The organization must divide up the responsibilities of each level into roles. Some possible roles will be described for each level. One person cannot do everything; instead, the responsibility must be shared among many at each level of leadership.

Employee Leadership

In a collaborative work system, leadership is not the sole province of managers and supervisors. Instead, empowerment creates a system of shared leadership at all levels. Empowerment plans (see Chapter 14) begin to define the process for sharing

Table 15.2. Employee Leadership Roles

Role	Description
Starpoints	Team members who take lead responsibility for dealing with their team's issues relating to a particular aspect (for example, quality, safety and health, administrative, training, customer service) for the team. Each team has a person fulfilling a starpoint role for each of the designated areas. Starpoints across teams for the same aspect (for example, safety and health) meet to address needs in their area of responsibility.
Boundary workers	Individuals who are members of more than one team or group who are responsible for communicating relevant issues from each team or group to the other team or group.
Integration teams	Representatives from multiple teams or groups who work together to integrate the work of the represented teams or groups. They may be responsible for elements such as prioritizing tasks, identifying problems, or determining how a change in one team or group affects another.
Liaisons	Members of one group or team who are responsible for acting as "ambassadors" by bringing issues to another group or team.

leadership, as employees take leadership roles through teams and groups. In a CWS, employees are encouraged to take on informal leadership roles by leading projects and decision making relevant to their areas of expertise and interest.

In addition to empowerment planning and informal leadership, employee leadership roles can be created to further share leadership. Some of these roles are listed in Table 15.2.

Table 15.3 lists employee leadership responsibilities in a collaborative work system.

Discussion

1. What should employee leadership look like in the CWS?

2. What kinds of new or different leadership roles can employees take in the CWS?

Table 15.3. Employee Leadership Responsibilities in a Collaborative Work System

Characteristic	Responsibilities
Develop organizational context	• Identify problems in the organization context from the employee viewpoint and make changes if possible or escalate issues to appropriate people • Starpoints identify issues from multiple teams and groups so common problems are found and can be addressed in that forum • Participate in support systems committees or other groups responsible for change in the organizational context, or share input with those leading the change • Develop relationships with people at all levels of the organization so that issues can be shared throughout when they occur
Build teams or groups	• Participate in the development of group norms and help remind group members of them in a proactive manner • Volunteer to communicate with customers and suppliers through visits, phone calls, and other methods • Volunteer for starpoint roles and meeting roles (for example, scribe, timekeeper, process observer) within the group • Bring up group performance issues in a constructive, proactive way with the group • Actively participate in the development of group goals, measures, and action plans
Support individual development	• Work with coach to identify opportunities for improvement • Provide positive and constructive feedback to the coach and other members of management • Provide positive and constructive feedback to group members on how their actions affect your work
Set direction	• Work to understand how your group fits in with the rest of the organization and help other group members understand • Participate in forums with all levels of the organization and share your perspective • Share problems in the work process with relevant others in the organization • Identify new innovations and ideas with appropriate others • Actively participate in the development of group goals
Actively support the CWS initiative	• Volunteer for starpoint roles • Participate in committees, focus groups, or other forums for discussion relevant to the CWS initiative • Show enthusiasm for the CWS initiative through words and actions • As a starpoint, participate fully and proactively in your role

Table 15.3.   (continued)

Characteristic	Responsibilities
Model collaboration	• Actively participate in meetings • Bring relevant issues and decisions to the team or group • Help other members of the group when needed • Ask others who are involved to help you make a decision • Follow up on action items assigned to you by the group • Be proactive about identifying problems and solving them • As a starpoint, work with starpoints from other groups to resolve common problems
Provide resources	• Help the group identify resources needs and share these with relevant people • Help the group identify resources that are not being used effectively • Help identify better ways of using resources (for example, new process, better vendor)
Integrate the organization	• As a starpoint, share relevant issues from your group with the starpoint group • Connect and communicate with other groups that your group works with on a daily basis • Share issues and needs with groups your group works with • Recognize other groups your group works with when they have done something well or something above and beyond the call of duty • Participate in liaison roles and integration teams when possible • Communicate between teams or groups if you are a member of more than one • Participate in cross-functional task forces when the opportunity arises • Communicate your group's progress and issues with all levels of management, formally and informally
Interface with the environment	• Volunteer to work with customers and suppliers by going on site visits or communicating in other ways • Understand regulations from outside agencies (such as OSHA and relevant others for your industry) • Communicate the point of view of the union to the organization and the point of view of the organization to the union if you are a union member; support collaboration between the union and the organization • Seek information about advances in your industry that may lead to new opportunities for your organization • Work to develop relationships with other sites and the corporate office as appropriate

(continued)

Table 15.3.   Employee Leadership Responsibilities in a Collaborative Work System (continued)

Characteristic	Responsibilities
Counsel and coach others	• Act as a sounding board for other group members with concerns • Get to know fellow group members personally • Provide constructive and positive feedback formally and informally to group members and the coach • Reinforce progress individually and within the group by identifying it and saying "good job" • Give a public "pat on the back" to group members who do something extra or do a particularly good job on something • Share ideas for improvement when identifying problems
Communicate and provide information	• As a starpoint, share relevant information about your group with the starpoint group • Communicate openly and honestly with group members and with the coach • Share relevant information with the group • Act as a resource to other group members when your expertise is needed
Lead performance management	• Participate actively in the development of group goals, measures, and action plans • Identify group areas for improvement and create processes for addressing them • Participate in benchmarking efforts with other groups in the organization or with other organizations • Participate in the development of your own goals, measures, and action plans • Provide feedback on performance issues to other group members • Participate in developing charts, graphs, and other ways of meaningfully displaying performance measures for your group

Coaches and Special Roles

Coaches and special roles of leadership are the first line of sight for teams and groups, and this level has the most daily interaction with teams and groups. Their actions either support or inhibit collaboration in teams and groups, so working with them to develop collaborative leadership skills is important (see Chapter 16 for development support systems for all levels). Development of coaches and special roles of leadership must align with the empowerment of teams, groups, and individuals (see empowerment planning in Chapter 14). Coaches and people in special leadership roles may participate in the CLT, management teams, and integration teams.

One person cannot effectively accomplish all of the responsibilities of the coach in the CWS, so special roles can be created to divide up parts of that responsibility. A list of special roles can be seen in Table 15.4. Each organization should consciously choose how to divide up these roles and act accordingly. Planning activities at the end of this chapter will facilitate the defining of leadership roles.

Table 15.5 lists the collective responsibilities of coaches and special roles in a collaborative work system.

Discussion

1. What should "coaches and special roles" leadership look like in the CWS?

2. What kinds of special roles do you want to create?

Executive Managers

Whether they know it or not, everyone in the organization looks to executive managers for their cues on what is important and what is not, so it is crucial that executive managers actively support the CWS initiative through their words and actions. Executive managers may work in management teams or independently with informal collaboration with other managers; they often create management teams of their own comprised of management members from multiple functions responsible for coordinating, integrating, and providing direction to other teams. Executive managers may also participate as members of the CLT or as champions or sponsors of that group.

As at the other levels of leadership, one executive manager cannot achieve all the responsibilities in a CWS alone. Instead, executive managers may each take a different focus, playing to their strengths and interests. For example, one might be the primary champion of the CWS initiative, while another focuses on creating performance management systems, and so on.

Table 15.6 lists the collective responsibilities of executive managers in a collaborative work system.

Table 15.4. Special Leadership Roles

Role	Description
Collaboration sponsor	Individual with no formal authority over groups or teams he or she assists, who acts as a mentor to teams or groups by checking on their progress toward developing their own processes, working with them to determine needs, championing them to other parts of the organization, and helping find resources to develop them.
Collaboration facilitator	Facilitates team and group processes in order to assist coaches to develop effective teams. This may include facilitation of meetings, conflict resolution, authority transfer, goal development, leadership emergence, and interpersonal cooperation.
Collaboration trainer	Develops, customizes, and presents training to support team and group development and performance improvement. Helps groups and teams identify training needs and develops processes for meeting those needs.
Collaboration consultant	Individual with expertise in collaboration who acts as resource to the CLT to help develop the CWS. Resource areas may include organization design, development of support systems, design of assessment of coaching behaviors, continued skill development, debriefing sessions, behavioral observations, and process suggestions.
Executive coach	Guides and supports coaches as they work to develop their teams and groups. May include assessment of coaching behaviors, continued skill development, debriefing sessions, behavioral observations, and process suggestions. May be done through a one-on-one relationship and/or a coaching group.
Integrator	Responsible for integrating groups and teams working on pieces of a whole product, process, or service.
Customer/supplier liaison	Responsible for developing customer and supplier relationships, and serving as liaison between groups in the organization and the customer or supplier.
Learning network developer	Supports the development of informal groups with similar educational interests and needs (such as engineers working on oil rigs). Responsible for forming the network, publicizing it, facilitating the group in determining its needs, and developing knowledge management systems for the group to use to create and share learning.
Community of practice supporter	Responsible for identifying naturally occurring communities of practice (for example, copy machine repair technicians) who informally come together to share their experiences and solve problems. Supports these communities of practice by creating physical and electronic spaces for them to occur and identifying and modifying any existing organizational policies or norms (such as "Don't let people stand around and talk; that's wasting time") hindering their existence, and creating new policies to support them.

Table 15.5.   Collaborative Responsibilities of Coaches and Those in Special Roles

Characteristic	Responsibilities
Develop organizational context	• Work on the system (the context outside the team or group), not just in the system (within the team or group) • Facilitate the accomplishment of work—become a "barrier buster" by identifying roadblocks and removing them (such as work processes that are no longer effective and policies that are hindering the group) • Figure out things they can change or influence others to change and thus improve the team or group
Build teams or groups	• Assist in the development of common work practices • Prepare teams to take on new management responsibilities and arrange training (formal and on-the-job) to make this possible • Help group determine training requirements, and provide training on team skills and understanding the business • Help group understand how to review their progress, set their goals, prioritize goals, and create action plans • Help the group create processes to determine what to do with changes such as new members and new policies • Help groups understand who their customers are and what they want, and establish processes for communicating with them • Be the group's champion and cheerleader to the rest of the organization—announce successes, communicate group progress • Develop processes such as conflict management, norm development, and dealing with poor performers and team disrupters in a constructive way; when necessary, step in and assist with these areas
Support individual development	• Work with individuals to identify development needs and ways to meet those needs • Understand how individuals contribute to the greater whole or the team, and help the group to understand that • Provide developmental opportunities in areas in which individuals are weak or strong or areas they are interested in pursuing • Show each individual the path to promotion • Motivate individuals to grow by talking to them, creating development plans, providing developmental feedback, and supporting them formally and informally • Teach group members how to champion each other • Deal with chronic poor performers and group disrupters in a constructive way, if at all possible; deal with them in other ways, if needed • Provide positive and constructive, formal and informal feedback on a regular basis

(continued)

Table 15.5.   Collaborative Responsibilities of Coaches and Those in Special Roles (continued)

Characteristic	Responsibilities
Set the direction	• Understand the "big picture" of organizational goals and strategy and relate them to their groups in a way that the groups will understand how they can help achieve the "big picture" • Create a vision that others find inspiring and motivating • Provide direction and help the group understand what they must do to be successful • Undertake long-term planning, while shifting responsibility for day-to-day and week-to-week planning to the group
Actively support the CWS initiative	• Develop a genuine understanding of the organizational design and goals for CWS • Participate directly or bring input to the CLT, committees, and groups leading the CWS initiative • Communicate the needs of coaches and those in special roles, as well as the needs of their groups, to the CLT • Quickly implement CWS initiative decisions • Continually provide upward and downward communication about the CWS initiative • Show enthusiasm for the CWS initiative through words and actions • Find ways to positively reinforce collaboration in groups, both formally (for example, compensation) and informally (for example, recognition) • Expect groups and the CWS initiative as a whole to succeed
Model collaboration	• Involve the group in decision making. When given an important decision to make, develop immediate response of "let's take it to the group" • Lead by example to motivate, present a positive attitude, project business image, challenge status quo, and act as a change agent • Serve as a role model for others by demonstrating the desired behavior of both team or group members and leaders • Participate in teams and groups • Ask for feedback from the team or group on a regular basis on a variety of issues and topics • Look for any way possible to recognize and reinforce collaboration • Be available to the group; take time to answer their questions, be seen by them on a regular basis, know what is going on, know group members personally • Act collaboratively in terms of own goals—work collaboratively with other coaches and departments and the CLT, and with customers

Table 15.5. (continued)

Characteristic	Responsibilities
Provide resources	• Find out what resources the group needs; lead the group in identifying their resource needs (such as training, information, money, physical work space, whatever they need to get the job done) • Provide resources or figure out who can • Reallocate the resources the group has but does not need • Ensure resources are being used in the right way by the right people • Help the group understand resources they have and how to use them
Integrate the organization	• Clarify roles between coaches and groups • Facilitate inputs and outputs from the team into the organization and vice versa • Facilitate communication among groups and work as the channel to the next level in the organization • Help the group determine when it needs to work with other groups and how to do that • Support development starpoints, when relevant (see employee leadership section in this chapter and Chapter 13) • Work with other coaches to ensure that collaboration is happening across the organization • Influence organization designers to make changes as needed • Work closely with the CLT on the CWS Initiative • Ensure that executives know what is going on—through informal conversations, communications during meetings, reports, and feedback when appropriate—and are responsive to collaboration
Interface with the environment	• Know what is going on with competitors in the general business community, communicate that to groups, and develop mechanisms for group members to communicate directly • Create processes of two-way communication with internal and external customers • Assess the changing business environment and how the group needs to respond to that • Actively maintain effective relationship with unions • Work with the group to develop new opportunities to meet the changing environment (for example, new products) • Know what is going on in the community, how the group affects it, and how the community affects the group • Understand pertinent regulations guiding the work process (for example, from government agencies), and share these with the groups • Work actively with suppliers and vendors to meet their needs and those of the group

(continued)

Table 15.5. Collaborative Responsibilities of Coaches and Those in Special Roles (continued)

Characteristic	Responsibilities
Counsel and coach others	• Help others identify and develop to their potential • Act as a sounding board • Facilitate decision making and problem solving • Assist with interpersonal issues and conflict management • Become an active listener • Take the ideas and complaints of group members seriously, and help group members take these to the proper place where ideas can be implemented or complaints can be heard and resolved • Support the career development of group members
Communicate and provide information	• Communicate and provide information on policies and procedures, administration and budget, and technical and operational practices • Identify external resources for further information when needed • Develop processes for communicating with customers and suppliers • Promote open and honest communication in all directions • Assist in improving communication within and between groups • Act as a resource for internal and external information • Encourage frequent communication and feedback • Provide member input upward; group may see things that top managers do not see
Lead performance management	• Ensure fair and consistent application (peer and group) of performance management processes • Assist with identification and resolution of performance issues • Assist with establishing peer or team goals and objectives • Track progress at organization, team/group, and individual levels, give feedback, follow up on that feedback • Hold the group accountable for both good and bad performance • Ensure that the group is rewarded formally and informally for performance • Hold regular meetings to assess group performance—with CLT, customers, other teams, other departments, and with team itself • Help the group figure out what is going wrong and what is going right, and implement lessons learned • Benchmark other teams and organizations to determine how the group is doing compared to others and what they can learn • Make performance visible on a regular basis through reports, charts, spreadsheets, and ensure group members understand these • Help group develop and redesign performance measures as needed; make sure you are tracking the right thing • Participate in appropriate committees to make changes to performance management systems

Table 15.6. Collaborative Responsibilities of Executive Management

Characteristic	Responsibilities
Develop organizational context	• Develop support systems to support collaboration • Ensure that all managers and coaches throughout the organization receive feedback on their performance from all levels • Tie managers' and coaches' pay and promotions to their ability to practice collaborative management principles • Develop feedback mechanisms that make everyone in the organization aware of the organization's progress toward its goals • Create environment where it is okay to make mistakes; take risks and learn from them, provide a safety net • Create environment where it is safe to say the "unsayable"
Build teams or groups	• Build the change leadership team (CLT) • Support the CLT • Ensure proper membership of the CLT • Give the CLT proper authority and power to make and implement decisions relevant to CWS effort • Make sure the coaches are trained appropriately • Build and develop management teams
Support individual development	• Provide training opportunities for the leaders in leading CWS • Hold leaders accountable for completing and implementing the CWS training • Help managers and coaches identify opportunities for improvement and development plans • Support the creation of development systems and opportunities for everyone in the organization
Set the direction	• Create an organizational vision and share it • Communicate regularly why you are doing CWS initiative (business issues and so forth) and what you expect to gain from it • Reinforce that the CWS initiative is not "flavor of the month" • Create an organization strategy that fits in with the corporate strategy • Hold the CLT and coaches accountable; are they doing what they say they will do and what they are expected to do? • Set the overall direction for the organization through goals • Create systems of accountability for organization goals • Share the organization direction and help everyone see how they fit into it
Actively support the CWS initiative	• Ensure foundational components (for example, design, CLT, support systems, culture, vision, strategy) support collaboration • Solicit feedback on the CWS initiative regularly • Expect the CWS initiative to succeed and convey that expectation through words and actions

(continued)

Table 15.6. Collaborative Responsibilities of Executive Management (continued)

Characteristic	Responsibilities
	• Be visible to the teams, coaches, and CLT; be out there on a regular basis to see what they are doing; ask! • Hold the CLT and coaches accountable; are they doing what they say they will do and what they are expected to do? • Sit in on CLT meetings; be there to show that you are there, listening, curious about how things are going • Be approachable to all levels by creating informal forums—open lunches, fireside chats, open-door policy
Model collaboration	• Ensure that individuals are given the opportunity to participate in decisions when their expertise is relevant • Model collaborative norms • Participate in or conduct training sessions on collaborative leadership • Model the behavior that they expect to see demonstrated throughout the organization (The way the decisions are made at the top sends a message to the rest of the organization as to whether there is a serious commitment to the CWS initiative.) • When possible and relevant, develop and participate in management teams • Solicit input from all levels of the organization in decision making, when appropriate • Receive feedback, and quickly act on that feedback • Get out of the office and be seen collaborating with others • Ask for input from people you normally wouldn't ask (first-line employees, teams) • Be willing to be wrong and be open to constructive criticism; don't think you are always right
Provide resources	• Provide work groups the resources (such as time, money, opportunity) they need to perform work • Allow collaboration—time for the CLT to meet, time for teams to meet, time to go to training, time to develop the teams • Provide money for collaboration—for training, supplies, education, team rooms and other facilities changes • Provide opportunities; let people sit in on meetings they normally would not be a part of, try doing different things, lead meetings, attend conferences, develop a new product; give them challenges, opportunities to share what they have learned
Integrate the organization	• Ensure that different areas of the company work well together • Create processes for identifying additional integration needs • Develop systems to support collaboration across the organization: "water cooler" spaces, starpoints, databases, e-mail, Web sites • Create processes to assess and modify organization design

Table 15.6. (continued)

Characteristic	Responsibilities
Interface with the environment	• Meet with customers and suppliers and share that information with relevant parties in the organization • Analyze developments in the business environment—new technology, global trends, competitors, customers' wants, new regulations, the economy—and share that information • Represent the organization; go to conferences, meet with customers, meet with businesses outside of normal operations, look for opportunities to develop new business • Work closely with corporate office, communicate with them • Develop ties to the community, create opportunities to enhance them • Work closely with any unions
Counsel and coach others	• Help identify career opportunities for managers and coaches • Mentor other managers • Coach management team
Communicate and provide information	• Share how the organization is doing, why it is doing what it is doing, decisions made and why, how that affects people • Be available to answer questions and provide guidance to leaders and team members • Solicit opinions on attitudes toward senior management ideas and overall company direction through surveys, task forces, and so forth • Hold regular communication meetings with groups throughout the organization • Communicate regularly through newsletters, Web sites, bulletin boards, and other means
Lead performance management	• Monitor how effectively the organization is operating through formal and informal channels such as financial and quality data, formal opinion surveys, direct information "hot lines," electronic mail, open-door policy, having lunch with employees on a regular basis • Create systems of accountability at all levels • Create structures for keeping managers and coaches accountable for both performance and developing their teams and groups • Measure performance at multiple levels (organization, business unit, department) and share that information • Track progress of the CWS initiative • Give feedback on regular basis to all levels • Develop systems of organization, team, and individual rewards and compensation and recognition • Create own goals and action plans and systems of accountability for self and share with others to model performance management

Discussion

1. What should executive manager leadership look like in the CWS?

2. What influence does the CLT have on shifting the leader role at the executive manager level?

Planning: Define Roles of Leaders at All Levels

Time Requirement: Approximately 3 hours, depending on the number of leader roles you choose to define

Supplies: Tables 15.2 and 15.4, Worksheets 15.1 and 15.2, flip chart, markers

Overview: Use this activity to determine which characteristics of collaborative leadership are most important for each of your leader roles and define those important characteristics in terms of tasks and behaviors. The result is a list of leader roles and their definitions.

Instructions

1. Develop a list of leader roles at all levels that you would like to implement or further develop in the CWS initiative. (Review Tables 15.2 and 15.4 for ideas.) List each leader role in the left column of Worksheet 15.1.

2. Review each of the leader roles. Determine the top three characteristics of collaborative leadership for each leader role at the highest level of collaboration, and indicate these with a checkmark on Worksheet 15.1. (Most likely each leader role will need to focus on each of the characteristics, but the objective of this activity is to pick the top three most important.)

3. Review completed Worksheet 15.1. Have all the characteristics been adequately covered? If not, why? Are they needed? If necessary, develop new roles to cover any holes.

4. Further define each leader role.

   - Create small groups of three to five people and divide up the leader roles among the small groups.

   - Each small group should complete Worksheet 15.2 for their assigned leader role(s). Make sure that each small group appoints a scribe to take notes on the worksheet. List the leader role in the left column, and list the three most important characteristics from Step 2 in the "characteristic" cells.

Worksheet 15.1. Characteristics of Collaborative Leadership at Each Level

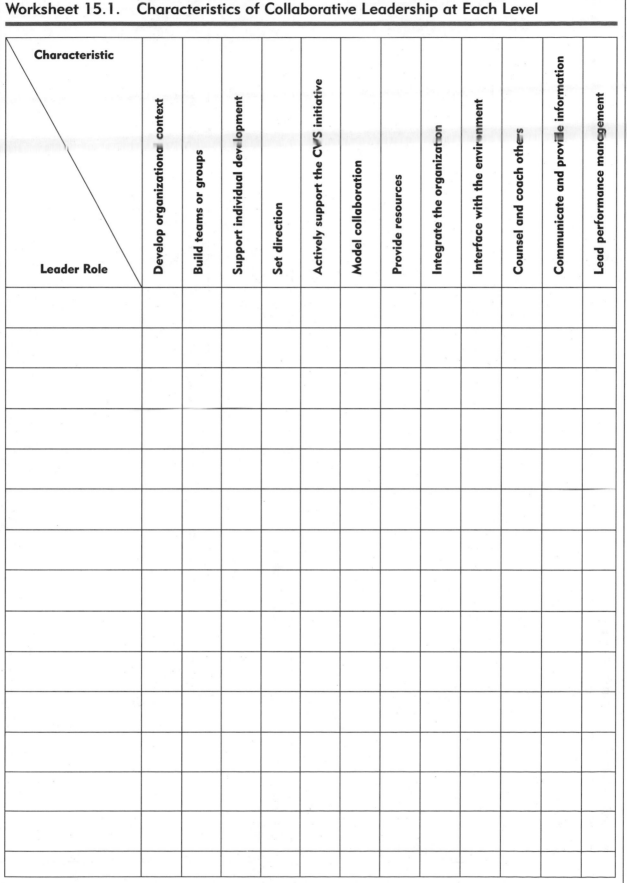

Leader Role \ Characteristic	Develop organizational context	Build teams or groups	Support individual development	Set direction	Actively support the CVS initiative	Model collaboration	Provide resources	Integrate the organization	Interface with the environment	Counsel and coach others	Communicate and provide information	Lead performance management

Worksheet 15.2.   Definitions of Leader Roles

Leader role:

Characteristic:

Tasks or behaviors:

Characteristic:

Tasks or behaviors:

Characteristic:

Tasks or behaviors:

Leader role:

Characteristic:

Tasks or behaviors:

Characteristic:

Tasks or behaviors:

Characteristic:

Tasks or behaviors:

Leader role:	Characteristic:	Tasks or behaviors:	Characteristic:	Tasks or behaviors:
Leader role:	Characteristic:	Tasks or behaviors:	Characteristic:	Tasks or behaviors:

- For each characteristic, define what that characteristic looks like for that leader role in terms of tasks and behaviors at the highest level of collaboration in the organization. Use previous material in the chapter for ideas.

5. Small groups share their results with the whole group. Make changes as needed.

6. Discuss next steps. Some ideas are listed below. Write action ideas on the action planning worksheet at the end of the chapter.

   - Confirm and revise the leader role definitions within the CLT with key decision makers and with groups of other employees.

   - Develop methods for communicating the leader role definitions to everyone in the organization.

   - Begin developing a leadership development plan to support the transition. (Some resources for this are listed at the end of this chapter and in Chapter 16.)

Identify Leader Roles to Support the Empowerment Plan

What Is a Leader Role Transition Plan?

- The leader role transition plan extends the empowerment plan (see Chapter 14) to the leader level.

- It serves to clearly define the new roles of leaders.

- The leader role transition plan shows leaders what their new roles will be once employees have become empowered to take some tasks traditionally belonging to the leader. When the leader knows that he or she will have a new role, he or she is more likely to support empowerment of employees.

Appropriate Level of Detail

Avoid being too detailed in your plan. Instead, create guidelines that can be tailored by each leader to fit his or her work. On the other hand, detail must be enough for leaders to understand your meaning.

Time Required for Development

A lot of time should be spent on the leader role transition plan, as it becomes a key piece of your CWS initiative. In addition to the entire CLT working on the plan, some time in small groups outside of regular meetings will be necessary. Development could take from two to six weeks or even more, depending on the circumstances (such as how much time CLT members devote to that work). When possible, either during or immediately following creation of the full draft of the empowerment plan, involve a cross-section of organizational leaders to review and modify it. Everyone in the planning process should be able to support the plan when it is complete so that they can show their support to others outside the process. The more up-front understanding of what you want the leader role transition to look like in your organization, the more likely you will be able to implement that vision.

A Living Document

No matter how much time you spend developing your leader role transition plan, some changes will be needed periodically. Create mechanisms for updating the plan as needed.

Certification

You may decide to create a certification program to support your leader transition plan. This may take the form of developing requirements for each phase of the leader role transition plan, then asking leaders to show proof of meeting the requirements to become certified in that phase.

Planning: Build a Leader Role Transition Plan

Time Requirement: Approximately 1 hour for each round

Supplies: Two or three flip charts, markers and pens, medium-sized sticky notes (approximately two pads per leader role to be discussed), masking tape and cellophane tape, copies of completed employee empowerment plan (developed in Chapter 14) for each participant, copies of completed Worksheets 15.1 and 15.2 for each participant

Overview: This activity helps create the leader role transition plan to support the employee empowerment plan previously created. This first draft just needs to be a high-level overview of how you want the leader role to develop over time. Later, you can further define and refine your leader role transition plan.

Instructions

1. Prepare for the activity.

   - Tape together six sheets of flip chart paper on a wall, as shown in the figure (dotted lines indicate each piece of flip chart paper).

   - Prepare the flip chart "wall" as shown in the figure. The number of phases should match the number in your employee empowerment plan. The diagram on the following page is for a four-phase plan, so you should adjust your heads accordingly if you have fewer or more phases.

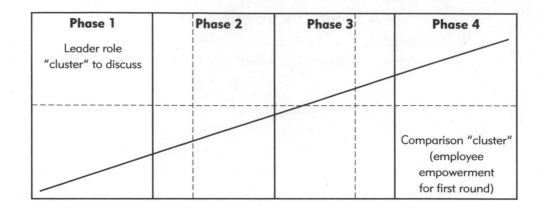

2. Determine different levels of leader roles to be discussed in this activity. Look at the leader roles listed in Worksheets 15.1 and 15.2. Cluster the roles into groups (employee leadership, coaches and special roles, and executive managers). The roles in these clusters will be reviewed together in this planning activity.

3. Start with the lowest level in the organization in which you want to plan leadership roles and then repeat the planning activity for each level moving upward. The result is a coordinated plan for leader role transition. We recommend the following rounds of the activity in this order (left side above the line/right side below the line):

   • Round 1—employee leadership/employee empowerment plan

   • Round 2—coaches and special roles/employee leadership

   • Round 3—executive managers/coaches and special roles

4. Begin the current round of this activity using the clusters of leader roles in the order determined in Step 3. Write the cluster to be discussed in this round on a sticky note and place it above the diagonal line, where "Leader role" is in the diagram above. Write the comparison cluster on another sticky note and place it below the diagonal line. In the first round, write tasks and behaviors for each phase of the employee empowerment plan on sticky notes and place them in appropriate spots below the diagonal line.

5. Look at the completed Worksheet 15.2 to find the leader role that you are reviewing in the current round of the activity. Write each task or behavior listed on a sticky note, one per note. Stick the notes on a flip chart (not the flip chart "wall") so the entire group can see them.

6. Move notes to the appropriate empowerment phase. The group should gather around the flip chart wall and work together to move each note into the appropriate phase of empowerment where that behavior or task begins. The leader role task or behavior should contribute to supporting the group below the diagonal line (in the first round, the employee). Put any sticky notes that are difficult into a separate "parking lot" flip chart to be discussed later. Please note, if you decide to move your flip chart wall, first tape down the sticky notes with cellophane tape so they will not fall off.

7. Ask for more sticky notes. Is there something missing? Are additional tasks or behaviors needed to support the "below the line" group in their phase of empowerment? Add new sticky notes to appropriate phases as needed.

8. Go back to Step 4 and repeat Steps 4 through 7 for each leader role cluster in the order determined in Step 3. When repeating the activity, move the previous leader role sticky notes to the appropriate phases at the bottom of the new chart and then write the new leader role on a sticky note to be placed at the top. The end result will be a leader role transition plan in which all levels of leadership are coordinated with each other and with the employee empowerment plan.

9. Congratulations! You have finished the first draft of your leader role transition plan! Now it is time to figure out the next steps. Some possibilities are listed below; determine the best steps for your organization. List any action items on the sheet at the end of this chapter.

   - Type the list into a computer file. This will make the information easier to maneuver and communicate. If possible, include all levels of the leader role transition plan and all levels of the employee empowerment plan in the same document so that everything can be seen at once. The result should be a coordinated plan where one level supports the next.

   - Confirm consensus on the leader role transition plan. This is a foundational document, so it is important that everyone be able to support it.

   - Begin to create ideas for implementing the leader role transition plan. Now that you have a foundation for what you want new leader roles to look like, you can decide how to create the conditions for transition to occur. Support systems development (see Chapter 16) is a critical mechanism for creating the conditions for leader transition.

   - Develop a system to add, modify, or delete items from the leader role transition plan. No matter how much effort and thought you put into your plan, changes will be needed. Treat the plan as a living document, and create mechanisms such as periodic reviews to adjust as needed.

   - Communicate to different audiences. Sharing the empowerment plan in ways that your different audiences understand is crucial to your success. Consider the level of detail and language necessary for your different audiences (employees, executives, and others) and adjust as appropriate. Go beyond written communication; consider using alternate formats, meetings, graphics, signs, and logos. Consider creating a communication plan for how you will share this information periodically.

Conclusion

The key question of this chapter is, "How should roles of leaders change in a collaborative work system?" Leadership in a CWS goes beyond traditional definitions, including all levels of the organization. While leaders must be able to apply different styles to different situations, there are some common skills and abilities that leaders must learn in order to support the transition to a CWS. Some of the characteristics of collaborative leaders are listed in Table 15.1. To support the transition to the collaborative work system, the role of the leader changes from a traditional command-and-control director to a collaborative supporter of the group.

Keys to the Chapter

- Leadership in a CWS encompasses the people in formal positions of power, such as managers and supervisors, but also includes workers.

- Leaders are responsible for designing and influencing change in systems, structures, and processes to support collaboration. Without their support, the CWS initiative is doomed to failure.

- In a traditional organization, there are three main levels of leadership: executive managers, middle managers, and direct supervisors. Little communication occurs between levels, and what communication does occur is predominantly top-down. In a CWS, the three levels of leadership are employee leadership, coaches and special roles, and executive managers. Lots of two-way communication occurs between levels. Understand and define leadership at all levels.

- Just because the middle management level of the organization no longer exists in a collaborative system, it does not mean the middle managers should be eliminated in the transition! Middle managers have a wealth of experience and knowledge—valuable intellectual capital—that will be lost if they are removed. Move former middle managers to new roles.

- The organization must divide up the responsibilities of each level of leadership into roles. One person cannot do everything; instead, the responsibility must be shared among many at each level of leadership, creating a shared system of leadership.

- The leader role transition plan extends the empowerment plan to the leader level, clearly defining the new roles of leaders.

Chapter Wrap-Up

- What ideas did this chapter trigger for you and your group? List them on the action planning worksheet at the end of this chapter.

- Review the ideas list. Which of these do you want to implement? List the action item, person or group responsible, and target due dates on the action planning worksheet.

- Were any significant decisions made? Include them at the bottom of the action planning worksheet.

- How can you communicate the pertinent material generated by your work on this chapter to different audiences? Discuss and consider adding action items based on your discussion.

- How can you use the resources list for additional help?

- What chapter should you go through next? Refer back to Guiding Assessment results in Chapter 3 for suggestions of next steps.

- What can you do tomorrow or within the next week based on what you learned in this chapter? Have each person share what he or she will do, and follow up.

- What is your biggest learning from this chapter? Ask each person to share. This is a nice way to end the session. Include any resulting ideas or action items on the action planning worksheet.

Resources

Beyerlein, M., Johnson, D., & Beyerlein, S. (Eds.). (1996). *Advances in interdisciplinary studies of work teams: Vol. 3. Leadership of teams.* Greenwich, CT: JAI Press.

Greenleaf, R. K. (1997). The servant as leader. In R. P. Vecchio (Ed.), *Leadership: Understanding the dynamics of power and influence in organizations.* Notre Dame, IN: University of Notre Dame Press.

Hackman, J. R. (2002). *Leading teams: Setting the stage for great performances.* Boston: Harvard Business School Press.

Manz, C. C., & Sims, H. P. (2001). *The new superleadership: Leading others to lead themselves.* San Francisco: Berrett-Koehler.

Pfeffer, J., & Veiga, J. (1999). Putting people first for organizational success. *Academy of Management Executive, 13*(2), 37–48.

Quinn, R. E., & Spreitzer, G. M. (1997, Autumn). The road to empowerment: Seven questions every leader should consider. *Organizational Dynamics*, pp. 37–49.

Rawlings, D. (2000). Collaborative leadership teams: Oxymoron or new paradigm? *Consulting Psychology Journal: Practice and Research, 52*(1), 36–48.

Tjosvold, D., & Tjosvold, M. M. (1998). *Leading the team organization: How to create an enduring competitive advantage.* Lanham, MD: Lexington Books.

Wilson, J., George, J., Wellins, R., & Byham, W. (1994). *Leadership trapeze: Strategies for leadership in team-based organizations.* San Francisco: Jossey-Bass.

Zaccaro, S. J., & Marks, M. A. (1999). The roles of leaders in high-performance teams. In E. Sundstrom (Ed.), *Supporting work team effectiveness: Best management practices for fostering high performance* (pp. 95–125). San Francisco: Jossey-Bass.

Action Planning and Summary Sheet

Ideas Generated from This Chapter

1

2

3

4

5

#	Action Item	Target Date	Person/Group Responsible
1			
2			
3			
4			
5			
6			

Significant Decisions Made

1

2

3

4

Align Support Systems

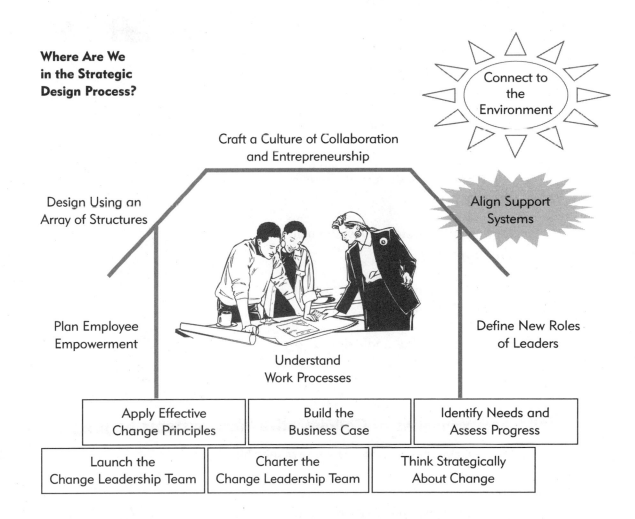

Connect to the Environment

Craft a Culture of Collaboration and Entrepreneurship

Design Using an Array of Structures

Align Support Systems

Plan Employee Empowerment

Understand Work Processes

Define New Roles of Leaders

Apply Effective Change Principles	Build the Business Case	Identify Needs and Assess Progress

Launch the Change Leadership Team	Charter the Change Leadership Team	Think Strategically About Change

Key Question of This Chapter

How can the organizational context support collaboration?

Quick Look

Overview

Organizational support systems are the infrastructure created to support the work and the people doing the work in the organization. Rewards and compensation, recognition, training, and performance management are examples of support systems. Through modifying and creating systems, collaborative work systems build cooperation and collaboration into the organizational context. The outcomes of this chapter include a draft of a support systems development plan, preliminary action steps and deadlines for support systems change, and preliminary plans for support systems committee composition and membership.

Chapter Plan

Topic				
Create the Context for Collaboration with Support Systems	✓	✓		
Use Support Systems in All Shapes and Sizes	✓		✓	✓
Align Support Systems with Your Environment	✓	✓		
Link Support Systems Development to Empowerment	✓			✓
Create Committees to Implement Support Systems Change	✓			
Continually Assess and Adjust Support Systems	✓			

Principles of Collaborative Work Systems Series

Align support systems to promote ownership

Align authority, information, and decision making

Design and promote flexible organizations that foster needed collaboration

Create the Context for Collaboration with Support Systems

Why Support Systems?

Using the human immune system as a metaphor, the organization often treats changes to the system like white blood cells do an intruding disease; it gathers the forces to surround the change and "kills" it. The existing organizational immune system can kill the CWS initiative before it can get started. Changing support systems to support collaboration is one way that the "immune system" is changed.

What Is a Support System?

The organizational context or environment can be defined through support systems. Support systems are the infrastructure created to support the work and the people doing the work within the organization. Reward systems and training and development systems are examples. Every organization has support systems, but in collaborative work systems, support systems must incorporate and reinforce collaboration and cooperation.

Organizational support systems should (Mohrman, Cohen, & Mohrman, 1995):

- Support the work being done in the organization

- Fit with the way the organization is designed

- Change to fit new logic when the organizational design changes

- Support desired behavior (in this case, collaboration)

Table 16.1 lists a wide variety of support systems and what they look like in a collaborative setting. Later in this chapter, a planning activity guides you through a review of the support systems in Table 16.1.

Traditional Systems vs. Collaborative Systems

Traditional support systems are set up to reinforce individual work and, often, competition between workers. CWSs require collaboration and cooperation, so systems must reinforce teamwork. For example, a traditional system typically bases pay solely on individual contributions, which sets up a situation in which individuals are competing for pay. In a CWS situation, if a team is instructed to work together on projects, yet the reward system is based on individual contributions (for example, the person with the highest sales numbers on the team gets a bonus), chances are quite high that the desired teamwork will not occur. Instead, to foster collaboration and cooperation, CWS-based reward systems need a component to reward team members for accomplishing team goals.

Table 16.2 characterizes the differences between traditional and collaborative systems (see also Mohrman, Cohen, & Mohrman, 1995).

The Empowerment Implementation Triangle

This chapter focuses on the development of collaborative support systems. The empowerment implementation triangle (Figure 16.1) shows that support systems are only one part of the equation. Support systems such as training, performance management, and

Table 16.1. Support Systems and Collaboration

Support System	Collaborative Applications
Goal-setting system Methods of establishing aligned goals (goals, priorities, and tasks)	• Align goals across organization levels (horizontal and vertical). • Facilitate shared understanding and common commitment to goals. • Give employees input into higher-level goals and responsibility for setting their own goals. • Use systematic goal-setting procedures. • Ensure clarity of goals. • Create processes for prioritizing goals when goal conflict occurs. • Create realistic goals, with some that require a stretch.
Performance measurement system Methods of identifying and measuring appropriate performance	• Measure what you value; what you measure is what gets done! • Use both formal and informal measurement. • Use measurements that are understandable, useful, available, and meaningful. • Use principles of valid measurement. • Measure what people have control or influence over. • Measure to improve performance, not to micro-manage, punish, or place blame. • Measure at multiple levels—individual, team or group, and organization. • Measure the intangibles (for example, "soft" data such as quality of decision making and communication between groups) as well as the tangibles (for example, "hard" data such as cost and quality).
Performance feedback system Methods (formal and informal) of relaying information regarding appropriate performance and other desired behaviors associated with performance	• Use both formal and informal feedback systems. • Only give feedback on things within that person's or group's influence. • Give feedback to members at all levels (individual, team, between-team, and organizational). • Create mechanisms for feedback that do not require a person to deliver it (for example, quality systems embedded in the task itself). • Create an atmosphere where people are open to feedback, value it, and make use of it for performance improvement. • Make time to listen, reflect on feedback, and make improvements accordingly (at individual, team, between-team, and organizational levels). • Ensure feedback is given in a timely manner. • Ensure that formal and informal feedback systems focus on the performance, not the personal characteristics, of an individual.
Reward and recognition system Methods of rewarding and recognizing performance and other desired behaviors (individual, team, business unit levels of performance)	• Highlight both intrinsic (for example, opportunities to learn new skills) and extrinsic (for example, pay) rewards. • Create rewards and recognition at individual, team, between-team, and organizational levels. • Align rewards and recognition to what is valued. • Ensure that rewards and recognition are fair (the procedure itself and consistent application of the procedure) and given in a timely manner.

Table 16.1. (continued)

Support System	Collaborative Applications
	• Ensure that employees share in the outcomes of the organization.
	• Create both informal and formal rewards and recognition.
	• Create meaning around rewards and recognition. Don't assume that something that is rewarding to you is rewarding for all. Ask people about what they want.
	• Recognize publicly.
	• Realize that sometimes recognition from peers is more important than gifts.
Financial system Financial systems to support collaboration, including the accounting and reporting systems	• Capture the value that teams add and make sure it is fed back to top strategic decision makers, the team itself, and anyone else who is relevant.
	• Share financial information with team members to give them the business knowledge.
	• Go beyond the traditional short-term focus of financial and accounting systems by creating long-term measures to give to long-term investors and support validity of CWS initiatives.
	• Financial and control systems must be changed so people (especially support groups) are reinforced for supporting teams.
Resource allocation system Processes for ensuring that teams get the resources they need to do the work	• Ensure that employees have the responsibility, accountability, and authority to get the resources that they need.
	• Establish assessment processes to determine where employees need additional resources.
	• Create new expectations of people providing resources (for example, the purchasing department). Reinforce these expectations with other support systems.
Communication system Methods for communication throughout the organization	• Create formal (for example, newsletters) and informal (for example, learning forums) mechanisms for communication.
	• Facilitate communication in all directions.
	• Manage the grapevine—the informal communication networks in your organization.
	• Value the "water cooler"—the informal sharing places in your organization.
	• Publish the progress of the CLT and CWS initiative in as many venues as possible (for example, bulletin boards, newsletters, e-mails, town hall meetings, Web sites, posters, T-shirts, and others).
	• Tailor the method of communication to each audience.
	• Communicate via integration mechanisms (see "Integration" later in this table).
	• Make CLT accessible to as many employees as possible.

(continued)

Table 16.1.   Support Systems and Collaboration (continued)

Support System	Collaborative Applications
Information system Methods for employees to get the information they need to perform effectively	• Use non-technical information systems, such as meetings within and across groups and whiteboards with current issues listed. • Make technology people-friendly; obtain input from people in creating the systems. • Create accountability in the information technology group (for example, measure how well the employees use the technology). • Make sure that teams have the tools in place (for example, computers where they can be used) to access technology. • Give employees access to all the information (for example, business accounting information) they need to contribute to overall performance, not just the information you think they need. • Deal with the realities of corporate-mandated systems while attending to the needs of employees. • Educate and influence corporate to institute enterprise-wide systems (for example, performance appraisal) that are flexible enough to meet the needs of teams.
Knowledge management system Processes for acquiring, organizing, sharing, and using knowledge	• Identify, capture, and share best practices. • Recognize that knowledge management is more than a database, but use technology whenever possible to store information and promote sharing. • Create mentoring programs to pair more experienced and knowledgeable workers with less experienced workers. • Remove barriers to sharing learning. • Create platforms that enable sharing; use a combination of technology, organizational structure and processes, and culture. • When using technology, use multimedia approaches to reach as many sensory levels as possible. • Recognize the value of unspoken knowledge and create mechanisms for translating it into spoken knowledge. • Use storytelling to share valued learnings. • Encourage teams to create shared databases.
Training system Methods for teams and individuals to identify and get the skills needed to perform (for example, interpersonal skills training, business skills training)	• Make training sessions serve as work sessions as well. • Balance technical, business, and social skills training. • Create processes that allow employees to determine their training needs and timing. • Build internal capacity to deliver and create training. • Consider carefully who should deliver the training—who is capable and who is best-suited to deliver the message.

Table 16.1. (continued)

Support System	Collaborative Applications
	• Take employees from where they are to where they need to be, without time as the sole focus.
	• Involve appropriate people in the development of training—for example, quality people in quality training.
	• If "off the shelf" solutions are used, tailor them to your needs.
	• Get help from outside sources (for example, consultants, local groups, and universities) if necessary.
	• Create processes to determine whether the training is working.
	• Match the type of training (classroom, mentoring, on-the-job, coaching, conferences, site visits, workshops) to the need.
	• Incorporate real feedback (from peers, bosses, and others) into training.
	• When possible, conduct team training in intact teams.
	• Help teams bring new members up to speed (by providing time, resources).
Selection system Processes for bringing new and transferred employees with the right skills into the right teams	• Create new succession planning mechanisms. • As teams gain expertise, give them an increased role in selection (interviews and other means). • If the team is involved in selection, its contributions must be in line with legal requirements for selection. Make sure the team has the resources available to deal with legal and policy issues (for example, through HR department assistance). • If team members are given a voice in selection, make sure they understand that their input is heard, and explain when a different decision is made. • Ensure diversity of perspective and expertise, and moderate the level of diversity so that team members can establish some cohesiveness, but not fall victim to groupthink. • Let teams have a role in determining competencies required for new team members.
Physical workspace and tools The actual spaces in which the employees and teams work; if it is a virtual team, then the "space" created by technology (for example, budgets, tools, and computers)	• Make sure employees have the tools they need and that they work properly. • Reorganize the workspace so that it is conducive to collaboration. • Allow employee input into redesign of workspace. • Recognize shared work issues and come up with joint solutions and norms (for example, using the same workspace for different shifts). • Ensure that teams have computers, storage space, and so forth for maintenance of team records and documents. • Provide proper training on tools to gain full value of the tool. • Create team meeting spaces. • When possible, locate team members near each other to promote informal communications.

(continued)

Table 16.1.   Support Systems and Collaboration (continued)

Support System	Collaborative Applications
	• When physical proximity is not possible, provide technology to simulate physical proximity as much as possible. • Provide employees with any special facilities needs.
Integration Methods for aligning, defragmenting, creating a holistic organization, capitalizing on the "between" spaces	• Integrate between teams so they cooperate instead of compete. • Ensure that between-support systems are aligned. • Ensure that multiple change initiatives are aligned in terms of complementary content and sequence. • Use integration mechanisms such as liaison roles, integration teams, and multiple team membership. • Periodically assess the alignment between all the parts. • Identify problem areas where pieces are not fitting together and do something about it. • Identify priorities and solve conflicts between parts.
Organization design Methods of looking at the organization as a whole, determining appropriate places for teams, and supporting them through support system design and culture (For more on organization design, see Chapter 13)	• The design of the organization sets the context for decisions in designing the teams. • Match the design to the environment and the type of work. • Design in flexibility and speed. • Create a few strict rules at the organizational level to guide design; too many rules create problems at lower levels. • Continually assess how the design is working and adjust appropriately. • Look for opportunities for using teams; then match the correct type of team to the opportunity. But remember that not all tasks are team tasks, so design for individuals when appropriate. • Design in ways that create between-team opportunities for adding value. Do not allow teams to become the new silos.
Team design At the team level, making sure the team has the inputs it needs to get the work done (For more on team design, see Chapter 13)	• Treat team as customer. Provide what is needed to get the job done. • Ensure appropriate team structure (for example, team leader, team facilitator, and others). • Ensure appropriate team membership (for example, correct skills and experiences to get the job done) and size. • Design appropriate individual jobs. • Ensure team design fits the task (for example, self-managing teams, task force, project team, cross-functional team). • Ensure effective decision processes and decision escalation paths. • Ensure role clarity (for example, by creating effective team charters that are revised as needed).

Table 16.1. (continued)

Support System	Collaborative Applications
Leadership system Formal and informal processes of distributing leadership throughout the organization, including supporting formally appointed leaders at all levels in learning the skills necessary to support collaboration (For more on the leadership system, see Chapter 15)	• Show formally appointed leaders how their roles should change to support collaboration, thereby increasing the chances that these leaders will support the CWS initiative. • Support the development of the characteristics of collaborative leadership (see Chapter 15). • Create momentum for change with senior manager support. • Preserve the expertise of the middle managers, even if the goal is a flatter organization. If the "middle" is eliminated, new roles might include sponsors, champions of change effort, consultants, integrator roles (vertical and horizontal), and customer/supplier liaison roles. • Transform traditional direct supervisors into coaches who help develop internal processes of teams and gradually transition some of their tasks to teams while taking on a more strategic role.

Table 16.2. Traditional vs. Collaborative Support Systems

Traditional	Collaborative
Systems are oriented toward the individual	Systems are collectively oriented
Systems are dependent on manager input only	Systems are open to input of all
Systems are accessible to managers only	Systems are accessible to all
Systems are inflexible and change slowly, if at all	Systems are flexible and capable of quick change
Systems are generic, "one size fits all"	Systems are tailored to meet the needs of each group
Groups frequently have to create "work-arounds" for systems	The needs of groups are always met by systems, eliminating the need for "work-arounds"

compensation must support employee empowerment or employees will get mixed messages about what is truly desired and revert to old habits. Expectations for how employee behavior and tasks should change as a result of empowerment should be identified and communicated through an empowerment plan. For more on creating an employee empowerment plan, see Chapter 14. Leaders must support employee empowerment and become more empowered themselves for employee empowerment to be effective. For more on the leader transition, see Chapter 15. The three parts of the triangle must be aligned for empowerment to occur.

Figure 16.1.   The Empowerment Implementation Triangle

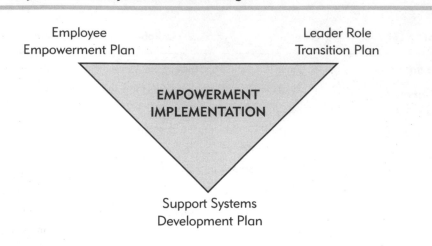

Employee
Empowerment Plan

Leader Role
Transition Plan

EMPOWERMENT
IMPLEMENTATION

Support Systems
Development Plan

Discussion

Refer to Table 16.2 to guide your discussion.

1. Review each item in the table. Which column characterizes your organization now? Give examples.

2. Review each item in the table again. Which column characterizes where you want your organization to be? Give specific examples of what that would look like.

3. What are the biggest gaps between where you are now and where you want to be?

4. What can the CLT do to close those gaps?

Use Support Systems in All Shapes and Sizes

Support systems come in all shapes and sizes. The deeper your understanding of the potential of different types of support systems, the more likely it is that you will be able to generate useful changes that will end up affecting performance.

Examine Accepted Systems and Less-Recognized Systems

Some support systems, such as reward and compensation, come readily to mind. Others, such as leadership and renewal, are just as prevalent in organizations, but are not always considered "systems." Similar to the old saying "What gets measured gets done," we believe that looking at less-recognized systems when planning change means the desired change is more likely.

Use Formal and Informal Systems

Organizations need support in place for all aspects of performance. It doesn't matter if it is formal, informal, or a combination, as long as you have sufficient support in some manner. For example, formal support may include performance appraisal systems that tie into compensation systems. Examples of informal support include informal methods of feedback such as in-the-moment critique and "how are we doing" reviews at team meetings.

Understand Individual, Team, and Organization Levels

Support can occur at individual, team, and organization levels. For example, in the rewards system, compensation may be necessary at all three levels—for meeting individual, team, and organizational goals. Most likely, all three levels of support are necessary for each support system, although the proportions may vary.

Planning: Collaborative Support System Review

Time Requirement: 45 minutes for each round of support system review

Supplies: Flip chart and markers for each small group, Worksheet 16.1

Overview: This planning activity helps participants further explore different support systems and begin creating a shared understanding of how the support systems apply to the participants' organization.

Worksheet 16.1.　Review of Collaborative Support Systems

Sample

Support system: ___Training System___

What is it?	Identify needs and develop means of providing basic skills to meet those needs.
Why is it important?	• Provides skills they don't otherwise have • Aids in transition to collaborative work system • Facilitates the development of abilities needed to support the responsibility, accountability, and authority of empowerment
What practices could we use?	• Just-in-time training • Cascading approach • Ongoing activity, not a one-time thing • New training, refresher training; continuous improvement • Participant evaluation, critique, feedback • Reinforcing skills learned • Processes to make sure skills have been transferred to the workplace • Use many appropriate forms of training—combination of classroom training, on-the-job training, and so forth • Develop processes for teams and individuals to identify their own needs and tell appropriate people so that those needs can be met

Worksheet

Support system: _____

What is it?

Why is it important?

What practices could we use?

Worksheet 16.1.   (continued)

Support system: _____

_____

What is it?

_____

Why is it important?

_____

What practices could we use?

Support system: _____

_____

What is it?

_____

Why is it important?

_____

What practices could we use?

Instructions

1. Form small groups of three to six people per group.

2. Assign one support system listed in Table 16.1 to each small group. If time is an issue, assign more than one support system per group (try to give them similar or complementary support systems).

3. Ask each small group to complete Worksheet 16.1 for each support system (make copies as necessary). A sample is provided.

4. Select a scribe from each group to capture the discussion results.

5. Each small group should take a turn reviewing its results with the entire group. The facilitator may want to reproduce the activity sheet on a flip chart to capture the discussion. Encourage the entire group to take notes during the discussion. Encourage clarifying questions.

6. Repeat Steps 1 through 5 until all the support systems are reviewed.

Assessment: A Closer Look at Your Organization's Support Systems

Time Requirement: Approximately 1 hour

Supplies: Assessment 16.1, flip chart, markers

Overview: Now that you have an understanding of what systems supporting collaboration look like, complete this assessment of your organization's current support systems.

Instructions

1. As a group, review the support systems listed in column 3 of Assessment 16.1. For each system, determine whether that support system is currently used in your organization and indicate yes or no in the far left column. If the support system is used, brainstorm examples of what that support system looks like in your organization and list them in column 2.

2. Next, decide whether each support system that the organization does use supports collaboration. Indicate yes or no in the far right column. If yes, indicate how.

3. Discuss the following questions:

   - Review the support systems not currently in use in your organization. Given what you have learned so far, should any of those support systems be developed?

   - Are the support systems currently in use clustered together in any way (for example, performance measurement and feedback are often conducted together)? Are these clusters valid? If not, how should they be changed?

   - Review the support systems that currently do not support collaboration. What preliminary ideas do you have for changing them to support collaboration?

   - Review the support systems that currently do support collaboration. What can you learn that can be transferred to support systems that do not support collaboration?

Assessment 16.1. Current Use of Support Systems

Currently Used?	Example in Organization	Support System	Does It Support Collaboration?
		Goal-setting system	
		Performance measurement system	
		Performance feedback system	
		Reward and recognition system	
		Financial system	
		Resource allocation system	
		Communication system	
		Information system	
		Knowledge management system	
		Training system	
		Selection system	
		Physical workspace and tools	
		Integration	
		Organization design	
		Team design	
		Leadership system	

Align Support Systems with Your Environment
Create Links to the External Environment

In an adaptive organization, employees must have access to the outside world. Incorporating these links into support systems is one way to ensure this access. For example, the learning system could incorporate databases that allow access to current newspapers and articles to ensure that employees have the most current data possible. (For more on connecting to the environment, see Chapter 10.)

Make the Support Systems Flexible

To deal with the quickly changing needs of the external environment, individuals and teams within the organization need to be able to change quickly. Support systems must adjust rapidly to meet and support these change requirements.

Link Support Systems to Strategic Goals

A crucial part of the environment that support systems must be aligned with is the strategic goals of the organization. Every system must be tied to those strategic goals. Every decision made should be based on the strategic goals. After all, the reason the organization is in business is to complete their work, and the strategic goals are the way completing the work is defined. If people at all levels are making decisions with the strategic goals in mind, then you have alignment.

Deal with the Realities of Your Environment

Whether we like it or not, some realities exist that play a role in the support systems change plans we make. The change leadership team must keep these realities in mind when planning change. One reality that often hinders support systems change is inflexible enterprise-wide systems that are mandated by the corporate office. It is up to the change leadership team and others in the organization to find creative ways to deal with demands of both enterprise-wide systems and needs of the CWS business unit.

In addition, the environment is always changing, so the change leadership team must be aware of changes so they can react appropriately and even predict needed changes ahead of time. Surprises such as economy shifts and corporate mandates occur all the time and kill CWS initiatives that are not flexible enough to deal with the surprises.

Discussion

1. What are the realities of your environment that you must deal with when planning support systems change?

2. What are the aspects of your environment to which you must attune to ensure success?

3. How will you stay attuned to these aspects?

4. How can each support system create links to the environment?

Link Support Systems Development to Empowerment

Support systems are so large that they are difficult to design and manage. One approach is the creation of a strategic design plan for support systems development that can link with the employee empowerment plan (see Chapter 14) and the plan defining the changing roles of leaders (see Chapter 15). This plan then becomes the guiding force for support systems development.

However, no matter how well the plans are laid out, realities always pose unforeseen challenges! The plan must be seen as a living document that can be changed to meet these challenges.

See Table 16.3 for an example of a partially completed strategic design plan for support systems development.

Note: Number of phases and primary phase expectations are determined by the organization's empowerment plan for teams. If the organization does not have an empowerment plan for teams, it would be wise to at least discuss with the group the number and types of phases of empowerment they would like to have in order to begin creating shared understanding of the foundation of the CWS initiative.

Table 16.3. Partially Completed Support Systems Planning Tool

Primary Phase Focus	Phase I Create the Foundation	Phase II Launch the Teams	Phase III Reinforce Team Habits	Phase IV Leap to High Performance
Support System: Performance	Develop informal feedback methods Develop informal reward system Discuss performance needs with team	Research team appraisal systems Review current appraisal system Discuss ideal appraisal system	Develop appraisal system for teams Determine integration needs Develop implementation plan	Implement new appraisal system Refine system as needed
Support System: Direct Supervision	Determine supervisor's role Select appropriate supervisors Provide initial training in teaming Provide resource information	Provide leadership training Develop informal feedback methods Address fears and concerns Create developmental plans	Develop appraisal system for supervisor Implement appraisal system	Review role of supervisor Continue development

Source: Harris & Bodner, 2003, p. 319. Used with permission.

Planning: Begin Planning Support Systems Change

Time Requirement: Approximately 1 hour per round for Steps 1 through 6; approximately 1 hour for Steps 7 and 8

Supplies: Flip chart and markers for each subgroup; Worksheet 16.2; copies of the empowerment and leader transition plans, if previously created; computer and projector or overhead projector and transparencies may be useful

Overview: In this activity, you'll begin planning the CWS support systems transition process.

Instructions

1. Divide the group into small groups of three to six people. Ask each group to select one or more support systems to focus on. Refer to the results of Assessment 16.1 to determine how these support systems may already be clustered, to give you guidance as to which to review together. Ask the group to consider appropriate selection of people for each group—that is, is there someone with particular expertise who needs to be in a particular group?

2. Have small groups brainstorm specific tasks that must occur within the support system category in order to align with the empowerment plan. Remind the groups that they will likely need to gather information from outside sources in order to make a good plan. Small groups may want to use computers or transparencies as methods for recording their results to share with others.

3. Small groups can then enter the tasks they brainstormed into the appropriate phase on Worksheet 16.2. Five phases are shown here as an example. Use the number of phases you have in your empowerment plan.

4. Small groups come back together to meet as a whole to debrief their progress. Some adjustment will occur here, as small-group members ask each other questions and make decisions about things such as:

   - Under which support system category does this task fall?

   - Which phase should contain this task?

   - Where do we have redundancies? Who should take responsibility?

   - Where do we need to integrate to pass off a piece of work from one group to the next? How can we do that?

5. This is an iterative process; alignment changes should continue to occur throughout planning and implementation. Remind the group that there is no "right" answer, but they need to come to a common agreement of the way they will proceed.

6. Capture the results of all the small groups into a master version of Worksheet 16.2. This is best captured in a computer file so that changes can be made easily. Distribute copies of the master version of Worksheet 16.2 throughout the process so everyone is on the same page.

Worksheet 16.2. Support Systems Planning Tool

	Phase I	Phase II	Phase III	Phase IV	Phase V
Primary Phase Focus					
Support system:					
Support system:					
Support system:					
Support system:					

7. Repeat Steps 1 through 5 until all the support systems have been covered.

8. As a whole group, put a tentative timeline on the empowerment plan so that everyone has a basic understanding of when the tasks of each phase need to be accomplished.

9. Go back into small groups to develop some tentative dates for tasks to be due.

10. The group as a whole meets to continue sharing and alignment of plans.

Create Committees to Implement Support Systems Change

Creating a successful context for collaboration requires intentional effort. The time and effort required to change support systems is huge, as it takes much more time to implement changes than to plan them. An "iceberg effect" happens when changing support systems. At first, only the tip of the iceberg above the water is seen, looking like relatively small changes. However, on further investigation, the extent of needed change that was hiding under the water is revealed. Be aware of the "iceberg effect" and create flexible plans that can be changed as more of the iceberg is unveiled. Realize that lots of energy will be required to make changes, revitalize by celebrating small successes, and be ready to hang in for the long haul.

The change leadership team cannot do it alone. Creating committees to address support systems is one way to focus that intentional effort and make the change manageable.

Determine Committee Membership

Committees should have representatives from affected stakeholders and include key implementers and decision makers of the support systems being changed. For example, the rewards support system committee would need someone from the department responsible for creating and implementing compensation system changes as a member. One way to do this is to ask the small groups that were working on support systems plans to make recommendations on who would be appropriate for working with support systems committees. Most likely, all members of the change leadership team should participate in some way on these support systems committees.

To promote momentum and promote integration of the support systems, identify an individual in each support system committee to act as chairperson and to be the spearhead of the effort. Some members of each committee should remain as long-term committee members. However, some rotation of members will help bring new ideas and energy to the project. Support systems committees and the change leadership team should determine some guidelines for membership rotation.

Determine Committee Responsibilities

The support systems planning tool becomes the "charter" for each of the committees.

Create Decision-Making Guidelines

Support systems implementation committees must understand their boundaries of authority, responsibility, and accountability. What decisions can the committees make on their own and which must be escalated back to the change leadership team? How will committees be made accountable for accomplishing their tasks?

Use Effective Change Principles

The support systems implementation committees are responsible for leading change, just like the change leadership team. Therefore, the change foundation elements reviewed in Part I of this workbook apply. In particular, support systems committees must assess the need for change, communicate changes within the organization, and become role models for the CWS initiative.

Integrate Support Systems Committees to Align Support Systems with Each Other

To maintain alignment, support systems committees must integrate within their groups and across all support systems committees. Here are some ideas on how this integration could occur:

- Key individuals of different support systems committees meet regularly to maintain alignment.

- Groups present at regular coordination meetings.

- Informal communication occurs regularly between groups (phone, e-mail, hall conversations, and so forth).

Early in the development of support systems, determine how integration will take place. Here are some questions to guide the development of your integration process:

- Which key members of each support system committee will meet regularly to maintain alignment?

- How often will they meet, and how?

- When, how, and how often will coordination meetings with all support systems committees occur?

- How else will you integrate support systems?

Continually Assess and Adjust Support Systems

Looking at support systems once as part of a CWS initiative is not enough. Support systems must be assessed periodically, and changes must be made to align to any other changes in the organization or organization's environment. Following are some questions to guide the development of a continual assessment and adjustment process:

- How often will each support system be assessed?

- Who will do the assessment?

- How often will the integration of support systems be assessed? Who will do the assessment?

- How will recommended changes determined through the assessment processes be implemented?

- Who will follow up to ensure that changes have been made?

Conclusion

The key question of this chapter is, "How can the organizational context support collaboration?" The organizational context, defined by commonly recognized support systems such as rewards and recognition and uncommonly recognized support systems such as integration and organization design, must be changed to support collaboration in order for the CWS initiative to succeed.

Support systems development must support the expectations for employee behavior change (see Chapter 14) and the leader role transition (see Chapter 15). Support systems are so huge that it will take a lot of effort to change them. Do not underestimate the time, effort, and resources required for successful change in support systems.

Keys to the Chapter

- Every organization has support systems, but in collaborative work systems, support systems must incorporate and reinforce collaboration and cooperation.

- Consider both recognized systems (such as rewards) and less-recognized systems (such as leadership and integration).

- Use both formal and informal aspects of systems. For example, in the performance feedback system, a formal aspect is yearly feedback on performance reviews and an informal aspect is "how are we doing" reviews at meetings.

- Support can occur at individual, team or group, and organization levels; it is likely that all three are needed in most situations.

- Link support systems development to the empowerment plan defining expectations for employee behavior and the leader role transition plan.

- Support systems are difficult to change. Create committees to lead change; involve those with relevant expertise, experience, and decision-making authority to implement change; and realize that support systems change takes time, effort, and resources.

- Support systems must be flexible and adaptable enough to meet the needs of the changing environment. Continually assess and adjust support systems.

Chapter Wrap-Up

- What ideas did this chapter trigger for you and your group? List them on the action planning worksheet at the end of this chapter.

- Review the ideas list. Which of these do you want to implement? List the action item, person or group responsible, and target due dates on the action planning worksheet.

- Were any significant decisions made? Include them at the bottom of the action planning worksheet.

- How can you communicate the pertinent material generated by your work on this chapter to different audiences? Discuss and consider adding action items based on your discussion.

- How can you use the resources list for additional help?

- What chapter should you go through next? Refer back to Guiding Assessment results in Chapter 3 for suggestions of next steps.

- What can you do tomorrow or within the next week based on what you learned in this chapter? Have each person share what he or she will do, and follow up.

- What is your biggest learning from this chapter? Ask each person to share. This is a nice way to end the session. Include any resulting ideas or action items on the action planning worksheet.

Resources

Campion, M. A., Medsker, G. J., & Higgs, A. C. (1993). Relations between work group characteristics and effectiveness: Implications for designing effective work groups. *Personnel Psychology, 46*, 823–850.

Eisenstat, R. A., & Cohen, S. G. (1990). Summary: Top management groups. In J. R. Hackman (Ed.), *Groups that work (and those that don't): Creating conditions for effective teamwork* (pp. 78–86). San Francisco: Jossey-Bass.

Fisher, K. (1999). *Leading self-directed work teams: A guide to developing new team leadership skills.* New York: McGraw-Hill.

Gross, S. E. (1995). *Compensation for teams: How to design and implement team-based reward systems.* New York: AMACOM.

Harrington-Mackin, D. (1996). *Keeping the team going: A tool kit to renew and refuel your workplace teams.* New York: New Directions Management Services.

Harris, C., & Bodner, S. (2003). Developing team-based support systems: Conceptual overview and strategic planning workshop. In M. Beyerlein, C. McGee, G. Klein, J. Nemiro, & L. Broedling (Eds.), *The collaborative work systems fieldbook: Strategies, tools, and techniques* (pp. 307–325). San Francisco: Jossey-Bass/Pfeiffer.

Janz, B. D., Colquitt, J. A., & Noe, R. A. (1997). Knowledge worker team effectiveness: The role of autonomy, interdependence, team development, and contextual support variables. *Personnel Psychology, 50*(4), 877–904.

Mankin, D., Cohen, S. G., & Bikson, T. K. (1996). *Teams and technology: Fulfilling the promise of the new organization.* Boston: Harvard Business School Press.

Manz, C. C., & Sims, H., Jr. (1995). *Business without bosses: How self-managing teams are building high-performing companies.* Hoboken, NJ: Wiley.

Mohrman, S. A., Cohen, S. G., & Mohrman, A. M., Jr. (1995). *Designing team-based organizations: New forms for knowledge work.* San Francisco: Jossey-Bass.

Sundstrom, E. D., & Associates. (1999). *Supporting work team effectiveness: Best management practices for fostering high performance.* San Francisco: Jossey-Bass.

Wilson, J., George, J., & Wellins, R., with Byham, B. (1994). *Leadership trapeze: Strategies for leadership in team-based organizations.* San Francisco: Jossey-Bass.

Action Planning and Summary Sheet

Ideas Generated from This Chapter

#	
1	
2	
3	
4	
5	

#	Action Item	Target Date	Person/Group Responsible
1			
2			
3			
4			
5			
6			

Significant Decisions Made

#	
1	
2	
3	
4	

## CHAPTER 17

Conclusion: Working Toward the Future

 ### Key Questions of This Chapter

What have we accomplished, what resources have we created, and what is our next goal?

 ### Quick Look

Overview

This chapter wraps up the work in the workbook. However, it is also designed to create a jumping-off point to the next step in the evolution of the CWS journey. Tools are provided here to enable the CLT to review the key learnings and decisions that occurred during the past weeks and months and use them as the basis for planning next steps. The implementation of a collaborative work system is never finished—it requires continual investment and focus. Outcomes from this chapter include a review of the activities in each chapter to determine what remains to be done, a review of key learnings as a basis for the next round of action planning, a new time-line, and an opportunity to measure progress using the Guiding Assessment introduced in Chapter 3.

Chapter Plan

Topic				
Review of the Workbook	✓		✓	
Create a CWS Initiative Handbook	✓	✓		
Address Key Questions from Each Critical Success Factor Chapter	✓			✓
Launch into the Future	✓		✓	✓

Principles of Collaborative Work Systems Series

Articulate and enforce "a few strict rules"

Treat collaboration as a disciplined process

Review of the Workbook

The foundation for the CWS initiative is now in place. A lot of progress has probably been made in constructing the parts of the CWS initiative. Do at least three things with your knowledge of that progress: (1) Notice it—it is easy to forget how far we have come on a long journey; (2) Celebrate it—congratulate yourself and your teammates on accomplishing some challenging goals; and (3) Use that information to complete the exercises in this chapter that help set the stage for the next phase in building your organization's collaborative capability.

By this point, the CLT will have worked through the three sections: Introduction; Part I: Create a Foundation for Change; and Part II: Align the Organization for Collaboration. In the Introduction section, you focused on an introduction to the workbook and techniques for using it (Chapter 1), reviewed the basic concepts of collaborative work systems (Chapter 2), including an activity to guide users through preliminary understanding of the extent of the change desired, and completed the Guiding Assessment tool (Chapter 3) that linked to the rest of the chapters in the workbook. Completing this Guiding Assessment provided the CLT with basic knowledge of the CWS concepts and some understanding of the prioritization of working through the chapters of the workbook.

After completing the Introduction, your CLT would have made a decision about what part of the workbook to move to next. You may have gone right into the next chapter or used the results of the Guiding Assessment to jump to a later chapter. Part I, Create a Foundation for Change, concentrated on creating a foundation for the collaborative work system initiative. Constructing the foundation starts by developing the change leadership team (Chapters 4 and 5), then by teaching how to think strategically about change and apply effective change principles (Chapters 6 and 7). Building the business case (Chapter 8) ensures approval from top leaders to ease the transition to Part II of this workbook. Finally, using assessment to identify needs and measure progress (Chapter 9) provides the tools necessary to understand whether the goals of the CWS initiative are being met.

Part II, Align the Organization for Collaboration, moves from the more internal change leadership team focus of creating the foundation for change to a broader organization focus on how to create the framework of plans to design or redesign your collaborative work system. Planning begins by understanding the environment outside the organization and creating ways to link and adapt to that environment (Chapter 10). Understanding current and ideal culture helps set guiding values and principles for the

CWS initiative (Chapter 11). Understanding the work of the organization provides an anchor for the rest of the initiative by ensuring that the real reason for organizations—conducting business—is the focus (Chapter 12); designing structures to best fit that work ensures an effective organization design (Chapter 13). Visualizing and planning what employee behavior looks like at the ideal level of collaboration through an empowerment plan (Chapter 14), defining the new roles of leaders to support employee empowerment (Chapter 15), and developing support systems to support employee empowerment and new leader roles (Chapter 16) all work together to reinforce collaboration.

Finally, this conclusion (Chapter 17) provides activities for pulling together all the material generated in the workbook.

Mechanisms for converting learning into practice were intentionally placed throughout the workbook to make it a useful tool. The many assessment and planning worksheets were designed to help your CLT get real work done on the CWS initiative while moving through the workbook. Use the next planning activity to assess progress on the assessment and planning worksheets in the workbook and determine whether these should be reviewed again.

Assessment: Review Chapter Products

Time Requirement: Approximately 1 hour

Supplies: Any outcomes or products created while completing workbook chapters, Assessment 17.1

Overview: Check your progress on the products created in each chapter, and determine whether these should be redone at some point.

Instructions

1. Create small groups of three or four people. Divide the chapters among the small groups.

2. In small groups, review chapter products for each assigned chapter, using Assessment 17.1.

   • Determine whether that product was completed. Indicate your answer in the Complete? column.

   • Make recommendations on whether there is a need to complete or revisit any of the products. Indicate your answer in the Need to Do or Redo? column.

3. Review small-group work in the whole group. Confirm or revise recommendations on need to do or redo the activity.

4. For any products needing to be completed or revisited, indicate when this will be done and who will be responsible for ensuring it will be done in the appropriate columns.

Assessment 17.1. Review of Chapter Products

Chapter	Type of Activity	Title of Activity	Complete?	Need to Do or Redo?	When?	Who?
2	Knowledge Building	Understand Different Types of Collaboration				
	Assessment	Identify Current Organization Type				
	Planning	Determine Collaborative Work System Target				
3	Assessment	The Guiding Assessment: Part I				
	Assessment	The Guiding Assessment: Part II				
	Assessment	Guiding Assessment: Further Analyze Your Results				
	Planning	Summarize the Pressures For and Against Change				
4	Assessment	Role Audit				
	Assessment	Effective Teams				
	Planning	Boundary Management				
	Assessment	Team Competency Audit				
	Planning	Improving Team Competencies				
	Assessment	Meeting Practices				
	Planning	Create a Meeting Agenda Form				

5	Planning	Define the Relationship with the Top Management Team			
	Planning	Statement of Work			
	Planning	Core Values			
	Planning	Developing the Code of Conduct			
	Planning	Managing the Sponsor			
	Assessment	CWS Initiative Stakeholder Expectations			
	Planning	Vision, Mission, and Name			
	Planning	Goal Setting			
	Planning	Identifying Measures for the CLT			
	Planning	Team Review			
	Planning	Assess Completeness of Charter			
6	Planning	Combine Strategic and Tactical Planning			
	Planning	Tactical and Strategic Planning for the CWS Initiative			
	Planning	Identify the Pain in the Organization			
	Planning	Develop a Vision for Change			
7	Assessment	Assess the Change Expertise of the CLT			
	Planning	Mapping Milestones			
	Planning	Identify Sources of Resistance to the CWS Initiative			
	Planning	Integrating with Other Initiatives			

(continued)

Assessment 17.1.   Review of Chapter Products (continued)

Chapter	Type of Activity	Title of Activity	Complete?	Need to Do or Redo?	When?	Who?
8	Planning	Checklist for the Business Case				
9	Assessment	Quality of Assessment Methods				
	Assessment	Within or Between Focus				
	Planning	Selection of Assessment Instruments				
10	Assessment	Elements of Environmental Awareness				
	Planning	Create Environmental Scanning Mechanisms				
	Planning	Act on Environmental Information				
	Planning	Develop Ways for All Members to Contribute				
11	Planning	Identify Current Culture				
	Assessment	Collaborative Culture				
	Assessment	Entrepreneurial Culture				
	Planning	Envision Ideal Culture, Part 1				
	Planning	Envision Ideal Culture, Part 2				
12	Planning	Identify Key Work Processes				
	Planning	Create a Work Process Map				
	Planning	Analyze the Work Process Map				
	Planning	Understand Customer, Supplier, and Regulator Requirements				

13	Planning	Understand Current Organization Structure
	Assessment	Collaborative Structure Utilization
	Planning	Understand Realities That Affect Future Organization Design
	Planning	Visualize Future Organization Structure
	Planning	Determine Where to Start Implementation
14	Assessment	Empowerment
	Planning	Identify Limits of Empowerment
	Planning	Build an Employee Empowerment Plan
15	Assessment	Collaborative Leadership
	Planning	Define Roles of Leaders at All Levels
	Planning	Build a Leader Role Transition Plan
16	Planning	Collaborative Support System Review
	Assessment	A Closer Look at Your Organization's Support Systems
	Planning	Begin Planning Support Systems Change
17	Assessment	Review Chapter Products
	Planning	Answer Key Questions
	Planning	Compile Action Planning Worksheets
	Planning	Create Master Timeline
	Guiding Assessment	Check Your Progress

Create a CWS Initiative Handbook

Although the results of Assessment 17.1 reflect that the CLT has accomplished a great deal in working through the workbook, an equal or greater number of other activities your team engaged in to work toward the vision of the CWS initiative probably exist. The entire set of outputs (plans, assessments, tools, and so on) created by the CLT can be collected, organized, and bound together in the CLT's own CWS Initiative Handbook. Consider it the CLT's project diary, a document where you can collect everything related to the CWS initiative. The handbook will provide a record of what has been accomplished and a toolkit for future work.

We hope your team has already been building this handbook in some form as you have progressed through the workbook and used forms of it to communicate the CWS initiative to others in the organization. If not, consider using the handbook as a living document to communicate both with CLT members (especially new CLT members) and others in the organization. Consider publishing one or more versions of the handbook in paper form or even on a Web site, so that it can be easily accessed. Assessment 17.1 can be used as one of the organizing mechanisms for your CWS Initiative Handbook.

Discussion

1. What else goes in the CWS Initiative Handbook?

2. Who will be responsible for pulling it together?

3. How can you distribute and communicate it?

Address Key Questions from Each Critical Success Factor Chapter

We dedicated a complete chapter to each of the questions in Table 17.1. In each of those chapters, your CLT completed planning and assessment exercises that increased your understanding of the key question and created ways of addressing the question at your worksite. As a summary, we present here a succinct statement answering each key question to aid in your review and recall of the workbook experience and its lessons. Your team should write out its own answers to each question. Your own answers will make sense to you, because they fit your situation. It is not a matter of right or wrong answers but of *useful* answers.

Planning: Answer Key Questions

Time Requirement: Approximately 2 hours

Supplies: Flip charts and markers for each small group, Table 17.1

Overview: In this activity, you'll spend some time reflecting on the key question for each chapter and develop answers for your organization. Then you'll communicate this material to others to share your progress and use the results to start thinking about the next step in the CWS evolution for your organization.

Instructions

1. Divide into small groups of three to five people and assign chapters to each group. Each group should then answer the key questions for its chapter(s). Use the answers in Table 17.1 to get you started.

2. Each group should then capture the results to the following two questions on flip chart paper—one page per question per chapter.

   • What are your top five learnings from the chapter?

   • How do these learnings apply to your CWS initiative?

3. Reconvene the whole team and have the subgroups report the results of their work on Steps 1 and 2.

4. Discuss and clarify the results. Reach agreement on a final set of answers and capture it on flip charts.

5. Capture the final results in the computer. Provide copies to everyone. Consider communicating the results of this activity to others in the organization.

6. Use the final set of answers as a reminder of what you learned and the principles you discovered. Referring to it will help you stay on track with what works in your organization. Edit the answers when learnings emerge. These are the vital few lessons that will help make your CWS initiative a success.

Launch into the Future

So your team has worked hard and completed the workbook. Congratulations! You will have learned a lot and completed a lot. Is the journey over? No! Action plans, phases, and steps can be achieved, but the journey never ends.

The work of the CLT is far from over. The review of learning and the identification of ways that those learnings link to action begins to lay the groundwork for the next round of the CWS initiative. At this point, the CLT will have learned a lot and done a lot. Congratulate yourselves! Celebrate this milestone as a team! Now begin to think about what remains to be done.

The vision for the CWS initiative is probably clearer now that you have accumulated experience in CLT activities. The achievement of that vision may seem just as far away, receding the way a rainbow does as you move nearer. The vision hasn't really

Table 17.1. Key Questions from Each Critical Success Factor Chapter

Chapter Number	Chapter Title	Key Question	Brief Answer
4	Launch the Change Leadership Team	How do we organize our group so we can effectively manage the strategic change process?	Create a team representing the whole organization, build competencies to match the scope of the CWS initiative, and create a meeting process that enables time and talent to generate maximum value.
5	Charter the Change Leadership Team	How will we work well together?	Share the experience of creating a team charter that captures the values, vision, and mission of the CWS initiative and the CLT in a way that communicates to CLT members and to others what you stand for and how you will work together.
6	Think Strategically About Change	How should the CLT think about the CWS initiative?	Take a strategic approach to planning the CWS initiative so that it aligns with the business strategy and creates a long-term framework for aligning and energizing the action steps of the CLT.
7	Apply Effective Change Principles	What enables a change plan to work?	Build the change management expertise of the CLT so that effective change principles are followed in designing and implementing the CWS initiative, thereby increasing the probability of short-term and long-term successes.
8	Build the Business Case	How can we use the business case to create support for the CWS initiative?	Make a business case for the CWS initiative that articulates the ways it will add value to the organization, align with other initiatives to leverage resources, and generate top management support.
9	Identify Needs and Assess Progress	How can we track our progress toward the CWS initiative vision?	Build quality into an ongoing assessment process so that information on progress and problems gathered from a variety of people using a variety of methods can enable a data-based decision-making process.

Table 17.1. (continued)

Chapter Number	Chapter Title	Key Question	Brief Answer
10	Connect to the Environment	How can we connect and adapt to our environment?	Intentionally creating environmental scanning mechanisms and processes for acting on that information will improve adaptability and contribute to long-term success of the organization.
11	Craft a Culture of Collaboration and Entrepreneurship	What kind of culture supports collaboration, and how can we move toward a collaborative culture?	In a collaborative culture, people want to work together, and work groups perform as if they own the business. Use culture as a way to understand current values of the organization, envision the ideal values, and use the ideal values as "signposts" for changes in the organization.
12	Understand Work Processes	What are the key work processes, and how can we better understand them?	Work encompasses the tasks to be completed for the business to thrive. An effective CWS initiative enhances the completion of work and anchors all the components of the initiative, especially the design of organization structure, with an understanding of the work.
13	Design Using an Array of Structures	What collaborative structures can be incorporated into our target organization design?	Organizational structure represents the way people are organized to carry out the work. In a CWS, structure is designed to support collaboration through groups, individuals, and integrating mechanisms.
14	Plan Employee Empowerment	What is empowerment, and how can empowerment plans be used to define it?	Empowerment means increasing authority, ability, and accountability of employees to accomplish their work. Empowerment planning is a method of laying out expectations for how employee behavior should change as a result of empowerment.

(continued)

Table 17.1.   Key Questions from Each Critical Success Factor Chapter (continued)

Chapter Number	Chapter Title	Key Question	Brief Answer
15	Define New Roles of Leaders	How should roles of leaders change in a collaborative work system?	Leadership in a CWS goes beyond traditional definitions, including all levels of the organization. While leaders must be able to apply different styles to different situations, there are some common skills and abilities that leaders must learn to support the transition to a CWS.
16	Align Support Systems	How can the organizational context support collaboration?	The organizational context, defined by commonly recognized support systems such as rewards and recognition and uncommonly recognized support systems such as integration and organization design, must be changed to support collaboration for the CWS initiative to succeed.

changed, but your understanding of it has. Many of the tools and activities in the workbook will assist with the next phase. Revisit them as needed.

The three activities that follow will help you launch your initiative into the future. This work could best be done in a one-day retreat offsite to minimize interruptions. Remember to use the resource lists at the end of each chapter for additional help.

Planning: Compile Action Planning Worksheets

Time Requirement: Approximately 2 hours

Supplies: Completed action planning worksheets from each chapter, Worksheet 17.1, computer and projector, flip chart and markers for each small group

Overview: Use this planning activity to compile material collected in the action planning worksheets at the end of each chapter. The result will be lists of action items and key decisions made and whether those have been confirmed. Include these documents in your CWS Initiative Handbook.

Instructions

1. Break into small groups of three or four CLT members representing a variety of stakeholder groups (for example, one top manager, one union representative, one person from a support system department like HR or IT) to work together with the completed action planning worksheets from the end of each chapter. Assign different worksheets to each group. Each group should determine progress on each action item, eliminate any items that are no longer relevant,

eliminate redundant items, and cluster those that go together. Capture the resulting set of action items on a flip chart.

2. Each small group shares its results with the rest of the CLT and obtains input for further refining the list of action items.

3. Create an electronic document to capture all of the action items that remain after the refinement work in Step 2. You may already have project management files and programs in place. If so, use them.

4. Have someone act as scribe and work at the computer inputting the action items. Ensure the computer is connected to a projector so all can see the list.

5. Consider adding columns to your electronic document to indicate relevant subparts of the action plan (for example, if committees have been formed, create a column where the relevant committee can be listed next to each action item).

6. Next, working as a whole group, compile the "Significant Decisions Made" sections of the completed action planning worksheets from each chapter onto Worksheet 17.1. Eliminate items that are no longer relevant or are redundant as you go.

7. Review the key decisions in Worksheet 17.1. In the "Confirmed?" column, indicate whether these decisions have been confirmed or not. If not, add the names of those who need to confirm and who is responsible for gaining confirmation in the appropriate columns.

8. Add key decisions needing confirmation to the electronic action items list created in Step 3.

9. Incorporate relevant material from this planning activity in your CWS Initiative Handbook.

Planning: Create Master Timeline

Time Requirement: 2 to 4 hours

Supplies: Electronic action items list from the previous activity, at least one pad of large sticky notes per subgroup, four or five flip chart pages, cellophane tape and masking tape, markers, computer and projector

Overview: Use this planning activity to take the results of the "Compile Action Planning Worksheets" activity and create a master timeline of all action plans. The timeline shows the history of the CWS initiative, its current state, and the planning milestones that can be identified for the future.

Instructions

1. Using the results from the final list of action items in the previous planning activity, create a master timeline. To do so, re-form the small groups from the previous activity and ask each group to write the name of each action item from its assigned chapters on a large sticky note.

2. Tape four or five flip charts on the wall next to each other. Draw a timeline across the flip chart pages and add dates, starting at the left with the date when the top

Worksheet 17.1.   Key Decisions Made

Decision	Confirmed?	If not, who needs to confirm?	Who is responsible for gaining confirmation?

management team decided to create a CLT and moving toward the present and the future on the right side of the line. Try putting today's date in the middle of the line—more pages may need to be added on the right or left of that.

3. Now each small group should place each sticky note in its appropriate spot on the timeline.

4. Each small group should then share with the rest of the CLT why it placed each sticky note on the timeline where it did and ask whether any adjustments are necessary.

5. When the report-out and adjustments are complete, the timeline is complete. It shows the history of the CWS initiative, its current state, and the planning milestones that can be identified for the future. Capture the timeline in the computer. Project management software makes this fairly easy. It can also be done in a spreadsheet or word processing program.

6. Publish the timeline. Make it public for the sponsor, top management team, and the rest of the organization. It maps the next phase of the CLT's work.

7. Incorporate relevant material from this planning activity into your CWS Initiative Handbook.

Guiding Assessment: Check Your Progress

Time Requirement: See Chapter 3 for estimates on completing the Guiding Assessment and compiling data; approximately 1 hour for discussion of results

Supplies: Previously completed Guiding Assessment; Assessments 17.2 and 17.3; Worksheets 17.2, 17.3, and 17.4; flip chart; different colored pens or markers

Overview: Check your progress using the Guiding Assessment in Chapter 3. Compare results of the first time the assessment was conducted with your current results to check on your progress, identifying gaps that have narrowed and gaps that need further attention.

Instructions

1. To distinguish between the two rounds of the assessment, call the first round Time 1 and second Time 2. If you want to conduct the assessment again later, continue the naming convention.

2. Complete Assessments 17.2 and 17.3. (These are the same as Assessments 3.1 and 3.2.) Follow the instructions in Chapter 3 for conducting the assessment.

3. Compile results at the critical success factor level using Worksheet 17.2, which is just another copy of Worksheet 3.3.

4. Using one color of pen, copy the results from Worksheet 3.4 to Worksheet 17.3.

5. Using a different color of pen, graph the results of the Time 2 assessment on Worksheet 17.3. Plot adjusted subscores on the graph. Use circles to plot the "where organization is now" adjusted subscores on the graph. Connect the circles with a solid line. Then use squares to plot the "where organization would like to be at highest level of CWS" adjusted subscores. Connect squares with a dotted line.

Assessment 17.2. Create a Foundation for Change: Progress Check

CSF #1: Launch the Change Leadership Team

Mark current state with a circle and desired state with a square.

#	Item	Low High	□ – ○	Workbook Pages
1-1	Key decision makers, key constituents, and members of the areas undergoing change are represented in the membership of the CLT.	1 2 3 4 5		62, 63, 65
1-2	CLT members understand their roles and responsibilities in the CWS effort.	1 2 3 4 5		62, 65, 73
1-3	The CLT exhibits the team attributes that are expected from other teams in the organization.	1 2 3 4 5		62, 67, 68, 71, 73, 75
1-4	The CLT membership has the knowledge, skills, and abilities needed to effectively lead the CWS effort (for example, knowledge of the business, knowledge of CWSs, ability to coach and mentor).	1 2 3 4 5		63, 73, 75
1-5	The CLT improves its capability through developmental opportunities and by supplementing with outside resources.	1 2 3 4 5		73, 75
1-6	The CLT works with others in the organization to implement plans instead of relying solely on its membership to make it happen.	1 2 3 4 5		81, 98
1-7	The CLT has effective meetings.	1 2 3 4 5		78, 79, 81
1-8	The CLT uses facilitators to help keep meetings on track or provide advice.	1 2 3 4 5		81

○ Raw Subscore CSF #1 =   □ Raw Subscore CSF #1 =

CSF #2: Charter the Change Leadership Team

Mark current state with a circle and desired state with a square.

#	Item	Low High	□ – ○	Workbook Pages
2-1	The CLT has a charter that guides its efforts and is supported by all members.	1 2 3 4 5		89, 117
2-2	The CLT has an explicit set of values and a code of conduct to guide its functioning.	1 2 3 4 5		94, 98, 99, 100
2-3	The CLT charter is periodically reviewed and modified as needed.	1 2 3 4 5		113, 117
2-4	The CLT has a clear, shared vision and mission.	1 2 3 4 5		90, 107, 108
2-5	The CLT has clear goals, measures of those goals, and action plans for achieving those goals, which are reviewed frequently.	1 2 3 4 5		110, 111, 113, 117

Assessment 17.2. (continued)

#	Item	Low High	☐ – ◯	Workbook Pages
2-6	The CLT has an effective relationship with the top management team and a strong sponsor.	1 2 3 4 5		90, 100, 101
2-7	The CLT has a clear decision-making process and a method for escalating decisions that are beyond its control to the appropriate decision maker.	1 2 3 4 5		96, 117
2-8	The CLT understands the expectations of the stakeholders in the CWS initiative (top management, employees, customers, suppliers, regulators, and so on).	1 2 3 4 5		101, 105

◯ Raw Subscore CSF #2 =   ☐ Raw Subscore CSF #2 =

CSF #3: Think Strategically About Change

Mark current state with a circle and desired state with a square.

#	Item	Low High	☐ – ◯	Workbook Pages
3-1	The CLT finds and manages the resources needed to support the CWS initiative.	1 2 3 4 5		126
3-2	The CLT has a big picture, long-term view of the CWS initiative but manages milestone to milestone.	1 2 3 4 5		125, 129, 134, 135, 137
3-3	The CLT identifies and manages the scope of the CWS initiative.	1 2 3 4 5		126
3-4	The CWS initiative is aligned with the business strategy of the organization.	1 2 3 4 5		125, 126, 133
3-5	The CLT uses its diversity to create a comprehensive framework for CWS implementation.	1 2 3 4 5		128, 138
3-6	CLT members understand the reasons for the change and communicate them to all stakeholders.	1 2 3 4 5		90, 107, 108, 126
3-7	The CLT communicates to all stakeholders its vision of how the organization will look when the CWS initiative is successful.	1 2 3 4 5		90, 107, 108, 126, 134, 135, 137
3-8	The CLT takes a deliberate and disciplined approach to planning the CWS initiative.	1 2 3 4 5		127, 138

◯ Raw Subscore CSF #3 =   ☐ Raw Subscore CSF #3 =

(continued)

Assessment 17.3.   Align the Organization for Collaboration: Progress Check

CSF #7: Connect the Organization to the Environment

Mark current state with a circle and desired state with a square.

#	Item	Low High	☐ – ○	Workbook Pages
7-1	Information about the organization's environment (for example, the economy, customers, new technology) is distributed to the right people to act on it.	1 2 3 4 5		214
7-2	Methods are in place to create awareness of the organization's outside environment.	1 2 3 4 5		210, 211
7-3	All members, not just top management, contribute to understanding and acting on information about the organization's environment.	1 2 3 4 5		217
7-4	The organization has processes in place to review and take necessary action on information from its environment.	1 2 3 4 5		214
7-5	Employees have open lines of communication with customers and suppliers.	1 2 3 4 5		210
7-6	Members of the organization try to anticipate changes in the organization's environment and respond proactively.	1 2 3 4 5		208, 210, 214, 218
7-7	All levels of the organization rapidly respond to work, supplier, and customer issues.	1 2 3 4 5		214
7-8	The organization quickly makes changes in response to changes in its environment.	1 2 3 4 5		208, 210, 214, 217

○ Raw Subscore CSF #7 =   ☐ Raw Subscore CSF #7 =

CSF #8: Craft a Culture of Collaboration and Entrepreneurship

Mark current state with a circle and desired state with a square.

#	Item	Low High	☐ ○	Workbook Pages
8-1	The organization has a culture that enhances collaboration and cooperation.	1 2 3 4 5		227
8-2	Different job functions work together without disruptive conflict.	1 2 3 4 5		229
8-3	Employees feel as though they are partners in the business.	1 2 3 4 5		227, 232, 233
8-4	People in the organization want to work together to solve problems.	1 2 3 4 5		227

Assessment 17.3. (continued)

#	Item	Low　　　High	□ – ○	Workbook Pages
8-5	Anticipating and meeting customer needs are priorities for all employees.	1 2 3 4 5		232, 233
8-6	The culture of the organization is periodically reviewed to evaluate needs for change.	1 2 3 4 5		224, 226
8-7	A vision of the ideal culture is communicated and understood by all employees.	1 2 3 4 5		224, 233, 236, 238
8-8	The ideal organizational culture is represented in a set of values that are used to guide decision making.	1 2 3 4 5		224, 238

○ Raw Subscore CSF #8 =　　　　　□ Raw Subscore CSF #8 =

CSF #9: Understand Work Processes

Mark current state with a circle and desired state with a square.

#	Item	Low　　　High	□ – ○	Workbook Pages
9-1	Key work processes of the organization (tasks necessary for the business to thrive) are identified and understood.	1 2 3 4 5		246, 247
9-2	Work processes are periodically reviewed and improved.	1 2 3 4 5		248, 249, 251
9-3	Organization structure is based on an understanding of work processes and the skills and abilities needed to perform them.	1 2 3 4 5		246, 248, 249, 251, 253, 265
9-4	Teams and groups are established around interdependent work processes.	1 2 3 4 5		248, 249, 251, 253
9-5	Members are organized around whole pieces of work (processes, products, or customers) instead of segmented work with many transitions between groups or departments.	1 2 3 4 5		248, 249, 251, 253
9-6	Change initiatives have business reasons and result in improving the business.	1 2 3 4 5		246
9-7	Customer, supplier, and regulator requirements are evaluated when analyzing work processes.	1 2 3 4 5		256
9-8	Work processes are redesigned to enhance collaboration when possible.	1 2 3 4 5		252, 253

○ Raw Subscore CSF #9 =　　　　　□ Raw Subscore CSF #9 =

(continued)

Assessment 17.3.   Align the Organization for Collaboration: Progress Check (continued)

CSF #10: Design Using an Array of Structures

Mark current state with a circle and desired state with a square.

#	Item	Low High	□ – ○	Workbook Pages
10-1	The organization design (for example, bureaucracy, organization using teams, collaborative organization) is appropriate for the organization's situation.	1 2 3 4 5		264, 269, 270
10-2	Organization structures (for example, departments, teams, individuals, different sites) facilitate, rather than hinder, the work.	1 2 3 4 5		246, 251, 264, 265, 275
10-3	The organization uses a combination of formal collaborative structures (for example, work teams, project teams, quality improvement teams) and informal collaborative structures (for example, informal learning networks).	1 2 3 4 5		264, 269, 273, 275
10-4	Different parts of the organization are integrated to enhance communication and cooperation and limit competition.	1 2 3 4 5		269, 273, 275
10-5	The organization structure uses individuals for individual work and groups or teams for work requiring collaboration.	1 2 3 4 5		269, 273, 275
10-6	Organization structure is periodically reviewed to identify strengths and weaknesses.	1 2 3 4 5		265
10-7	Organizational realities (for example, corporate policies, union contracts, and government regulations) are taken into account when attempting to change organizational structure.	1 2 3 4 5		265, 273, 275
10-8	Well-thought-out plans are created when implementing changes in organization structure.	1 2 3 4 5		275, 279

○ Raw Subscore CSF #10 =   □ Raw Subscore CSF #10 =

Assessment 17.3. (continued)

CSF #11: Plan Employee Empowerment

Mark current state with a circle and desired state with a square.

#	Item	Low High	☐ – ○	Workbook Pages
11-1	Decisions are made at the lowest level of the organization possible.	1 2 3 4 5		288, 292
11-2	Employees have the power and freedom to manage tasks and make relevant decisions.	1 2 3 4 5		288, 292
11-3	Individuals and groups are answerable for accomplishing assigned tasks.	1 2 3 4 5		288, 292
11-4	Members have the information and skills needed for effective decisions and task completion.	1 2 3 4 5		288, 292
11-5	Leader behavior (sharing power, information, decision making) supports employee empowerment.	1 2 3 4 5		288, 292
11-6	Different groups and individuals have empowerment levels that match their skills, authority, and experience.	1 2 3 4 5		292, 294, 299
11-7	Limits on empowerment are identified, communicated, and understood.	1 2 3 4 5		292, 294, 299
11-8	Employee empowerment expectations are planned systematically and communicated so that everyone understands them.	1 2 3 4 5		294, 299

○ Raw Subscore CSF #11 =   ☐ Raw Subscore CSF #11 =

CSF #12: Define New Roles of Leaders

Mark current state with a circle and desired state with a square.

#	Item	Low High	☐ – ○	Workbook Pages
12-1	Leaders are collaborative coaches rather than command-and-control directors.	1 2 3 4 5		308, 310
12-2	Leadership is spread to all parts of the organization, including those who are not in formal positions of power.	1 2 3 4 5		308, 313, 314
12-3	Two-way communication occurs between all levels of leadership.	1 2 3 4 5		313
12-4	Leaders understand how their roles will change over time as employees are empowered.	1 2 3 4 5		308, 313, 332, 333

Assessment 17.3.   Align the Organization for Collaboration:
                           Progress Check (continued)

#	Item	Low High	☐ – ○	Workbook Pages
12-5	New leadership roles (such as coaches, sponsors, facilitators) are created to correspond with the empowerment of employees.	1 2 3 4 5		313, 314, 318, 328, 332, 333
12-6	The organization consciously considers how to divide up leadership responsibilities among different leadership roles.	1 2 3 4 5		318, 328, 332, 333
12-7	Roles and responsibilities of leaders are clearly defined and understood at each level of leadership.	1 2 3 4 5		314, 328
12-8	Employees have formal leadership roles (team leaders) and informal leadership roles (leading projects, making decisions).	1 2 3 4 5		313, 314, 332, 333

○ Raw Subscore CSF #12 =   ☐ Raw Subscore CSF #12 =

CSF #13: Align Systems to Support Collaboration

Mark current state with a circle and desired state with a square.

#	Item	Low High	☐ – ○	Workbook Pages
13-1	Organizational systems (for example, accounting, rewards, leadership, training) support collaboration and cooperation.	1 2 3 4 5		341, 349, 352, 357
13-2	The organization uses a variety of systems to support collaborative practices.	1 2 3 4 5		349, 352
13-3	Organizational systems support and reinforce employee and leader empowerment.	1 2 3 4 5		341, 355, 357
13-4	Organizational support systems do not contradict one another.	1 2 3 4 5		357, 359
13-5	Organizational support systems are continually assessed and adjusted as needed.	1 2 3 4 5		354, 360
13-6	The organization makes the most of both formal aspects (annual performance reviews) and informal aspects ("how are we doing" meetings) of support systems.	1 2 3 4 5		349
13-7	Organizational systems have appropriate individual, team/group, and organization components.	1 2 3 4 5		349
13-8	Efforts are made to change organizational systems to support collaborative practices.	1 2 3 4 5		357, 359, 360

○ Raw Subscore CSF #13 =   ☐ Raw Subscore CSF #13 =

Worksheet 17.2. Guiding Assessment Scoring Summary

CSF #	○ Raw Subscore	Number of Items		○ Adjusted Subscore	□ Raw Subscore	Number of Items		□ Adjusted Subscore
1		÷ 8	=			÷ 8	=	
2		÷ 8	=			÷ 8	=	
3		÷ 8	=			÷ 8	=	
4		÷ 8	=			÷ 8	=	
5		÷ 8	=			÷ 8	=	
6		÷ 8	=			÷ 8	=	
7		÷ 8	=			÷ 8	=	
8		÷ 8	=			÷ 8	=	
9		÷ 8	=			÷ 8	=	
10		÷ 8	=			÷ 8	=	
11		÷ 8	=			÷ 8	=	
12		÷ 8	=			÷ 8	=	
13		÷ 8	=			÷ 8	=	

Worksheet 17.3. Critical Success Factors Graph

○ Where Organization Is Now   ☐ Where Organization Would Like to Be

Part I   **Part II**

Time 1 Color =

Time 2 Color =

Adjusted Subscore

5

4

3

2

1

#1 #2 #3 #4 #5 #6 #7 #8 #9 #10 #11 #12 #13

Critical Success Factors

Worksheet 17.4.   Chapters to Review

Critical Success Factor/Chapter	Need to Review?	Review Order
Launch the Change Leadership Team		
Charter the Change Leadership Team		
Think Strategically About Change		
Apply Effective Change Principles		
Build the Business Case		
Identify Needs and Assess Progress		
Connect to the Environment		
Craft a Culture of Collaboration and Entrepreneurship		
Understand Work Processes		
Design Using an Array of Structures		
Plan Employee Empowerment		
Define New Roles of Leaders		
Align Support Systems		

6. Discuss the graph, using the following questions:

   - Compare results of Time 1 and Time 2. What progress have you made? What work remains? How can you use this measure to share progress with others?

   - Focusing on Time 2, what are the biggest gaps between where you are now and where you want to be? Why? What are the next steps for addressing those gaps?

   - Again focusing on Time 2, what are the smallest gaps? Why? What successful ideas can you transfer from these smaller gaps and apply to the larger ones?

   - Do you agree with the results? Why or why not?

   - What can you do immediately to close the Time 2 gaps?

7. Use what you have learned through the analysis to develop a plan for reviewing the workbook.

8. Using Worksheet 17.4, review each CSF (each of which corresponds to a workbook chapter) and determine whether that CSF/chapter needs to be addressed. Indicate yes or no in the "need to review?" column.

9. Identify the order in which to address the chapters by ranking them in the Review Order column. Determine the order by considering the largest gaps in your Guiding Assessment, priorities that have already been determined in your discussions, and sequencing issues—for example, does one chapter have to come before another? The workbook order was developed to ensure flow from one chapter to the next, but can be modified to meet the needs of your organization.

10. Review Worksheet 17.4 after completing each chapter to determine where to go next and adjust the workbook plan accordingly.

Conclusion

The key questions of this chapter are, "What have we accomplished, what resources have we created, and what is our next goal?" Now that you have finished the workbook, a framework for the foundation of the CWS initiative is in place. Do not forget to notice the progress and celebrate your success! Spend time reflecting on the journey so far. However, while action plans, phases, and steps can be achieved, the journey to collaborative work systems never ends. The reflection on the journey so far helps to lay the groundwork for the next round of the CWS initiative. Building collaborative capability is a continual process.

The vision for the CWS initiative is probably clearer now that you have accumulated experience in CLT activities. Many of the tools and activities in the workbook will assist you with the next phase. Revisit them as needed. Use the Guiding Assessment to check your progress and set new targets for the next phase in the evolution of the CWS journey.

Keys to the Chapter

- Take time to notice CWS initiative progress and celebrate it. Reflect on your progress by reviewing the key questions from each chapter, extracting learnings, and applying these to your CWS initiative.

- If you have not done so already, consider creating a CWS Initiative Handbook in which everything related to the CWS initiative can be collected, organized, and distributed, to preserve the history of the initiative and communicate it to all.

- Compile action items and key decisions made, to create a master timeline reflecting the journey so far and the journey yet to come.

- Use what you have learned to set the stage for the next phase in building your organization's collaborative capability. Use the Guiding Assessment to check your progress and set new targets for the next phase in the CWS journey.

- Realize that the journey to a CWS never ends; constant focus and investment is needed to move to the next phase of evolution.

MICHAEL M. BEYERLEIN, PH.D., is director of the Center for the Study of Work Teams (www.workteams.unt.edu) and professor of industrial/organizational psychology at the University of North Texas. His research interests include all aspects of collaborative work systems, organization transformation, work stress, creativity/innovation, knowledge management and the learning organization, and complex adaptive systems. He has published in a number of research journals and has been a member of the editorial boards for *TEAM Magazine, Team Performance Management Journal,* and *Quality Management Journal.* Currently, he is senior editor of a JAI Press/Elsevier annual series of books, *Advances in Interdisciplinary Studies of Work Teams.* In addition, he is co-editor, with Steve Jones, of two ASTD case books about teams and has edited a book on the global history of teams, *Work Teams: Past, Present and Future.* He has been involved in change projects at the Center for the Study of Work Teams with such companies as Boeing, Shell, NCH, Advanced Micro Devices, Westinghouse, and Xerox and with government agencies such as the Bureau of Veterans Affairs, Defense Contract Management Agency, the Environmental Protection Agency, and the City of Denton, Texas.

JAMES R. BARKER, PH.D., is director of research and professor of organizational theory and strategy in the Department of Management at the U.S. Air Force Academy. His research interests focus on the development and analysis of collaborative control practices in technological and knowledge-based organizations. His research projects include collaborations with scientists at the Los Alamos and Sandia National Laboratories and with scholars at the University of Melbourne and the University of Western Australia. Dr. Barker's work has appeared in a number of professional journals, including *Administrative Science Quarterly, Journal of Organizational and Occupational Psychology,* and *Communication Monographs.* His book *The Discipline of Teamwork* is available from Sage Publications. He won the 1993 Outstanding Publication in Organizational Behavior award from the Academy of Management and the 1999 *Administrative Science Quarterly* Scholarly Contribution Award for his research on self-managing teams. He has lectured on teamwork in organizations at many universities and organizations, including the Sloan School of Management at the Massachusetts Institute of Technology and the University of Western Australia. He served as assoicate editor of the *Western Journal of Communication* and on the editorial boards of *Administrative Science Quarterly, Journal of Organizational Change Management*, and *Management Communication Quarterly.*

SUSAN TULL BEYERLEIN, PH.D., holds a B.A. in English from the University of Oregon, an M.S. in general psychology from Fort Hays State University, and a Ph.D. in organization theory and policy with a minor in education research from the University of North Texas, Denton. Since 1988, she has taught a variety of management courses as an adjunct faculty member at several universities in the Dallas area, with a focus on strategic management at both undergraduate and MBA levels. Dr. Beyerlein has served as a research scientist/project manager with the Center for the Study of Work Teams at the University of North Texas and has been a recipient of research grant awards from the Association for Quality and Participation, the National Science Foundation, and corporate donors. Since 1995, she has co-edited the JAI Press/Elsevier annual book series entitled *Advances in Interdisciplinary Studies of Work Teams* and during the same period has served as an ad hoc reviewer for *Academy of Management Review.* She has published book reviews on contemporary business offerings in *Business and the Contemporary World,* and her work has also appeared in *Structural Equation Modeling: A Multidisciplinary Journal, Teams: The Magazine for High Performance Organizations* (UK), *Journal of Management Education, Empirical Studies of the Arts,* and *Multiple Linear Regression Viewpoints.* She is a member of the Academy of Management, Phi Kappa Phi National Honor Society, and Beta Gamma Sigma—the honor society for collegiate schools of business.

MICHAEL M. BEYERLEIN is director of the Center for the Study of Work Teams (www.workteams.unt.edu) and professor of industrial/ organizational psychology at the University of North Texas. His research interests include all aspects of collaborative work systems, organization transformation, work stress, creativity/innovation, knowledge management and the learning organization, and complex adaptive systems. He has published in a number of research journals and has been a member of the editorial boards for *TEAM Magazine, Team Performance Management Journal,* and *Quality Management Journal.* Currently, he is senior editor of a JAI Press/Elsevier annual series of books, *Advances in Interdisciplinary Studies of Work Teams,* and the Pfeiffer Collaborative Work Systems series. In addition, he has been co-editor with Steve Jones of two ASTD casebooks about teams and has edited a book on the global history of teams, *Work Teams: Past, Present and Future.* His most recent books are *Beyond Teams: Building the Collaborative Organization, The Collaborative Work System Fieldbook,* and *The Collaborative Work System Casebook.* He has been involved in change projects at the Center for the Study of Work Teams with companies such as Boeing, Shell, NCH, Advanced Micro Devices, Raytheon, First American Financial, Westinghouse, and Xerox and with government agencies such as Veterans Affairs, the Defense Contract Management Agency, the Environmental Protection Agency, and the City of Denton.

CHERYL L. HARRIS is a consultant and researcher affiliated with the Center for the Study of Work Teams (www.workteams.unt.edu) at the University of North Texas, where she is finishing a Ph.D. in industrial/organizational psychology. She recently completed a year of research at the Center for Creative Leadership. She has written chapters for *The Collaborative Work System Fieldbook, The Collaborative Work System Casebook, International Handbook of Organisational Teamwork and Cooperative Working,* and *Team-Based Organizing,* a volume in the Advances in Interdisciplinary Studies of Work Teams series. Recent projects include leading a team of consultants in facilitating the redesign of an organization into a team-based organization, development of an online system for assessing collaboration in organizations (www.workteams.unt.edu/assessment.htm), design and delivery of workshops for those leading the change to collaborative work systems, and presentations at numerous conferences. She has worked on change projects at the Center for the Study of Work Teams with such organizations as Westinghouse, Millennium Chemicals, the Veterans Administration, United Way, UNT Systems Center at Dallas, Wellmark International, and Boeing. Her research interests include all aspects of collaborative work systems (especially organizational support systems for collaboration), whole-systems methods of organization change, organization design, and learning in organizations.

INDEX

a = assessment; *f* = figure; *p* = planning activity; *t* = table